God's Timetable

God's Timetable

The Book of Revelation and the Feast of Seven Weeks

Daniel F. Stramara Jr.

☙PICKWICK *Publications* • Eugene, Oregon

GOD'S TIMETABLE
The Book of Revelation and the Feast of Seven Weeks

Copyright © 2011 Daniel F. Stramara Jr. All rights reserved. Except for brief quotations in critical publications or reviews, no part of this book may be reproduced in any manner without prior written permission from the publisher. Write: Permissions, Wipf and Stock Publishers, 199 W. 8th Ave., Suite 3, Eugene, OR 97401.

All Scripture quotations are from the New Revised Standard Version unless noted otherwise.

New Revised Standard Version Bible: Catholic Edition, copyright © 1989, 1993, Division of Christian Education of the National Council of the Churches of Christ in the United States of America. Used by permission. All rights reserved.

Revised Standard Version of the Bible, Apocrypha, copyright © 1957; The Third and Fourth Books of the Maccabees and Psalm 151, copyright © 1977, Division of Christian Education of the National Council of the Churches of Christ in the United States of America. Used by permission. All rights reserved.

Scripture quotations marked (NIV) are taken from the Holy Bible, New International Version®, NIV®. Copyright © 1973, 1978, 1984 Biblica, Inc.™ Used by permission of Zondervan. All rights reserved worldwide. www.zondervan.com

Pickwick Publications
An Imprint of Wipf and Stock Publishers
199 W. 8th Ave., Suite 3
Eugene, OR 97401

www.wipfandstock.com

ISBN 13: 978-1-60899-638-4

Cataloging-in-Publication data:

Stramara, Daniel F., J.

God's timetable : the Book of Revelation and the Feast of Seven Weeks / Daniel F. Stramara Jr.

xvi + 186 p. ; 23 cm. Including bibliographical references and indexes.

ISBN 13: 978-1-60899-638-4

1. Bible. N.T. Revelation — Criticism, interpretation, etc. I. Title.

BS2825 S79 2011

Manufactured in the U.S.A.

In Memoriam
Dedicated in loving memory of my little whelp,

Daniel Francis Duke Stramara III

17 April 2003

"Dan is a lion's whelp,
that leaps forth from Bashan."
Deut 33:22

Contents

Foreword / ix

Preface / xi

Acknowledgments / xiii

Abbreviations / xiv

1. Introduction / 1
2. Jewish Apocalyptic Literature / 7
3. The Liturgical Meanings of the Feast of Weeks and the Lectionary / 22
4. Revelation as an Apocalyptic Pentecost Commentary / 32
5. The Historical, Religious, and Political Contexts / 86
6. Gematria and Some Underlying Hebrew Plays on Words / 106
7. Recapitulation: Re-envisioning Revelation / 137

APPENDICES:

A: Jewish Liturgical Readings for the Feast of Weeks / 145

B: The Ancient Empires and Their Major Rulers / 147

C: The Hasmonean and Herodian Dynasties in Israel / 149

D: Chronology of the Jewish War (66–70) / 151

E: Chiastic Structure of the Book of Revelation / 154

Bibliography / 163

Subject Index / 169

Acient Document Index / 177

Foreword

MAKING PLAIN THE MEANING of the many numbers, names, and incredible images of John's vision is no small feat. Daniel F. Stramara Jr. has done just that, at least for this reader. And his first move is perhaps the most ingenious and yet simple one: to observe this imagery on a first-century Jewish canvas.

Stramara demonstrates how the elements that the Apocalypse employs follow the sequence of the Jewish calendar; more specifically, the liturgical readings and their interpretations in other Jewish literature of the time. The texts that the visionary cites or alludes to are associated with the Scripture readings leading up to and immediately following Shavu'ot, the Festival of Weeks, of the seven sevens of the Jubilee sequence. This dynamic is attested in the *Book of Jubilees*, no less, as well as in other contemporary Jewish literature. In addition to being the Feast of First-Fruits, this festival is the Feast of Harvest: it is not hard to see that the Seer's theme is God's harvest of the righteous ones from Israel and nations, of the winnowing of the wheat from the chaff. Moreover, Pentecost/Shavu'ot is the celebration to recount God's revelation of the Torah (God's covenantal "Teaching" to guide Israel among the nations) on Mt. Sinai.

John delivers a story of those who celebrate the Lord of the cosmos over the lord of the empire, of those who are faithful to the commandments of Israel's God instead of compromising them in the service to Caesar and the appearance of imperial power in the present age. That is precisely the kind of religio-political countercultural message one might expect to arise in the context of the Jewish Revolt of the late 60s and its aftermath, in this case, among Jewish groups in Asia Minor concerned about the meaning of God's revelation to humankind in Jesus Christ who must wrestle with the implications of these events in their own local contexts.

In this way, Daniel Stramara has hit upon a new way to decode the cryptic language that would have resonated with a Jewish audience in the first century CE. More than that, he explains how he has arrived at his conclusions—however clever and complex (e.g., can decoding gematria or aligning figurative kings and kingdoms be otherwise?)—in surprisingly plain language that anyone interested in understanding this message can follow.

But beware, reader, Stramara's conclusions come at a price. For this reading to have made sense to John and his audience, they must have understood themselves to remain practicing members of first-century Judaism, albeit within a subgroup movement that believed that Jesus was the Messiah of those who observe Jewish ways of life, including ways of marking time and reading the Scriptures as well as decoding them in the service of its Lord—not of Judaism's end or transformation into something else. This requires the later reader to suppose that John did not understand his convictions as superior or opposed to Judaism in the ways that Christianity came to understand itself. Rather, the author sees himself speaking for Judaism as the way of righteousness that should be practiced by his audience—including those who are not Jews, but who are now members of this Jewish movement. They must endure those who seek to harm them and remain set apart from the ways of their neighbors, trusting that things will turn out other than how they presently seemed to be, that the arrival of the storm signals the dawning of a new day, one that will bring the awaited harvest for the faithful.

Is that probable, or even plausible? I urge the reader to put any reservations on hold for a time, or at least half a time, and give this reading a chance to play itself out. When the "counting" is completed, you will discover a satisfying, perhaps even perfect, surprise.

Mark D. Nanos
Soebbing Visiting Scholar
Rockhurst University
Shavu'ot 5770—19 May 2010

Preface

I BEGAN THIS WORK as an article in which to explore how the Feast of Weeks, which consists of seven weeks, might have had some influence upon the Book of Revelation. The Feast of Weeks—known as Pentecost—is the Harvest Feast, and harvest metaphors (as well as sets of seven) operate in the Apocalypse. As I studied the historical context of the book and compared it to preceding and contemporaneous Jewish apocalypses I was struck by the similarities and then postulated that perhaps the main corpus of the Book of Revelation was in fact more so a Jewish apocalypse that had been Christianized than a primarily original Christian apocalypse. As I immersed myself in the Jewish liturgical readings for the Feast of Pentecost, known by Jews as Shavu'ot, I was amazed at the correspondence between the Jewish lectionary and the Hebrew Scriptures cited and alluded to in the Book of Revelation.

Obviously, the article grew into a book in which to test and present my hypothesis and findings. This book takes the lay as well as academic reader through the historical Jewish background to the Book of Revelation and the new insights that are "revealed" through this lens. Many previously unnoticed Hebrew plays on words and numerological possibilities are brought to light.

Finally, I posit that John, the Christian seer, re-envisioned the message of the Jewish Apocalypse in the light of the Risen Lord Jesus, proclaiming him as the fulfillment of the Jewish apocalyptic expectation.

Christian Pentecost—23 May 2010

Acknowledgments

I would first of all like to thank my loving wife, Clare, who was both patient and supportive during my writing of this book and getting it ready for publication. Originally it was simply to have been an article, but as I pursued my research and commenced writing, the ideas necessitated exposition within a book. My wife is a real saint, especially since we were planning to spend lots of time together during the summer when I first wrote this! I also want to thank my baby daughter, Julianna, whose smiles and giggles at the time kept me focused on what is really important in life. You are a profound joy to me, "puddin'." Of course, there are also my loving parents, Daniel and Audrey Stramara, who have encouraged and supported me throughout life—thank you.

In the academic arena, special thanks go to Wilburn T. Stancil, Professor of Theology at Rockhurst University, who read the manuscript and provided valuable feedback. Also, Dr. Mark D. Nanos was kind enough to read my work from a Jewish point of view and provide comments. Of course, the ideas and opinions in this book are mine and I alone bear responsibility for the contents, for better or for worse.

I also wish to thank Rockhurst University for the Presidential Grant which allowed me to work on this project during the summer of 2003.

A special thank you goes to the staff at Greenlease Library at Rockhurst University, in particular to Verna Rutz, who secured various books and articles for me through interlibrary loan. Also, our faculty secretary, Renee McGautha, was a help regarding typesetting and encoding issues.

Finally, I wish to thank Chris Spinks and the team at Pickwick Publications of Wipf and Stock Publishers for bringing this work to fruition.

Abbreviations

AB	Anchor Bible
ANF	*Ante-Nicene Fathers*, A. Roberts and J. Donaldson, eds., 10 vols. (Peabody, MA: Hendrickson, 1994)
GCS	Die Griechischen Christlichen Schriftsteller der ersten (Leipzig: Hinrichs, 1897–1969)
JB	Jerusalem Bible
LCL	Loeb Classical Library
LXX	Septuagint
NABR	New American Bible Revised
NEB	New English Bible
NIV	New International Version
NJB	New Jerusalem Bible
NPNF2	*Nicene and Post-Nicene Fathers*, 2nd ser., P. Schaff and H. Wace, eds., 14 vols. (Peabody, MA: Hendrickson, 1994)
NRSV	New Revised Standard Version
OTP	*The Old Testament Pseudepigrapha*, J. H. Charlesworth, ed., 2 vols. (Garden City, NY: Doubleday, 1983–1985)
RSV	Revised Standard Version

ANCIENT JEWISH SOURCES

Deuterocanonical Books/Apocrypha

Bar	Baruch
Bel	Bel and the Dragon (Dan 14)
1/2 Esd	1/2 Esdras
1/2 Macc	1/2 Maccabees
Sir	Sirach
Tob	Tobit
Wis	Wisdom

Dead Sea Scrolls

CD	Cairo Genizah copy of the *Damascus Document*

Josephus

Ant.	*Antiquitates judaicae* (Jewish Antiquities)
B.J.	*Bellum judaicum* (Jewish War)
C. Ap.	*Contra Apionem* (Against Apion)

Philo of Alexandria

Contempl.	*De vita contemplativa* (On the Contemplative Life)
Decal.	*De decalogo* (On the Decalogue)
Leg.	*Legum allegoriae* (Allegorical Interpretations)
QE	*Quaestiones et solutiones in Exodum* (Questions and Answers on Exodus)
Somn.	*De somniis* (On Dreams)
Spec.	*De specialibus legibus* (On the Special Laws)

Pseudepigrapha

2 Bar.	*2 Baruch* (Syriac Apocalypse)
3 Bar.	*3 Baruch* (Greek Apocalypse)
1 En.	*1 Enoch* (Ethiopic Apocalypse)
2 En.	*2 Enoch* (Slavonic Apocalypse)
Jub.	*Jubilees*
Ps.-Philo	Pseudo-Philo, *Liber antiquitatum biblicarum*
Sib. Or.	*Sibylline Oracles*

Rabbinic Literature

ʽ*Abod. Zar.*	*Avodah Zarah*
b.	*Babylonian Talmud*
Ber.	*Berakhot*
Bik.	*Bikkurim*
ʽ*Ed.*	*Eduyyot*
Ḥag.	*Hagigah*
m.	*Mishnah*
Meg.	*Megillah*
Midr.	*Midrash*

xvi *Abbreviations*

Pesaḥ.	*Pesahim*
Roš Haš.	*Rosh HaShanah*
S. ʿOlam Rab.	*Seder Olam Rabbah*
Šabb.	*Shabbat*
Sanh.	*Sanhedrin*
Sop.	*Sopherim*
t.	*Tosephta*
Taʿan.	*Taʾanit*
Tanḥ.	*Tanhuma*
y.	*Jerusalem Talmud*

EARLY CHRISTIAN SOURCES

Hist. Ecc.	Eusebius of Caesarea, *Historia ecclesiastica* (Church History)
Adv. Haer.	Ireneaus, *Adversus haeresis* (Against Heresies)
Dial. Trypho	Justin Martyr, *Dialogus cum Trypho* (Dialog with Trypho)
Comm. Joh.	Origen, *Commentarium in Johannem* (Commentary on John)

OTHER GRECO-ROMANS SOURCES

Hist.	Dio Cassius, *Historiae Romae* (Roman History)
Sat.	Juvenal, *Satirae* (Satires)

Suetonius, De vita Caesarum (On the Lives of the Caesars)

Cal.	*Gaius Caligula*
Cl.	*Divus Claudius*
Dom.	*Domitianus*
Gal.	*Galba*

Tacitus

Ann.	*Annales*
Hist.	*Historiae*

1

Introduction

Trying to divine the inspiration behind the Book of Revelation is like using a dowsing rod to discover a major artesian well: perhaps several aquifers can be detected, but the underlying source escapes the dowser. Each commentator applies sound (and perhaps at times not so sound) criteria to tap into what is buried in the text—a text which claims to be a revelation of what was hidden. Many streams of thought have been explored and have produced various results in trying to slake the thirst of the avid reader and interpreter. It was quite fortuitously that I stumbled upon what I now consider to be the main wellspring of the currents of thought running throughout the Book of Revelation. I am convinced that the thematic source of the contents and structure of the Book of Revelation is the Feast of Pentecost, the Feast of [Seven] Weeks that celebrates the harvest as well as God's revelatory action.[1] The "divining rod" I employed was that of analyzing extra-biblical apocalyptic literature written before the Book of Revelation, primarily the *Book of Jubilees*, and then reading the Book of Revelation as a liturgical text embedded in Jewish midrashic (expository) thought.

To sound the depths of my hypothesis, in this treatise I will 1) set forth the major importance of the Feast of Weeks in the *Book of Jubilees* and its theology at Qumran, as well as in literature contemporaneous to that of the Book of Revelation; 2) discuss the liturgical meaning of Pentecost as understood before and soon after the first century CE; 3) unpack the Jewish liturgical readings for the Feast of Weeks; 4) reveal these liturgical texts in the Book of Revelation and then exegete the passages accordingly; 5) review the Book of Revelation in the historical

---

1. This will be explored in depth below. To alert the reader, the following designations are all for the same liturgical feast day: Feast of Weeks, Feast of First-Fruits, Harvest Feast, Feast of Shavu'ot, Pentecost.

context of Jerusalem and the Jewish War 66–70 CE ; 6) explore some possible gematria and Hebrew plays on words in the text; and 7) recapitulate my thesis and draw conclusions to see if it "holds water."

Anyone casually acquainted with the Book of Revelation realizes that it is filled with seven sets of various items: seals, trumpets, angels, bowls, plagues, et cetera. Several scholars have tried to structure the book accordingly.[2] The text is likewise replete with images of the temple, altar, priests, incense, hymns, Ark of the Covenant, and offerings.[3] Demonstrably a liturgical understanding is integral to the work. But was there a liturgical feast that gave rise to the conception of the apocalypse itself? Håkan Ulfgard as well as Barbara Snyder have argued that the Feast of Tabernacles helps to unlock the meaning.[4] This issue will be reviewed below, but I believe the Feast of Weeks, a liturgical celebration of the harvest in seven sets of seven and the commemoration of the giving of the Torah, most aptly resonates with the thematic presentation throughout the whole work. I believe Pentecost is the well, the "Well of the Oath," feeding the various streams of thought.[5]

The number of books, articles, and sermons ever composed on the Book of Revelation must number as the stars of heaven. So why produce yet another book? The main reason is to test my hypothesis; to see what you the reader and scholars say about my re-evaluation of the Book of Revelation. Though other authors have explored somewhat similar avenues, I have come up with a fairly novel approach. Based on my research, I contend that the main section of the Book of Revelation (now part of the New Testament canon) was originally a Jewish apocalypse, at least in its oral stage—though I do not rule out an original written version.[6] Many

---

2. For a survey of various views see Beale, *Book of Revelation*, 108–51; as well as Ford, *Revelation*, 46–50.

3. For authors excavating liturgical aspects within the text see Prigent, *L'Apocalypse et liturgie*; and O'Rourke, "Hymns of the Apocalypse."

4. See Ulfgard, *Feast and Future*; and Snyder, "Combat Myth in the Apocalypse." Beale (*Book of Revelation*, 141–44) provides a useful synopsis and analysis of Snyder's presentation.

5. The *Book of Jubilees* references the "Well of the Oath" when expounding on the Feast of Weeks; see *Jub.* 22:1; 16:10–13; 44:1–4. It does so because there is a play on words in Hebrew between "oath" (*shevu'ot*) and "weeks" (*shavu'ot*).

6. I originally wrote this manuscript in 2003, totally oblivious to Marshall's book, *Parables of War: Reading John's Jewish Apocalypse*. Sadly, I didn't even happen upon it (and read it) until doing final editing (2010) in preparing my manuscript for this publication. I say, sadly, because his contention that the Book of Revelation is a Jewish apocalypse seems to have been overlooked. I have, however, taken a markedly different

Jewish works were lost to the mainline Jewish tradition but preserved by Christians. For example, the works of Philo and Josephus were both unknown to Jewish scholars until the sixteenth century.[7] In fact, what Christians call *4 Ezra* (also known as *2 Esdras*) was originally a Jewish apocalypse taken over by Christians. For all present-day Christians, *4 Ezra* is part of the Apocrypha (or Pseudiepigrapha depending upon your classification). Nevertheless, copies of this book ended up in some medieval Latin Bibles as well as in Syriac, Ethiopic, and Armenian Bibles. Thus the hypothesis that what we now call the Revelation of St. John was an earlier Jewish work taken over by a Christian editor (who added chapters 1–3 and tacked on an epilogue) is not totally implausible.

But whatever one's views are regarding the authorship of the Book of Revelation, this treatise argues that the original author, that is to say authoritative source behind the revelation, was deeply influenced by Jewish theology and the liturgical readings for the Feast of Weeks. This Feast is also known in Hebrew as Shavu'ot, as the Harvest Feast or the Feast of First-Fruits, and in Greek as Pentecost.

From the outset, it is imperative to define what I mean by the terms "Jew" and "Christian," and the concomitant adjectives. *In the religious sphere, I am defining a Jew as someone of any ethnic background who espouses monotheism and a belief that God's covenantal love is revealed through the books and teachings of the Torah (Law) and the Prophets. Such believers adhere to various degrees of Torah observance and utilize a variety of practices. I am defining a Christian as someone of any ethnic background who espouses monotheism and a belief that this One God sent Jesus of Nazareth as Messiah (Anointed One = Christ in Greek) to inaugurate the Messianic Age by his resurrection from the dead. Such believers adhere to various degrees of Torah observance, utilize a variety of practices, and believe in various levels of Jesus' divine status.* Thus one can be a Torah observant Jew (whether ethnically a Jew or not) and have faith in Jesus as the Christ.[8]

---

approach and interpretation in this book. Marshall comes primarily from a religious studies perspective while I from a historical theological point of view, though the two are not intrinsically at odds. Marshall's book is valuable in highlighting several commentators' presumptions against anything Jewish being positive.

7. See Sandmel's "Foreword for Jews."

8. For the Apostle Paul who saw no conflict with Torah observance and faith in Jesus, see the following seminal works by Nanos: "Paul and Judaism: Why Not Paul's Judaism?"; "The Myth of the 'Law-Free' Paul Standing between Christians and Jews";

Before moving into my argument in earnest, I provide here an overview of how I shall develop it. Chapter 2 introduces the reader to apocalyptic thought in general, and then explores Jewish apocalyptic literature. This helps us to contextualize the writing of the Book of Revelation. I especially analyze the *Book of Jubilees*, which was widely used at Qumran by the Dead Sea Community and which re-envisions Israel's history around the Feast of Weeks.

Chapter 2 also investigates the Jewish understanding of the Feast of Weeks before the second century of the Common Era. Besides as an offering of first fruits to God, this Feast was also a celebration of God's giving the life-giving Law to Moses and of God's act of self-revelation itself. Many Jewish apocalypses were built off of this motif.

Chapter 3 reviews the practice of having assigned readings for every Sabbath in the synagogue. I then uncover the actual readings used during the Jewish liturgy for the Feast of Weeks. These readings pre-date the various synagogue lectionaries and go back to before the first century BCE.

Chapter 4 presents an exegesis of the Book of Revelation in light of the Jewish liturgical readings for the Feast of Shavu'ot. This is the heart of the book. Building on the lectionary readings uncovered in chapter 3, this chapter demonstrates that the author of Revelation purposefully utilized the readings from the Law, the Prophets, and Writings specific to that feast day. Additionally, the theological and liturgical themes of the Harvest Feast appear throughout the corpus of the Book of Revelation. In short, the Book of Revelation is a Jewish apocalyptic midrash. That is to say, it is a commentary on the Feast of Weeks that is interpreted as God's timetable: a set of seven weeks. This midrash, an exegetical commentary, is thoroughly steeped in Jewish theology and expects the End of Time to be close at hand. The earlier *Book of Jubilees* had already shown that all of Israel's major events in history happened on the Feast of Weeks. The conclusion of history on that Feast makes perfect sense. With this insight, chapter 4 offers solutions to many hidden riddles found in the Book of Revelation.

Chapter 5 situates the Book of Revelation in the historical context of Jewish history, particularly those events that had previously taken

---

The Mystery of Romans: The Jewish Context of Paul's Letter; "What Was at Stake in Peter's 'Eating with Gentiles' at Antioch?"; and *The Irony of Galatians: Paul's Letter in First-Century Context*.

place on Pentecost. Pentecost was a politically charged festival. The major event in Israel's history during the first century CE was the Jewish War, which lasted three and a half years from 66–70 (regarding Jerusalem). The Book of Revelation is then reread through this lens.

Chapter 6 unlocks the hidden meaning of numbers and names. Everyone is familiar with the mark of the Beast: 666, which is also the name of a man. This is explored in depth in regard to the Feast of Weeks. In the ancient world, both Hebrews and Greeks did not have separate symbols for numbers. They used the letters of their alphabet to designate what we call ciphers (1, 2, 3 etc.). Consequently, letters carried a numerical value and could be added up. In chapter 6, numerous Hebrew plays on words and hidden numerological mysteries are revealed. This chapter, building upon chapter 4, demonstrates that the Book of Revelation, although presently preserved in Greek, had a thoroughly Jewish mind behind it that made various plays on words and crafted numerological symbols in Hebrew and Aramaic.

Chapter 7 draws conclusions from all the evidence assembled. The reader and scholarly world is invited to evaluate whether I have objectively tested my hypothesis and produced valid results. The book itself is an "intellectual exercise." It is the fruit of "enjoying thinking for the sake of thinking." Like any scientist, I came up with a hypothesis and then tested it. I began this book, originally as an "intellectual exercise," an "academic curiosity," just to see where it would lead me. Is this thought plausible? Does this avenue of investigation lead anywhere? Much to my amazement, I found evidence convincing me that understanding the Jewish theology behind the Feast of Weeks unlocks the meaning of the Book of Revelation as never before.

But as with any scientific hypothesis, it needs to be tested by others and reduplicated. I ask the scholarly community, as well as the general public, to scrutinize my theory, and to see if my insights make sense. Obviously I am persuaded that they do or I would not have attempted to publish them. But I am also persuaded that "no prophecy of scripture is a matter of one's own interpretation" (2 Pet 1:20). The JB and NEB translations bring out even more so how interpretation is never a matter for an individual alone.

To aid the reader, I have supplied several appendices. Appendix A provides all the liturgical readings for the Jewish Feast of Shavu'ot used before the second century CE. Appendix B charts out the ancient empires and their major rulers. Appendix C chronologues the Hasmonean and Herodian dynasties in Israel. Appendix D provides a timeline of major events during the Jewish War. Finally, Appendix E presents a brief analysis of the chiasms operative in Rev 2–3, 4–11, and 12:1—22:7.

My goal was to make this book as readable and yet as scholarly as possible for a wide audience. Hopefully I have achieved this and you will enjoy re-evaluating the Book of Revelation in a new light.

2

Jewish Apocalyptic Literature

WHAT IS AN APOCALYPSE?

IN ORDER TO APPRECIATE the Book of Revelation, the work needs to be situated in its historical context. Before the Book of Revelation was even written, a whole body of Jewish literature had arisen that spoke of God's intervention in the affairs of Israel, rescuing them from their persecutors; in the End, God will have the final victory. This body of literature is called apocalyptic. A study group of the Society of Biblical Literature came up with this definition: "'Apocalypse' is a genre of revelatory literature with a narrative framework, in which a revelation is mediated by an otherworldly being to a human recipient, disclosing a transcendent reality which is both temporal, insofar as it envisages eschatological salvation, and spatial insofar as it involves another, supernatural world."[1] The term eschatological refers to the end of time. Nevertheless, the readers of the apocalypse are addressed in their present situation and encouraged to have faith because God will triumph in the end; this end, however, is believed to be quite imminent, coming very soon. In common parlance, an apocalypse says: "God knows what you're going through. Hang in there; it won't be long now. Have faith." Apocalypses are words of encouragement; they are inspirational.

PROPHECY VERSUS PREDICTION

By its very nature, apocalyptic literature is *prophetic*, rather than predictive. The Greek verb *prophēteuō* comes from the roots *pro* and *phēmi*, which literally mean "to speak on behalf of another." The prophet is literally a "spokesperson" for someone, in this case God. The prophet delivers

1. J. Collins, "Introduction," 9.

the word of the Lord, in other words presents God's point of view on a subject. Most often, the prophet reveals a divine perspective on current events that might have been hidden from others. The Hebrew prophets delivered a theological and moral spin on social issues and political happenings. The prophet and prophetess as such rarely predicted future events, but rather commented on current and forthcoming realities, delivering the word of the Lord to that particular situation. Thus there is a marked difference between prophecy and prediction, a theological spin on a current situation, and a divine foretelling of distant future events.[2]

In apocalypses, one can find many "prophecies" that are really statements after the fact, many times providing details; but when it comes to future events, the prophet is more vague and paints a picture with broader brush strokes. Likewise, because the prophet is speaking from God's eternal point of view which is instantaneous, most often, time sequences in apocalypses have been collapsed, and what for us had happened in the past can be presented as a future event, and what has not yet taken place can even be presented with certitude as already finished, a definite fact. Thus the inspired seer presents his listeners with a prophetic interpretation of their present situation as well as immediate future. All of this is done in the light of how God has acted and been faithful in the past. The God of yesterday is the same today and forever. In short, "he'll do it again."

MAIN TRAITS OF APOCALYPTIC LITERATURE

Apocalyptic literature usually has most of the following twenty-four characteristics operating within it to some extent. Apocalypses are written during an *age of political and social upheaval*. They address the current issues which are experienced as tumultuous. The centerpiece of the drama is the *persecution of God's holy ones*. The saints are being unjustly assaulted by a *diabolical enemy*, some ruler who appears to embody evil itself. The answer or consolation to this crisis comes through a *prophetic vision or dream* and thus is filled with *symbolic imagery*. Just like in any dream, one thing represents something else and the interpreter needs to make associations in order to divine the latent meaning. The symbols and imagery also rapidly change and merge into one another. The vision or prophetic dream is communicated through an *angel, a messenger of God*. Consequently, the vision is a divine revelation, a new inspired

---

2. See Boring, *Revelation*, 23–26.

insight into the present situation and what is soon to take place. Most often the message not only works through symbols and metaphors but *numerology* as well. Numbers are wrapped in a special significance and symbolic meaning. They are endowed with an aura of a divine timetable and/or heavenly pattern.

The antagonist in the apocalyptic book is usually presented in the guise of a *beast, some animal figure, which represents a political institution*. The empire is experienced as overwhelming and devouring, out of control, thus there is an *urgent need* for *divine intervention*. Apocalypses pulse with a sense of *urgency* and imminence. God needs to break into the current situation and bring deliverance and salvation. The matter is very clear; the issues are black and white; a *dualism* is operative. There are two camps and two perspectives. "It's us against them." The *reign of evil and sin* must be dealt with. The tyranny must be addressed. Hence the prophet is inspired to realize that the warfare going on is actually part of a *cosmic battle* between Good and Evil, holiness and wickedness. In the midst of the terror and conflict, a *holy remnant* will be saved. They might be decimated, but they're not annihilated. These holy ones view their lives as an *offering to God*. Sometimes this requires more than just personal sacrifices; there is a call to witness even to the point of death.

Thankfully God is quite aware of the dire situation and will execute *divine judgment and retribution*. Not only does God judge the matter, but the Lord exacts justice by way of punishment and reversal. This inaugurates the *restoration of the saints' well-being*. Resolution of the problem not only entails a cessation to the hostilities, but a fresh infusion of well-being and divine blessing. The cosmic battle that is played out on the earthly plane causes the believers to experience the immediacy of the drama which convinces them that they are living in the *Last Days*. The End of Time is close at hand. Yet in the midst of this overwhelming darkness, the *Divine Glory* triumphs. God's glory and victory culminates in the saints' experiencing (or at least being promised) *heavenly beatitude and resurrection*. Relief and bliss are right around the corner. The resurrection need not, however, be physical and literal, but can also simply be metaphorical. What seemed wiped out and dead is now revived and enlivened by the life-giving power of God. A *new world is ushered in*; a new age is soon to dawn which releases the faithful from the shadows and old oppressive constructs. Ultimately, the believer's consolation lies in the fact that God is eternal and transcends time. Thus the faithful will also eventually share in this dimension of *eternal transcendence of time*. The present situation and immediate future can be transcended, risen above, in the Spirit. The apocalypse presents things from God's perspective. *History is re-envisioned* and interpreted according to God's *divine timetable*.

These twenty-four characteristics are almost always operative in apocalyptic literature to various degrees and extents.[3] All of these attributes can be discerned in the Book of Revelation.

THE *BOOK OF JUBILEES* AND THE FEAST OF WEEKS

Feast of Covenants

The *Book of Jubilees*, which predates the Book of Revelation, shares the apocalyptic perspective by rewriting Jewish history from a divine perspective. Stressing God's timetable and the unfolding of history according to the sacredness of time itself, the *Book of Jubilees* is a masterful reconception of Jewish history through the lens of the biblical notion of the jubilee: seven sets of seven years. The author enumerates the events of Israel according to this liturgical chronology. The book itself purports to be written by Moses and is received on the sixteenth of the third month, the Feast of Weeks according to the calendar used in the book and by the Qumran community.[4] For the author of the *Book of Jubilees*, the Feast of Weeks is the most important feast and is of paramount theological significance. The title of the book itself bears this out: "This is The Account of the Division of Days of the Law and the Testimony for Annual Observance according to their Weeks (of years) and their Jubilees throughout all the Years of the World just as the Lord told it to Moses on Mount Sinai."[5] *Jub*. 1:1 specifies the date when Moses received this revelation: the day of Pentecost. The *Book of Jubilees*, written in the mid second century BCE, already associates the giving of the Torah, as well as covenant renewal, with the Feast of Weeks.[6] Why? Because the

---

3. For a good synopsis of contemporaneous Jewish apocalypses see Lupieri, *Apocalypse of John*, 13–25.

4. CD 16:3–4 references the *Book of Jubilees*; see J. Collins, *Apocalypticism*, 24–25.

5. All quotations from the *Book of Jubilees* are from the translation by Wintermute, found in *OTP* vol. 2. See also *Jub*. 1:26–29.

6. See Wintermute, *Book of Jubilees*, 43–44; and VanderKam, *Textual and Historical Studies*, 283–84.

feast itself is heavenly and eternal. "This feast was celebrated in heaven from the day of creation until the days of Noah," and from henceforth (*Jub.* 6:18). Noah was the first man on earth to celebrate the Feast of Weeks. That he and his descendants must keep the feast in perpetuity "is ordained and written in the heavenly tablets" (*Jub.* 6:17).

In fact, according to the *Book of Jubilees*, the Feast of Weeks is the Feast of Covenants. It was celebrated in heaven at the beginning of creation (*Jub.* 1:29; 6:18) and thus included Adam. The Noahic Covenant was sworn by oaths (*shevu'ot*) on the Feast of Shavu'ot, the Feast of Weeks (*Jub.* 6:17–22). The covenant that God made with Abram as found in Gen 17:1–16 is related as having taken place on the same date as the "Feast of the First-fruits of the harvest grain" (*Jub.* 15:1; 14:20). This Abrahamic Covenant instituted the practice of circumcision (*Jub.* 15:11), and those who refuse circumcision are the "sons of Beliar" (*Jub.* 15:33), the offspring of Satan as it were. Finally, the Mosaic Covenant was also made on the Feast of Weeks (*Jub.* 1:1, 6:11–14, 20–22). Therefore, for the author of the *Book of Jubilees*, the Feast of Weeks is the celebration of God's covenantal love and promises; it is when the People of God swear an oath to be faithful to their God.[7]

The theological revisionist of Jewish history also presents major events in the lives of the Patriarchs as occurring on the Feast of Shavu'ot. Abraham experienced God, received a revelation and entered into a covenant with him that very day. Consequently, "Isaac was born on the feast of the firstfruits of the harvest" (*Jub.* 16:13). Isaac and his progeny were thus destined to "become a kingdom of priests and a holy people" (*Jub.* 16:18), a liturgical theme of the Feast of Pentecost.[8] The last feast that Abraham, the father of the faith, celebrates is that of Shavu'ot, during which time he blesses his children and dies that same day (*Jub.* 22:1—23:10). Judah, likewise, is born to Jacob and Leah on this festal occasion (*Jub.* 28:15).[9] Jacob continues to keep the feast and subsequently has a

---

7. This practice of swearing an oath (*shevu'ot*) on Shavu'ot is also found in *Jub.* 29:5–8, where Jacob and Laban swear an oath of truce.

8. The idea of a kingdom of priests comes from the liturgical reading for Pentecost from Exod 19; this will be explored below, especially with regard to its usage in Revelation.

9. For the author, this probably has messianic overtones. The author focuses his book around Moses and thus the revisionist history ends with its protagonist. However, the author was probably aware of the tradition that stated that King David was born and died on Pentecost; see below. Judah's birth on the Feast of Weeks is a foreshadowing of what God will do in coming Jubilees.

vision on Shavu'ot in which God assures him that it is safe to go down to Egypt to see his son Joseph. God will make Israel a great people in Egypt and then bring them back. Finally, God promises Jacob that he will be buried in his homeland (*Jub.* 44:1–6). This was the revelation of the Feast of Harvest—that Jacob's seed would flourish and be restored to its ancestral land. The God of Abraham, Isaac, and Jacob is the God of the Feast of Weeks. In short, almost all of the major events in Israel's history happened on the Feast of Shavu'ot.

The author does not downplay the Law of Moses; to the contrary, he highlights it as God's covenantal revelatory act taking place precisely on this feast. The God of Moses is the same God of Abraham, Isaac, and Jacob. The Torah (Law of Moses) is to be followed and the Passover is to be celebrated (*Jub.* 49:1–23), but it is to be appreciated in the light of the eternal liturgical Feast of Weeks, which predestines the history of Israel. The author has literally re-counted the history of Israel in blocks of forty-nine years, emphasizing the Feast of [Seven] Weeks throughout his midrash, his spiritual commentary. The book concludes with God discoursing with Moses about the Sabbath and its importance as liturgical rest on the seventh day, in light of the Jubilee, seven times seven years. In short, the Jubilee Year is the crowning Sabbath.

The Jubilee Year as Apocalyptic Time

The author then cryptically alludes to the future when Israel shall achieve its final Sabbath rest. The covenant with Moses was struck forty-nine jubilees after the creation of Adam (*Jub.* 50:4).[10] Thus the Mosaic Covenant is delivered to God's people on the Feast of [Seven] Weeks at the square of a jubilee. From the time of the Mosaic Covenant, "jubilees will pass until Israel is purified from all the sin of fornication, and defilement, and uncleanness, and sin and error. And they will dwell in confidence in all the land. And then it will not have any Satan or any evil one. And the land will be purified from that time and forever" (*Jub.* 50:5). In other words, the end will come at some measurement of a jubilee,

---

10. The verse actually states "forty-nine jubilees from the days of Adam until this day and one week and two years." Recall that weeks and years are figurative measurements of seven. How to account for this "extra" week and two years, rather than a perfect forty-nine jubilees? Adam and Eve sinned and were banished from Eden exactly seven years = one week and in the second month counting from the day they were placed in Eden; see *Jub.* 3:15–32. It appears that the Law of Moses was thus given forty-nine jubilees after the sin of Adam. The Torah is a life-giving corrective.

the year in which ancestral land is restored and debts are wiped out. The author expects the conclusion of God's covenant with Israel to take place on Shavu'ot, the Feast of Weeks; then will come the end of history. In bookend fashion, the writer has already opened the *Book of Jubilees* with this panoramic vision of salvation history. God tells Moses, "Write down for yourself all of the matters which I shall make known to you on this mountain: what was in the beginning and what will be at the end, what will happen in all of the divisions of the days which are in the Law and testimony and throughout their weeks of years according to the jubilees forever, until I shall descend and dwell with them in all the ages of eternity" (*Jub.* 1:26). The beginning of time and the end of time are determined by the timetable of the Feast of Weeks, embodied par excellence in the Year of Jubilee.

The book is prophetic, rather than predictive. It presents a prophetic interpretation of the theology of time: time has a liturgical significance marking the cycle of life and the necessity of giving thanks to God for first-fruits. What is sown comes to fruition and is reaped with gratitude to the Creator. During the seven sets of seven years, whatever is lost through indebtedness or held in bondage is to be restituted during the Jubilee Year (Lev 25:8–46). The Year of Jubilee is the year of redemption, the liturgical time of God's salutary action.[11]

Jub. 1:29 picks up on what was hinted at in verse 26 and expounds on this mystery of the restoration at the Jubilee Year, the numerical square of the Feast of Weeks. The verse states: "And the angel of the presence, who went before the camp of Israel, took the tablets of the division of years from the time of the creation of the law and testimony according to their weeks (of years), according to the jubilees, year by year throughout the full number of jubilees, from [the day of creation until] the day of the new creation when the heaven and earth and all of their creatures shall be renewed according to the powers of heaven and according to the whole nature of earth, until the sanctuary of the Lord is created in Jerusalem upon Mount Zion." In short, the apocalyptic new creation will be inaugurated on the Feast of Weeks, the Feast of First-Fruits, when the time is fully ripe. The temple will be permanently re-established so that the fruits of the harvest may be presented before the Lord, and the

---

11. The Gospel of Luke presents Jesus of Nazareth as reading from Isa 61:1–2, a passage that proclaims the year of favor of the Lord, the Jubilee Year. Jesus applies it to his own ministry; Luke 4:16–22.

eternal covenant previously celebrated by Noah, Abraham, Isaac, Jacob, and Moses, and all Israel may be concluded in thanksgiving.

The *Book of Jubilees* is liturgically apocalyptic. History itself is predetermined by God's liturgical cycle, which will be concluded with a final Feast of Harvest. According to the author of Jubilees, of the three great pilgrimage feasts (Passover, Pentecost, and Tabernacles), the first historically to be celebrated was the Feast of Pentecost, when Noah offered up the first-fruits and swore an oath to God. Philo likewise considered the Feast of Weeks to be the most important Jewish celebration.[12] For the *Book of Jubilees*, creation commences with the Feast of Weeks and will be consummated on that Feast, thus establishing a new creation (*Jub.* 1:29; 6:18).[13] The author's apocalyptic agenda is not primarily religio-political, but rather one of liturgical spirituality consisting of purity and fidelity to the covenant. His re-envisioning of Israel's history attempts to solicit a faith response from the reader to trust in God's providential timing. Just as the Feast of Weeks has been celebrated in heaven from the beginning of creation and has marked the salvation history of Israel, the Feast of Weeks will be concluded on earth with the restoration of Israel at the end of time, thereby inaugurating the new creation.

The Book of Jubilees *and Qumran*

The one community that saw itself as the True Israel of God and believed the eschaton was imminent was the Qumran Community. Numerous scholars deem the community to be apocalyptic in nature.[14] The monastic settlement at Qumran dates back to around the time of John Hyrcanus, the nephew of Judas Maccabeus.[15] John became high priest in 135 BCE and many rejected him for his alliances with the Seleucid Empire.[16] The *Book of Jubilees* was composed soon after the Maccabean period, an era fraught with apocalyptic speculation and expectation. The Qumran Community held the book in high esteem; at least fourteen, if not fifteen, copies have been discovered there.[17] The

---

12. See Philo, *Spec.* 2.176.

13. While the author does not explicate this point, creation itself is the first-fruit of God.

14. See J. Collins, *Apocalypticism*, 10, for a list.

15. See Hempel, "Qumran Community."

16. The Seleucid Empire succeeded that of the Macedonian and lasted from 323 to 64 BCE.

17. See J. Collins, *Apocalypticism*, 24.

Damascus Document itself presents a prophetic re-interpretation of history and suggests an imminent end, undoubtedly influenced by the *Book of Jubilees* which it cites.[18]

Significantly, for the believers of the Dead Sea Community, the Feast of Weeks was the most important theologically.[19] On this day they would receive new members and renew their covenant with God, celebrating the Torah.[20] Multiple copies of the apocalyptic books Daniel and *1 Enoch* were found at Qumran. Understandably, the community mused upon the seventy weeks of years.[21] Such a theological reflection upon the Feast of Weeks and an apocalyptic understanding of the Jubilee within Palestine at the beginning of our era, must be factored into the *Sitz im Leben* for the writing of the Book of Revelation.

THE HARVEST FEAST IN CONTEMPORARY APOCALYPTIC LITERATURE

To appreciate the Book of Revelation, one must read it in the historical milieu out of which it arose. The exact date of its writing, whether before 70 CE or circa 96 CE, is inconsequential to my thesis. The second century BCE through the second century CE will serve as the parameter of the contemporary religious thought patterns.

Therapeutae's Liturgical Celebration

The theological reverence for the Feast of Weeks was not limited to the Qumran Community. The Therapeutae of Egypt likewise celebrated the Feast of Weeks with great solemnity and considered it their primary feast.[22] Philo points out how in their Pentecost celebration they dressed in white robes and imitated the Song of Miriam, sung at the Exodus.[23] The Therapeutae's eschatological views, however, are unknown. Nevertheless, they were a counter-cultural community, dedicated to creating a new so-

---

18. See ibid., 10 and 24–25. CD 16:3–4 is a quotation from the title of the *Book of Jubilees*.
19. See Noack, "Day of Pentecost."
20. See Potin, *Fête juive de la Pentecôte*, 124; VanderKam, "Shavu'ot," 2:872; and Weinfeld, "Pentecost as Festival," 12.
21. See Collins, *Apocalypticism*, 11, 14.
22. See Philo, *Contempl.* 65–90; and Potin, *Fête juive de la Pentecôte*, 126–28.
23. See Philo, *Contempl.* 90; and Hayward, "Therapeutae."

ciety centered upon study of the Torah. They liturgically connected their commemoration of Pentecost with the Exodus and appropriate Torah readings and commentary. Unfortunately, not much is known about this community that separated itself from the world for the sake of spiritual revelation.

1 Enoch

One of the most influential apocalyptic writings is *1 Enoch*. It must be noted, however, that *1 Enoch* is silent with regard to the Feast of Weeks despite its calendrical sections. Nevertheless, in the *Apocalypse of Weeks* (*1 En.* 93:1–10; 91:11–17), written shortly before 167 BCE, the completion of the seventh week figures prominently as the time of sevenfold divine instruction (*1 En.* 93:10).[24] The metaphor of harvest as judgment does appear, however, in the section known as the *Book of Parables* (*1 En.* 31–71), written between the second and first century BCE.[25] The advancing Parthian troops, sent as God's judgment against sinful Israel, trample upon the land as upon a threshing floor (*1 En.* 56:6); although no liturgical timetable is given for this harvesting.[26]

4 Ezra and the Feast of Weeks

The work that closely approximates the writing of the Book of Revelation is *4 Ezra*, also known as 2 Esdras. This text was originally a Jewish apocalypse, subsequently Christianized by way of a preface (chs. 1–2) and epilogue (chs. 15–16). It dates from the late first century CE.[27] J. Van Goudoever places the central body of *4 Ezra* shortly after 70 CE.[28] He reconstructs the underlying calendar employed in the text and concludes, "For the writer of the Ezra Apocalypse, the Feast of Weeks has an 'eschatological' feature. He 'commemorates' at this feast that the twelve tribes shall be gathered together in the future (after the twelve parts of the 'world-age' have passed)."[29] Here he is following the Syriac version of

---

24. For the dating see VanderKam, *Enoch*, 63, and his comments page 70.

25. For the dating see Isaac, *1 Enoch*, 6–7.

26. The early-second-century-CE apocalyptic work *2 Baruch* also utilizes the harvest allusion for universal judgment; see *2 Bar.* 22:5; 70:2.

27. See Metzger, *4 Ezra*, 517–24. Also see Stone (*Fourth Ezra*, 9–10) who concludes that it was written during the reign of Emperor Domitian, 81–96 CE.

28. See Goudoever, *Biblical Calendars*, 95.

29. Ibid., 102, see also his comments on page 103.

4 Ezra 14. In the beginning of the Jewish corpus, the eschatological event is compared to a harvest and the time of threshing (*4 Ezra* 4:26–39). The canonical precedents for this metaphor are several, but the text in Joel 4:9–17 is particularly poignant. What the author of *4 Ezra* does, howbeit, is link the final judgment and harvest with the Feast of Weeks.

The Gospels and the Harvest

In the Christian Scriptures, other parallels to harvest imagery may be found. John the Baptist is reported as saying about the one who will execute the coming retribution: "His winnowing fork is in his hand, and he will clear his threshing floor and will gather his wheat into the granary; but the chaff he will burn with unquenchable fire" (Matt 3:12).[30] This message must have been core to the Baptist's preaching because it is retained in the Lukan account (Luke 3:17), which provides other dicta of the prophet not found in the Matthean text. The specification of the wheat harvest delimits this metaphor to the Feast of Weeks, when this particular grain was gathered and offered as the first-fruits. It appears that John the Baptist likewise associated the final harvest of the world with the Feast of Shavu'ot. Several scholars have linked him with the Qumran Community.[31]

Jesus of Nazareth is also depicted as delivering an eschatological parable employing images of sowing and reaping (Matt 13:24–30, 36–43). The parable is clearly explained: "The harvest is the end of the world" (Matt 13:39, my translation). The parable utilizes the scene of storing wheat in the barn (Matt 13:30). Was there an underlying Pentecost motif at work here, causing the association? I do not believe one can argue conclusively, however, it is quite plausible. There is yet another parable that betrays a connection between the Feast of Weeks and the end of time.

> As it was in the days of Noah, so it will be at the coming of the Son of Man. For in the days before the flood, people were eating and drinking, marrying, and giving in marriage, up to the day Noah entered the ark; and they knew nothing about what would

---

30. All quotations from the Christian Bible are from the New Revised Standard Version unless noted otherwise.

31. For a good survey and bibliography of the scholarship regarding John the Baptist and his connection with the Qumran Community (pro and con) see Webb, "John the Baptist."

> happen until the flood came and took them all away. That is how it will be at the coming of the Son of Man. Two men will be in the field; one will be taken and the other left. Two women will be grinding with a hand mill; one will be taken and the other left. (Matt 24:37–41 NIV)

Why this odd juxtaposition between Noah and men in the fields and women at grindstones? The *Book of Jubilees* attributes the first Feast of Weeks, the offering of first-fruits, to Noah, who celebrated it after coming out of the ark (*Jub.* 6:1–18). We have already seen how before the first century CE the Feast of First-Fruits had ripened into an eschatological event recalling God's first judgment of the earth. With this liturgical context in mind, the women at the grindstones milling the grain and the men in the fields—presumably harvesting—makes perfect sense. The whole of the parable deals with the eschatological meaning of the Feast of Weeks. One will be chosen as a first-fruit offering acceptable to the Lord, another will not.[32] Purposely making a play on words, history will grind to a halt at the Harvest Feast.

Harvest was a metaphor employed by Jesus on several occasions.[33] He said, "The harvest is plentiful, but the laborers are few; therefore ask the Lord of the harvest to send out laborers into his harvest" (Matt 9:37; Luke 10:2). Luke's setting for this dictum is more clearly eschatological than Matthew's is. Luke correlates it to the end-time judgment (see Luke 10:1–16). The text in Matthew is more elusive because the verse is followed by the commissioning of the Twelve who are sent out (Matt 9:37—10:36), albeit the selection ends with dire predictions of judgment. The Gospel of John likewise presents Jesus using the harvest motif for eternal salvation (see John 4:34–38). The passage at first appears veiled. But upon closer reading one realizes the import of Jesus' saying, "My food is to do the will of him who sent me and to complete his work. Do you not say, 'Four months more, then comes the harvest?'" (John 4:34–35). Seed was sown in the winter, the last month of the year before the spring rains. "Four months later" places one in the third month of the year, namely Sivan, when the Feast of Weeks is celebrated. In other words, the final harvest is the completion of God's work. This is not just

---

32. I believe I am the first to make this connection.

33. In Luke 12:16–21 harvest figures in a parable about death and personal judgment. In Matt 24:31 the Son of Man sends his angels to gather his chosen ones from the ends of the earth.

a mere matter of missionizing, of evangelization; it is the weighty matter of the eschatological harvest, the completion of God's creation.

While Jesus' utilization of the harvest analogy is always eschatological in thrust, it is not necessarily all the time colored by an apocalyptic understanding of the Feast of Weeks, but rather reflects a generalized theological tradition based out of the prophets, especially Joel. Notwithstanding, the parable relating to Noah and the Flood and the men in the fields, and the women grinding grain, is best understood as emerging out of the Jewish correlation of the Feast of Weeks with Noah and the Final Harvest as found in the *Book of Jubilees*. The saying in John 4:34–35 regarding the four months and the harvest is also aptly interpreted as referring to the Harvest Feast.

Is there a rabbinic tradition as well that associates the end-time judgment with the Feast of Pentecost? The Mishnah, written around the second century CE, reports that Rabbi Johanan b. Suri (who flourished between 120–140 CE) taught that the judgment of the unrighteous will last from Passover to Pentecost, at which time all will be consummated.[34] The saying does not explain the reasoning behind this belief, but one can safely wonder whether the Feast of Weeks is not at least partially at play here. Pentecost is the conclusion of the Passover mystery, because its very dating is determined by that of Passover.

THE FEAST OF WEEKS AS A FEAST OF REVELATION

But the Feast of Weeks is also a celebration of God's revelation. God makes a covenant with Noah on that day and gives the theophanic sign of the rainbow (*Jub.* 6:15–17). God appears to Abram in a vision as El Shaddai on the Feast of Weeks, and reveals his covenantal promise to him and all his seed (*Jub.* 15:1–10). Note the agricultural metaphor at work here. The birth of Isaac providentially falls on the Feast of First-Fruits, after God appeared to Abraham and Sarah (*Jub.* 16:12–13); Isaac is their first-born son—the fruit of their old age. On the Feast of Shavu'ot, just before Abraham dies, he prophesies over his grandson Jacob, blessing all his seed (*Jub.* 22:1–24). Later in life, Jacob experiences a divine theophany on the liturgical commemoration, and God predicts the return of Jacob's progeny from the land of Egypt, making them a great people (*Jub.* 44:4–6). And finally, Moses receives the revelation on Mount Sinai

---

34. *M. Ed.* 2.10; also see Goudoever, *Biblical Calendars*, 183–84.

on the Feast of Weeks (*Jub.* 1:1; 6:11–14). For the author of the *Book of Jubilees*, Pentecost is the liturgical time of God's self-revelation.[35]

This is reflected in Luke's recollection of the early Christian community as well (see Acts 2:1–41). Not only do the disciples re-experience the tongues of fire of Sinai,[36] but Peter is also inspired to give an eschatological interpretation of Joel's prophecy regarding the Great Day of the Lord; he then exegetes passages from the Psalms in a messianic sense. For the early Christian community, Pentecost is a day of christological revelation.

The same correspondence between divine revelation and the Feast of Weeks is also true for other authors. According to the Syriac and Ethiopic versions of *4 Ezra* 14:48, the prophet finishes writing down his revelations on "the seventh year of the sixth week, five thousand years and three months and twelve days after creation."[37] I am indebted to Goudoever for pointing out the significance of this calculation, namely the liturgical time. He concludes, "Both in the Book of Jubilees and the Ezra Apocalypse, the Feast of Weeks plays an important role as a feast of Revelation, viz. new Revelation."[38]

Another apocalyptic work of interest is *2 Enoch*. The dating of this work is fraught with difficulties because the earliest manuscripts date from the fourteenth century CE. However, the work contains no quotations or obvious borrowings from the Christian canon and exhibits several affinities with writings found at Qumran. Consequently, F. I. Andersen dates it to the late first century CE.[39] Goudoever claims that it is contemporaneous with *4 Ezra* and *2 Baruch*.[40] Significantly, in the Second Revision of *2 Enoch*, Enoch is born and ascends to heaven on the sixth of Sivan (*2 En.* 68:1–3), which is the date for the Feast of Weeks according to rabbinic Judaism.[41] The exact date when Pentecost should be celebrated was highly debated among various Jewish groups such as

---

35. I had independently come to this conclusion, and was happy to discover that Goudoever's analysis (see *Biblical Calendars*, 106) confirms my own.

36. See Weinfeld, "Pentecost as Festival," 13–18; and Goudoever, *Biblical Calendars*, 228–35.

37. See Metzger, *4 Ezra*, 555, note "p"; or 2 Esd 14:48 NRSV, note "x."

38. Goudoever, *Biblical Calendars*, 106.

39. See Andersen, *2 Enoch*, 91–97.

40. See Goudoever, *Biblical Calendars*, 112.

41. Also see ibid., 115.

the Qumran Community, the Pharisees, Sadducees, and Samaritans, all depending upon their interpretations of the biblical injunction found in Lev 23:9–16.[42]

It is noteworthy that in the Slavonic Revision of *2 Enoch*, Enoch finishes writing down all of his revelations on the fifteenth of the third month, which is the eve of the Feast of Weeks according to the calendar in the *Book of Jubilees*. Whatever the case may be, the writer of *2 Enoch* and possible redactors all wish to firmly associate Enoch and his revelations with the Feast of Pentecost, whether by means of his birth and translation into heaven, or the date on which he finished composing his works. After analyzing these apocalypses, Goudoever avers,

> The Feast of Weeks is ... the feast of Revelation. In the *Book of Jubilees* the contents of this book are revealed to Moses at the Feast of Weeks. The fourth Ezra (a second Moses) wrote down 94 books on III/3, thus within the 50 days; the Feast of Weeks is in that book an apocalyptic feast of Revelation. In the Enoch Apocalypse, Enoch wrote down the 360 books on the Feast of Weeks.[43]

I concur. In fact, the author of *2 Enoch* appears to teach that the fullness of apocalyptic revelation is achieved on the Feast of Weeks when Enoch completes his inspired production of 360 books.[44]

That the Feast of Shavu'ot is imbued with a revelatory character is also attested in Pseudo-Philo's *Biblical Antiquities*, written in the first century CE. The work is thoroughly Jewish, originally written in Hebrew, and of Palestinian provenance.[45] At the time of this feast, Joshua receives a prophetic dream reviewing Israel's history (*Ps.-Philo* 23:1–13). Thus by the late first century CE, there is a substantial tradition relating the Feast of Weeks as a Feast of Divine Revelation with apocalyptic import. Given such a theological mindset, the Book of Revelation must be analyzed within this context. Prophetic revelation should occur on the Feast of Pentecost or be intrinsically connected to it.

---

42. See Jacobs, "Shavuot," 422–23 for a brief overview, as well as Goudoever, *Biblical Calendars*, 18–29.

43. Goudoever, *Biblical Calendars*, 114, see also 140.

44. See Potin, *Fête juive de la Pentecôte*, 126.

45. See Harrington, *Pseudo-Philo*, 297–302; and Goudoever, *Biblical Calendars*, 116. Potin (*Fête juive de la Pentecôte*, 126) dates it to soon after 70 CE.

3

The Liturgical Meanings of the Feast of Weeks and the Lectionary

THE BIBLICAL BACKGROUND

First-Fruits

THE FEAST OF WEEKS at first was primarily an agricultural celebration, giving God thanks for the first-fruits of the harvest (Exod 34:22).[1] Thus it was also known as the Day or "Feast of the First-Fruits" (Exod 23:16; Num 28:26), or simply the "Feast of Harvest" (Exod 23:16). The rituals for the Feast of Weeks are set forth in Lev 23:9–22 and Num 28:26–31. As such, it is a day of sacred assembly, one of the three pilgrimage festivals. Because of the reckoning, the Feast of [Seven] Weeks always follows fifty days after Passover and also came to be known as Pentecost (Tob 2:1; 2 Macc 12:32). Already within the Deuteronomic Code, the Feast of Weeks is linked with the Exodus event. After stipulating how the Feast is to be commemorated and enjoining the Israelites to take care of the stranger, orphan, and widow, the passage concludes: "Remember that you were a slave in Egypt, and diligently observe these statutes" (Deut 16:12).

The text in Deut 26:1–11 expounds even further upon the offering of first-fruits which would apply to the Feast of Harvest. The person offering the gifts must say, "Today I declare to the LORD your God that I have come into the land that the LORD swore to our ancestors to give us" (Deut 26:3). What is significant here is the verb "swore" from which comes the noun *shevu'ot*, a close homonym of Shavu'ot. The person

---

1. Besides Potin's magnum opus, see Kretschmar, "Himmelfarht und Pfingsten." This article extensively studies the origins of the Feast of Pentecost and integral themes.

offering the first-fruits is then to continue with the following poignant synopsis of Jewish history.

> A wandering Aramean was my ancestor; he went down into Egypt and lived there as an alien, few in number, and there he became a great nation, mighty and populous. When the Egyptians treated us harshly and afflicted us, by imposing hard labor on us, we cried to the LORD, the God of our ancestors; the LORD heard our voice and saw our affliction, our toil, and our oppression. The LORD brought us out of Egypt with a mighty hand and an outstretched arm, with a terrifying display of power, and with signs and wonders, and he brought us into this place and gave us this land, a land flowing with milk and honey. So now I bring the first of the fruit of the ground that you, O LORD, have given me. (Deut 26:5–10)

Demonstrably, the offering of first-fruits is integrally joined with Israel's salvation history. Central to this motif is the Exodus story. This text eventually became an important segment of the Haggadah for the Passover Meal.[2]

Given the contextualization of first-fruits within the book of Deuteronomy, soon after the Babylonian Exile the celebration of the Feast of Weeks was situated within the Exodus motif.[3] Because the Harvest Festival falls in the third month, and in Exod 19:1 one can misread the text as, "In the third month, after they had departed Egypt, on that day the children of Israel came to the wilderness of Sinai,"[4] the author of the *Book of Jubilees* places Moses' reception of the Torah on the Feast of Shavu'ot. This correlation is also made because at Mount Sinai Israel made covenantal oaths (*shevu'ot*) with God. As seen above, for the Qumran Community, Pentecost is an annual renewal of covenant with God and a celebration of the giving of the Torah.

---

2. Unfortunately, I have not been able to determine the earliest date of its usage in this regard.

3. For an excellent study of the Feast of Weeks see Potin, *Fête juive de la Pentecôte*. To my knowledge, Potin does not make the correlation between the Feast of First-Fruits and Deut 26:1–11, stipulating how they are to be offered.

4. The verse actually means three months after leaving Egypt, hence roughly eighty-four days after Passover, not forty-nine; however, see Noack ("Day of Pentecost," 84–85) who argues the third month meant including the counting of the first month of Nisan, and thus Siwan is obtained. Also see Goudoever, *Biblical Calendars*, 57.

King Asa and Covenant Renewal

This connection between the Feast of Weeks and covenant renewal probably dates back even further in history, namely to 896 BCE. The chronicler records King Asa as calling an assembly in the third month and renewing the covenant with God (2 Chr 15:1–15). Several scholars see this as relating to the Feast of Weeks.[5] A few points need to be drawn out from this passage. King Asa is responding to an apocalyptic prophecy delivered by Azariah. Speaking of Israel's apostasy, the prophet declares,

> For a long time Israel was without the true God, and without a teaching priest, and without law; but when in their distress they turned to the LORD, the God of Israel, and sought him, he was found by them. In those times it was not safe for anyone to go or come, for great disturbances afflicted all the inhabitants of the lands. They were broken in pieces, nation against nation and city against city, for God troubled them with every sort of distress. (2 Chr 15:3–6)

The focus is upon Israel's separating itself from the life-giving Law (Torah), as well as lacking proper instruction from the priests.

There are consequences for these actions on the socio-political level, even to an international extent. God's "afflicting" Israel conjures up memories of how God afflicted Egypt. Therefore, "When Asa heard these words, the prophecy of Azariah son of Oded, he took courage, and put away the abominable idols from all the land of Judah and Benjamin and from the towns that he had taken in the hill country of Ephraim" (15:8). This nationwide renunciation of idolatry was then ratified by a solemn assembly in Jerusalem in the third month. Given that Shavu'ot was the only pilgrimage feast in the third month, it seems most likely that this is when the "great numbers of Israelites" had assembled in Jerusalem. Significantly the text states that they sacrificed to God "seven hundred oxen and seven thousand sheep" (15:11). Note the multiples of seven, which would coincide with the seventh week celebration after Passover. "They entered into a covenant to seek the Lord, the God of their ancestors, with all their heart and with all their soul. . . . They took an oath to the Lord with a loud voice, and with shouting, and with trumpets, and with horns. All Judah rejoiced over the oath, for they had sworn it with all their heart" (15:12, 14–15). This solemn making of *shevu'ot* most

---

5. See VanderKam, "Shavuot," 871; Goudoever, *Biblical Calendars*, 53; and Goulder, *Evangelists' Calendar*, 194.

probably was a renewal of the Mosaic Covenant sworn on the Feast of Shavu'ot. For this reason and others, Jean Potin and Michael Goulder believe that Pentecost was the Festival of Law-Giving before the Common Era.[6] Furthermore, Goulder claims "There is considerable evidence that a part of the ritual of Pentecost in O.T. times was the hewing down of a tree, as the symbol of the destruction of heathen worship." He cites as one example this instance of Asa hewing down the terebinths.[7]

EXAMPLES IN JEWISH LITERATURE

We have already seen that the *Book of Jubilees* and Qumran community reckon this feast as one of covenant renewal. Another witness to such a theological tradition is Pseudo-Philo's *Biblical Antiquities*, written in the first century CE. While not specifying the date as the Feast of Weeks, Moses receives the Torah on this day according to the Pharisaic dating system (*Ps.-Philo* 11:1–3). Later, Joshua summons all Israel at Shiloh and renews the covenant of the Law on the date of the Feast of Weeks according to the Qumran Community (*Ps.-Philo* 23:2).[8] Was the author trying to account for both traditions regarding the dating of Shavu'ot? Regardless, the Feast of Pentecost is one of covenant making and renewal.

Unfortunately, the earliest source of rabbinic thought in general is the Mishnah, dating from the second century CE. The tradition that the Torah was given on Pentecost goes back at least to Rabbi ben Chalaphta who thrived around 150 CE.[9] But the Babylonian Talmud recounts an early debate between R. Akibah (late first century CE) and R. Jose the Galilean as to whether the Torah was given on the Feast of Weeks (*m. Yoma* 4b).[10] Obviously, rabbis were aware of such a tradition. Around 270 CE, Rabbi El'azar affirms, "All were agreed regarding the Feast of Weeks that we likewise need the 'for us', because it is the day on which the Torah was given."[11] This quote is illustrative, for not only does Rabbi El'azar reflect an earlier rabbinic tradition, but he also cites a discussion of Deut 26:3 ("swore to our ancestors that he would give for us") and

---

6. See Goulder, *Evangelists' Calendar*, 212.

7. See ibid., 194.

8. See Goudoever, *Biblical Calendars*, 119, 140; and Potin, *Fête juive de la Pentecôte*, 126.

9. See S. *'Olam Rab.* 5; and Potin, *Fête juive de la Pentecôte*, 131, 300.

10. See also Noack, "Day of Pentecost," 81.

11. *M. Pesaḥ.* 68b.

verse 6 ("The Egyptians ill-treated us") in regard to the Feast of Harvest. This association between the giving of the Torah and the Feast of Weeks becomes standard in rabbinic thought, and the present Jewish liturgy of Shavu'ot reflects this theological understanding.

Because of the Qumran community's emphasis on the Feast of Weeks as the renewal of the Mosaic Covenant and subsequent rabbinic statements found in the Mishnah, Potin attests: "already at the beginning of our era, the rabbinic tradition had attached to this Feast the recollection of the events at Sinai."[12] Moshe Weinfeld also argues that before the destruction of the temple, the Feast of First-Fruits is a Festival of Torah-Giving.[13] Later in his seminal book Potin affirms: "One must conclude that Pentecost had been considered as a Feast of the Covenant (Alliance) by the second, and perhaps even by the third century BC."[14] Accepting this to be the case, does the liturgy itself for the Feast of Harvest shed light on this theological tradition?

ANCIENT JEWISH LITURGICAL READINGS

Synagogue Readings

Before one can analyze any correlation between the Feast of Weeks and liturgical readings, the question of how one can specify and date such passages used during public worship must be addressed. Given that the Book of Revelation was written sometime in the first century CE, this delimits our timeframe. Jacob Mann was the first to attempt a reconstruction of synagogue readings before the destruction of the temple.[15] The bases for such an attempt are several, but quotations from the Christian Scriptures will contextualize the matter at hand. The Gospel of Luke portrays Jesus in the synagogue, being handed a scroll of the prophet Isaiah which he then opens and expounds upon (Luke 4:16–28). Luke likewise records James as stating, "From early generations Moses has had in every city those who preach him, for he is read every Sabbath in the synagogues" (Acts 15:21 RSV). In fact, Paul and his companions used this Jewish practice as a platform for evangelization. "After the reading of the law and the prophets, the officials of the synagogue sent them a message, saying, 'Brothers, if you have any word of exhortation for the people, give

---

12. Potin, *Fête juive de la Pentecôte*, 131.
13. See Weinfeld, "Pentecost as Festival."
14. Potin, *Fête juive de la Pentecôte*, 301.
15. See Mann, *The Bible as Read and Preached in the Old Synagogue*.

it'" (Acts 13:15; cf. v. 27). The custom of weekly reading from the Torah is attested to by Josephus as well as Philo.[16] Thus by the first century CE, liturgical readings in the synagogue from the Law and Prophets was normative. Charles Perrot argues that there is archaeological evidence for this practice as well.[17]

Nevertheless, can one verify which readings were assigned to which days? Michael Fishbane declares, "A continuous cycle of Torah readings (with many specifically designated ones) was in practice in the Land of Israel near the beginning of our era—possibly already in the first century C.E."[18] Scholars debate, however, if there was an annual cycle of readings or a triennial lectionary operative in Palestine.[19] Perhaps, in fact, instead of there being a cycle lasting three and a half years, a seven year cycle actually was employed.[20] Whatever the case maybe, the choice of Torah readings (sedarim) and passages from the Prophets (haphtarot) most probably varied from region to region.[21] Naomi Cohen has cogently demonstrated that regarding the Sabbath readings from the seventeenth of Tammuz to Yom Kippur, Philo (ca. 20 BCE—50 CE) used the same cycle of readings from the Prophets as found in the *Pesikta de Rav Kahana*, dating from the fifth century CE to the seventh at the latest.[22] Since the prophetic readings for regular Sabbaths as found in the fifth century CE were already in force by the first century, then surely the prescribed readings for major Feast Days were established as well.

Feast Day Lectionary

So where does this leave us in our investigation? Before Cohen's research, Joseph Heinemann pointed out the dangers in presuming there was a fixed lectionary cycle of Sabbath readings; however, he acknowledges that the readings for the major Feast Days were fixed by the first

---

16. See Josephus, *C. Ap.* 2:18 section 175; and Philo, *Somn.* 2:127.
17. See Perrot, "Reading of the Bible," 137, 150.
18. See Fishbane, *Haftarot*, xxi.
19. For an overview of the whole situation see ibid., xix–xxx; and Wacholder, "Prolegomenon." Also see Goulder, *Evangelists' Calendar*, 20.
20. See Fishbane, *Haftarot*, xii; and Na'eh, "Sidrei Keri'at ha-Torah."
21. Once again see Fishbane, *Haftarot*, xix–xxx; Perrot, "Reading of the Bible," 139; and Wacholder, "Prolegomenon."
22. See Cohen, *Philo's Scriptures*, 55–69.

century CE.²³ After a thoroughgoing and stringent analysis, Ben Wacholder even states, "It is possible to argue that the custom of reciting the related Pentateuchal passages on the festivals dates back to the time of Ezra."²⁴ Perrot, stressing the cultic aspects of the Feast Days, likewise dates the liturgical practices and lections back to temple worship, and thus does not "question the great antiquity of the festal readings."²⁵ Hence while scholars rightly debate whether one can accurately delimit which readings occurred on which Sabbath, all are agreed that the liturgical readings for the Feasts were well-established before the destruction of the temple in 70 CE.²⁶ This, of course, has momentous bearing on the investigation at hand: the liturgical readings for the Feast of Shavu'ot.

The Jewish Liturgical Texts for Pentecost

The earliest stipulation of liturgical readings for the various Feast Days is found in the Mishnah, dating from the second century CE. Woefully there is no tractate in the Mishnah devoted to Shavu'ot. Perhaps the Feast became too controversial due to its eschatological mantle and apocalyptic aura; thus no rabbinic agreement could be reached on certain matters.

The Torah reading for the Feast of Weeks according to *m. Meg.* 3.5 was to be Deut 16:9–12. The Toseftah (*t. Meg.* 3.5) and the Jerusalem Talmud (*y. Meg.* 74b) cite Exod 19–20 as the appropriate Pentecost readings.²⁷ The Babylonian Talmud (*b. Meg.* 31ab) appears to compromise. The Feast of Harvest is here accorded two days of liturgical observance; on the first day one reads Exod 19:1—20:23 and on the second Deut 16:9–12.²⁸ The Mishnah also recollects an early seder that bears on our exegesis of the Book of Revelation. R. Simeon ben Eleazar (140–165 CE)

---

23. See Heinemann, "Triennial Lectionary Cycle," 46. Morris also expresses caution in his book, *New Testament and Jewish Lectionaries*.

24. See Wacholder, "Prolegomenon," xv.

25. See Perrot, "Reading of the Bible," 146.

26. For scholars who have tried to excavate probable cycles of readings see Goulder, *Evangelists' Calendar*; Finch, *Synagogue Lectionary*; and Guilding, *Fourth Gospel and Jewish Worship*.

27. See Potin, *Fête juive de la Pentecôte*, 141.

28. See Goulder, *Evangelists' Calendar*, 63.

The Liturgical Meanings of the Feast of Weeks and the Lectionary 29

states that Ezra commanded that Lev 26 be read before Pentecost (*m. Meg.* 31b).[29]

Obviously one could rightly question how fixed indeed were the liturgical readings for the Feast of Weeks. For my analysis, however, the weight of the argument will lie in that these readings are in fact influential upon the composition of the Book of Revelation. These will be explored at length in the following section, but suffice it to point out here that the parallels with Exod 19 have been noted by many commentators without their being aware of the liturgical background to its usage.

The lections from the Prophets, haphtarot, are also specified. *B. Meg.* 31a advises Hab 3, which figured among some rabbis whereas others held to Ezek 1–2. According to *m. Meg.* 4.10, R. Judah (about 150 CE) defended the reading of Ezek 1 as haphtarah for Pentecost, whereas R. Juda ha-Nasi wished to exclude it from recitation in the synagogue because the passage was too susceptible to fantastic interpretations and mystical flights of fancy. *T. Meg.* 4.34 takes the middle ground and states the chariot passage may be read in Hebrew, but no translation should be provided. On the other hand, *m. Hag.* 2.1 allows a commentary by an approved wise elder.[30] An alternate reading was that of Zeph 3.[31] Anyone casually acquainted with the Book of Revelation will immediately see the correlation between Ezek 1–2 and Rev 4–5. The texts from Habakkuk and Zephaniah also come into play in the Apocalypse.

The liturgical selections from the Writings are far more fluid. These are also called haphtarot. According to *Sop.* 18.3 (which has Palestinian influences), one sings Ps 29 for Pentecost. Yet in *Sop.* 29, Pss 1 and 119 are also listed.[32] *B. Meg.* 31a has Ps 68 for the Feast of Weeks.[33] The influence of the Psalms on the Book of Revelation has been noted by others and will be explored below, as well as the other readings from the Ketuvim, the Writings.

Because Ruth speaks of the harvest, it too is read at Pentecost (*m. Šabb.* 15c).[34] Goulder argues that the Book of Tobit was read between

---

29. See Potin, *Fête juive de la Pentecôte*, 139.
30. See ibid., 189–91.
31. See Perrot, "Reading of the Bible," 147.
32. See Goulder, *Evangelists' Calendar*, 212.
33. See Goudoever, *Biblical Calendars*, 201.
34. See Goodman, *Shavuot Anthology*, 2; Perrot, "Reading of the Bible," 147; Jacobs, "Shavuot"; as well as Goulder, *Evangelists' Calendar*, 184–86.

Passover and Pentecost.[35] In fact, Tob 2:1 states that the drama that is to follow began to unfold on the very Feast of Pentecost. The Book of Tobit then would be a spiritual story leading up to the Feast of Weeks. Goudoever likewise makes parallels between Tobit and Pentecost.[36] For those not readily familiar with Tobit, the book closes with an apocalyptic vision of the New Jerusalem as a bejeweled city. Besides Tobit being preserved in the Septuagint, four Aramaic fragments and one in Hebrew were found at Qumran, evincing that some Palestinian Jews utilized Tobit as well.[37]

Given this brief introduction to the lectionary readings for the Feast of Weeks, one might be amazed that the Book of Daniel does not factor in. As Gregory K. Beale underscores, any proper interpretation of the Book of Revelation must take into account the integral influence of Daniel.[38] This seeming shortcoming in the Danielic liturgical influence is happily remedied when looking at the Targum of Hab 3, which expounds on Daniel's four kingdoms. But most significantly, Goulder convincingly demonstrates how the Aramaic sections of Daniel were a Pentecost midrash built on Gen 41 which is read on the tenth sidra in his reconstruction of the annual Nisan cycle of readings, just on or about the Feast of Pentecost.[39] Whether due to the Habakkuk Targum or the Aramaic Pentecost midrash on Daniel, the Book of Daniel does in fact play a role in the liturgical literature for the Feast of Harvest.

Needless to say, one will never know definitively if all of these liturgical readings obtained for the Feast of Weeks in the first century CE; the earliest testimony is from the second century. Nevertheless, as other scholars have claimed, the liturgical readings for the major feast days were long fixed. The remarkable correspondence between these readings and the Book of Revelation makes it seem quite probable that they were in fact used during the first century. As in most cases with historical studies, one must be satisfied with probability rather than modern certitude.[40]

35. See Goulder, *Evangelists' Calendar*, 132–33.
36. See Goudoever, *Biblical Calendars*, 87–88.
37. See Fitzmyer, "Tobit."
38. See Beale, *Book of Revelation*, 137–60 *et passim*; and his "Influence of Daniel."
39. See Goulder, *Evangelists' Calendar*, 192.
40. In my analysis, quotations from and references to the Talmud, Targums, Mishnah and other rabbinic literature are merely by way of showing correspondence, not arguing

In the subsequent chapter, I will evince that the various liturgical readings used for the Feast of Weeks within the synagogues deeply impacted the apocalyptic vision of the Book of Revelation. The Apocalypse, filled with liturgical symbolism, is itself a liturgical midrash on the Feast of Weeks understood as God's consummation of the ancient and eternal covenant resulting in the Final Harvest.

---

for a non-extant earlier work that impacted Revelation. Nevertheless, the circumstantial evidence is quite compelling, pointing to an oral tradition and liturgical practice that pre-dates the composition of Revelation. The role of oral tradition should not be discountenanced when Judaism (as well as early Christianity) placed so much importance in it. Cohen's work clearly shows the congruence between Philo's use of the haphtarot for general Sabbath readings and that found in the *Pesikta de Rav Kahana*. The lectionary for major feast days must have been established long before the first century CE.

4

Revelation as an Apocalyptic Pentecost Commentary

THE COMPOSITION OF THE BOOK OF REVELATION

No matter what one's views are regarding the authorship of the Book of Revelation, my theory regarding the liturgical context out of which the corpus arose still obtains. Whether there was one writer, or one writer and a final redactor, or an underlying author in the sense of authoritative source whose ideas were subsequently given stylus and style, and perhaps even then later edited and prefaced—whatever the case may be—at the initial stages the liturgical context of the Feast of Weeks deeply formed the conception and articulation of the Apocalypse. For the sake of simplicity and clarity in writing style, in this treatise I will employ the term "author" to refer to the inspired mind of the original composer, without barring, however, the psychological mindset of any disciple who might have later edited his revered teacher's work. Despite the plethora of theories regarding the identity of the author, there is universal agreement that the author had a Palestinian Jewish background.[1]

Accepting this as fact, we are now able to investigate the Palestinian liturgical tradition that would have influenced the writing of the Book of Revelation. The book itself has long been recognized as a free-flowing collage of verses and one-word references to well-known texts found in the Hebrew Scriptures, the Tanakh (Torah, Nevi'im, Ketuvim = Law, Prophets, Writings). Tabulations on the exact number of citations from the Tanakh vary anywhere from 150 to 635 depending upon the applied

---

1. For the various theories see Collins, *Crisis and Catharsis*, 25–53; Beale, *Book of Revelation*, 34–36; Ford, *Revelation*, 28–37; and Aune, *Revelation*, xlvii–lvi (while it was published in three volumes, Aune's commentary has consecutive pagination, therefore citations to it do not specify volume number).

criteria.[2] Most often the author of Revelation only employs phrases at best, or freely makes verbal connections relying upon allusion and familiarity with the Law, Prophets, and Writings. A further question concerns whether the author used the Hebrew text or a Greek translation. R. H. Charles argues that he followed the Hebrew version because the Greek of the Book of Revelation significantly departs from the LXX.[3] Other scholars have followed suit, marshalling evidence, and the majority of commentators concur.[4]

APPRECIATING THE BEAUTY OF THE APOCALYPSE

Because the Book of Revelation is such a rich tapestry of scriptural threads, many imbued with apocalyptic hues, it is difficult to know where and how to approach the subject matter. As with any tapestry, one needs to step back to appreciate the grandeur of the effect the artist wished to achieve. Close-up inspection might reveal intricacies in the weaving technique and the colors employed to create a particular subtlety, but then the overall impression of the work is lost from one's point of view. To tease out the theological threads running throughout the Book of Revelation, I will take a varied approach, sometimes going chapter by chapter while drawing attention to other panels in the tapestry, and on other occasions I will focus more so on the underlying theme rather than the depiction in a sequential passage. And like any tapestry, sometimes the same theological theme is portrayed yet again from a different angle or with a varying twist.

The Exodus Epic

Central to the Feast of Weeks is the Exodus motif. The story line is basic, yet filled with archetypal intrigue and excitement. God's chosen people are persecuted by an evil tyrant, bent on their subjugation to his heathen realm. Hearing the cries of his beloved children, God intervenes by raising up a charismatic leader endowed with the mantle of God's power and authority. Conflict naturally ensues, but the people are miraculously

2. See Beale, *Book of Revelation*, 76–99; Boring, *Revelation*, 27–28; and Thompson, *The Apocalypse and Semitic Syntax*.

3. See Charles, *Revelation of St. John*, 1:lxvi–lxxxii.

4. For various catalogues of commentators see Aune, *Revelation*, clix–ccvii; Beale, *Book of Revelation*, 100–107; Witherington, *Revelation*, 11–12; and Thompson, *The Apocalypse and Semitic Syntax*.

delivered and God enters into a formal covenant with his newly chosen people who promise to worship him accordingly. God promises them bounty and security in his kingdom, with unfading eternal glory. The people then give God thanks for the first-fruits they now enjoy.

The plot itself clearly runs throughout the Book of Revelation and needs no detailed substantiation. Notwithstanding, the liturgical texts behind the scene merit inspection. According to *y. Meg.* 74b and the Palestinian Toseftah (*t. Meg.* 4.5), the prescribed reading for the Feast of Weeks is Exod 19–20. *B. Meg.* 31ab likewise honors such a tradition while also advocating Deut 16:9–12. Demonstrably, by the second century CE, the Exodus sedarim had been canonized for this feast. In fact, a quote from this text appears far earlier in the *Book of Jubilees* written in the second century BCE. "Isaac was born on the feast of the first-fruits of the harvest. And Abraham circumcised his son on the eighth day. He was the first one circumcised according to the covenant which was ordained forever" (*Jub.* 16:13–14). This covenant itself, made with Abram, was compacted on the Feast of Weeks, and decreed the need for circumcision (*Jub.* 15:1–16). The author of *Jubilees* explicates the blessing of Isaac's seed, that one would be particularly consecrated to the Lord, namely Levi, "so that he might become a kingdom of priests and a holy people" (*Jub.* 16:18). The author of *Jubilees* purposefully situates this excerpt from Exod 19:6 ("But you shall be for me a priestly kingdom and a holy nation") within his exposition concerning Isaac's being born on the Feast of Weeks.

As mentioned previously, Noah was the first to celebrate this feast and in the passage referring to this, the author of the *Book of Jubilees* weaves in the covenant with God made at Sinai and alludes to Exod 19:1.[5] This resonance between Exod 19:6 and the Feast of Weeks as presented in the *Book of Jubilees* is strong evidence that the pericope from Exod 19–20 was already in force as a Pentecost liturgical text by the second century BCE.

The author of the Book of Revelation likewise makes use of Exod 19:6 as well as other parts of chapters 19–20. The apocalyptic drama and corpus of the book commences in Rev 4. Because some scholars view chapters 1–3 as a prologue to the vision, I will treat the appearance of Exod 19:6 in Rev 1:6 further below. I myself am of this opinion. Nevertheless, for those commentators who treat Revelation

---

5. See *Jub.* 6:11 and note Wintermute's column of biblical parallels.

as a continuously flowing work by one author, the citation from Exod 19:6 so soon within the book corroborates the centrality of the liturgical aspect of the Feast of Weeks as the thematic viewpoint running throughout the whole book.

REVELATION 4–5: THE THRONE VISION

For the ease of the reader, pertinent passages from the Book of Revelation and the Hebrew Scriptures are supplied below.[6]

> After this I looked, and there in heaven a door stood open! And the first voice, which I had heard speaking to me like a trumpet, said, "Come up here, and I will show you what must take place after this." At once I was in the spirit, and there in heaven stood a throne, with one seated on the throne! And the one seated there looks like jasper and carnelian, and around the throne is a rainbow that looks like an emerald. Around the throne are twenty-four thrones, and seated on the thrones are twenty-four elders, dressed in white robes, with golden crowns on their heads. Coming from the throne are flashes of lightning, and rumblings and peals of thunder, and in front of the throne burn seven flaming torches, which are the seven spirits of God; and in front of the throne there is something like a sea of glass, like crystal.
>
> Around the throne, and on each side of the throne, are four living creatures, full of eyes in front and behind: the first living creature like a lion, the second living creature like an ox, the third living creature with a face like a human face, and the fourth living creature like a flying eagle. And the four living creatures, each of them with six wings, are full of eyes all around and inside. Day and night without ceasing they sing,
>
>> "Holy, holy, holy
>> the Lord God the Almighty,
>> who was and is and is to come."
>
> And whenever the living creatures give glory and honor and thanks to the one who is seated on the throne, who lives forever and ever, the twenty-four elders fall before the one who is seated on the throne and worship the one who lives forever and ever; they cast their crowns before the throne, singing,
>
>> "You are worthy, our Lord and God,
>> to receive glory and honor and power,
>> for you created all things,

---

6. A list of the liturgical readings for the Feast of Weeks and a synopsis is supplied in Appendix A. As noted before, quotations are from the NRSV.

and by your will they existed
and were created."

Then I saw in the right hand of the one seated on the throne a scroll written on the inside and on the back, sealed with seven seals; and I saw a mighty angel proclaiming with a loud voice, "Who is worthy to open the scroll and break its seals?" And no one in heaven or on earth or under the earth was able to open the scroll or to look into it. And I began to weep bitterly because no one was found worthy to open the scroll or to look into it. Then one of the elders said to me, "Do not weep. See, the Lion of the tribe of Judah, the Root of David, has conquered, so that he can open the scroll and its seven seals."

Then I saw between the throne and the four living creatures and among the elders a Lamb standing as if it had been slaughtered, having seven horns and seven eyes, which are the seven spirits of God sent out into all the earth. He went and took the scroll from the right hand of the one who was seated on the throne. When he had taken the scroll, the four living creatures and the twenty-four elders fell before the Lamb, each holding a harp and golden bowls full in incense, which are the prayers of the saints. They sing a new song:

> "You are worthy to take the scroll
> and to open its seals,
> for you were slaughtered and by
> your blood you ransomed for God
> saints from every tribe and
> language and people and nation;
> you have made them to be a
> kingdom and priests
> serving our God,
> and they will reign on earth."

Then I looked, and I heard the voice of many angels surrounding the throne and the living creatures and the elders; they numbered myriads of myriads and thousands of thousands, singing with full voice,

> "Worthy is the Lamb that was slaughtered
> to receive power and wealth and
> wisdom and might
> and honor and glory and blessing!"

Then I heard every creature in heaven and on earth and under the earth and in the sea, and all that is in them, singing,

> "To the one seated on the throne
> and to the Lamb

> be blessing and honor and glory and might
> forever and ever!"
> And the four living creatures said "Amen!" And the elders fell down and worshiped. (Rev 4:1—5:14)

The prophetic vision in chapter 4 ushers the seer into the heavenly throne room where he sees what the prophet Ezekiel had previously envisioned (see Appendix A). To refresh the reader's memory, for every major Jewish Feast there is a selection from the Torah, collectively known as the sedarim, followed by an appropriate passage from a Prophet—these texts are known as the haphtarot. Readings are also chosen from the Writings, and these are also referred to as haphtarot.

This heavenly scene is steeped in the merkabah tradition, the chariot throne of YHWH.[7] The textual precedent is Ezek 1, the haphtarah for the Feast of Weeks; this will be studied shortly. The apocalyptic corpus in the Book of Revelation opens with a re-envisioning of the prophetic pericope for the Feast of Pentecost. Embedded within this mystical midrash on Ezek 1 is a citation from Exod 19:6, from the Pentecost sedarim. The fullness of the throne vision means that the redeemed of God will serve the One as originally intended when Israel entered into a covenant with the Holy One. God stated the purpose of the Sinai event right up front: "you shall be for me a priestly kingdom and a holy nation" (Exod 19:6). The Lamb brings God's initial vision to fulfillment.

But before the author of the Book of Revelation even depicted the reminiscence from Ezek 1—the designated prophetic reading for the Feast of Weeks, and incorporated Exod 19—the appropriate text from the Law of Moses, he opened the throne scene with an excerpt from Dan 2:28—"what is to come." The book of Daniel is ranked among the Writings in the Tanakh, and has been argued as a Pentecost midrash. Not only is Dan 2:28 reflected in Rev 4:1, other segments from Daniel are found in Rev 4–5 as well. Strikingly, an allusion to Ruth 4:17–22, the appropriate scroll reading for the Harvest Feast, is found in Rev 5:5. Likewise Rev 5:13 might echo Ps 150:6, one of the possible Psalms for Pentecost. In short, the opening vision presented in chapters 4–5 is grounded in all three sets of liturgical lections for the Feast of Weeks. The chances of this occurring unintentionally in the space of a mere twenty-five verses are miniscule. Consequently, this passage is an apocalyptic midrash on the eschatological meaning of the readings for the Feast of Weeks.

7. See Afzal, "Wheels of Time"; and Davila, "Dead Sea Scrolls."

The Book of Daniel and the Feast of Weeks

Now that an overview of the "first panel of the tapestry" has been provided, let's tease out the significance of the threads from Daniel. The Aramaic sections of the Book of Daniel are considered by Goulder as a Pentecost midrash. In his book *The Evangelists' Calendar: A Lectionary Explanation of the Development of Scripture*, Goulder convincingly argues the case by comparing the sedarim for the Sabbaths leading up to Pentecost with the thematic development in Daniel.[8] Goulder is premising his argument upon a reconstruction of the sedarim according to a Nisan cycle. Such a precise cataloguing of readings is hard to prove definitively, but his hypothetical lectionary produces insightful results. Even if one were to discount Goulder's assessment in assigning Daniel to a Pentecost lection, irrefutable proof is at hand to warrant Daniel's inclusion in the Feast of Weeks motif. *B. Meg.* 31a specifies Hab 3 as the haphtarah reading, because the chapter is a reflection on the Exodus theophany. For our present purposes, the point to be made is that the Targum of Habakkuk contains a very interesting spin. According to the Targum numeration, 3:17 reads:

> For the kingdom of Babel will not endure;
> It will not exercise its power over Israel;
> The kings of the Medes will be killed;
> The powerful rulers of Greece will not prosper;
> The Romans will be destroyed;
> They will not gather the remaining bits of Jerusalem.[9]

This section of the Targum is a commentary on Israel's political situation and is dependent upon the four kingdoms mentioned in Daniel.[10] The Habakkuk haphtarah for the Feast of Weeks has been merged with the Daniel Pentecost midrash.

But when was this Targum written? Potin concludes, "Perhaps, then, one can admit that it had been composed when Jerusalem could possess the conviction that she would not be destroyed again, either before 70, or before 135, in this atmosphere of eschatological fever where the people could only hope to receive their salvation by the personal intervention

---

8. See Goulder, *Evangelists' Calendar*, 191–204.
9. See Potin, *Fête juive de la Pentecôte*, 169, my translation.
10. See ibid., 181.

of God." [11] No matter the precise dating, this Targum would either be antecedent to or at least contemporaneous with the writing of the Book of Revelation. Demonstrably there was a theological tradition already at work linking Daniel's apocalypse to the Habakkuk reading for the Feast of Weeks.

Habakkuk and Daniel

But is there earlier evidence connecting Daniel to Habakkuk? Quite curiously there is—and I believe I am the first to solve a puzzling occurrence in Dan 14:33–39—part of a work classified separately by Protestants in the Apocrypha as *Bel and the Dragon*. This story appears in both the Septuagint and the Theodotion version and dates before the second century BCE. Scholars argue for an underlying Aramaic version.[12] As previously stated, the Aramaic sections of Daniel are a midrash for the Feast of Weeks, a feast that denounces idol worship. This is the very theme of Dan 14. In this particular story, which commences at verse 23, there was a great dragon in Babylon that people reverenced, treating this idol as a living god. Not only does Daniel refuse to recognize the Dragon as a living god, but he even destroys the Dragon. Subsequently, the protagonist is thrown into a den containing seven ravenous lions. Note the number seven. In verses 33–39, the prophet Habakkuk miraculously appears into the story line. How to account for this?

According to the Babylonian Talmudic tradition, Hab 3 was to be read at the Feast of Weeks, celebrating the harvest. Thus in haggadic fashion Dan 14:33–34 relates, "Now the prophet Habakkuk was in Judea; he had made a stew and had broken bread into a bowl, and was going into the field to take it to the reapers." The setting is the preparation of a meal during the harvest.[13] Next Habakkuk is literally seized by the Spirit and inserted into Daniel's situation in Babylon where he is beset by the seven lions in a pit. They are wishing to devour him as a meal and Daniel himself has been without food for six days. Habakkuk miraculously appears and gives Daniel his meal, a meal meant to be eaten at the harvest. Habakkuk shouted, "'Take the food that God has sent you.' Daniel said, 'You have remembered me, O God; you have not forsaken those who

---

11. See ibid., 182.

12. See Moore, *Daniel, Esther, and Jeremiah*, 23–34 and 117–49.

13. Tob 2:1 also draws attention to the meal at Pentecost. *Jubilees* likewise reflects a celebratory meal at the Feast of Weeks (*Jub.* 22:4; 29:7).

love you'" (14:37–38). Daniel was condemned to death because he resisted idolatry and managed to destroy the Dragon of Babylon. On the seventh day, Daniel was delivered.

The liturgical celebration can be none other than the Harvest Feast, seven weeks after Passover. Daniel is surrounded by seven beasts for seven days, miraculously preserved and sustained by God, finally to be released on the seventh day. Therefore, by the second century BCE, a Jewish tradition existed linking the prophet Daniel with Habakkuk in the setting of the harvest season in the liturgical context of fighting idolatry. This analysis corroborates Goulder's claim that the Aramaic sections of Daniel are written with the Feast of Weeks in mind. The parallels between Dan 14/Bel and the Book of Revelation are interesting, but these will need to be articulated later.

In conclusion, the Targum of Hab 3 reflects usage of the Book of Daniel in connection with the Feast of Weeks; Goulder has presented a strong case for the Aramaic sections of Daniel being a Pentecost midrash; and the text from Dan 14 evinces the linkage between Habakkuk and Daniel in the context of the harvest. Consequently, the Book of Daniel will be treated throughout the rest of this analysis as part of the liturgical literature employed in connection with the Feast of Weeks.

CHAPTERS 4–5: ANALYSIS

The One on the Throne

The first scriptural parallel to Rev 4 comes from Daniel. In fact, the phrase "what is to come" in Rev 4:1 comes directly from Dan 2:28 "There is a God in heaven who reveals mysteries, and he has disclosed to King Nebuchadnezzar what will happen at the end of days." Beale has unpacked the significance of this quote as well as the influence of Daniel upon Revelation.[14] It is beyond the purview of this treatise to provide an extensive exegetical analysis, especially where the work of other scholars will suffice.[15] The goal is simply to substantiate a correspondence between the liturgical readings for the Feast of Weeks as well as associated practices and how these impacted the composition of the Book of Revelation. The Book of Revelation itself is a pastiche of biblical phrases and images. Rev 4:2 has woven within itself a snippet from Ezek

---

14. See Beale, *Book of Revelation*, 158–59, 314–19; and his *Use of Daniel*.
15. I recommend the works of Beale and Aune.

1:3 and 2:2, namely, "the Spirit possessed me" (subsequently followed by a throne vision).[16] Because Rev 4's dependence upon Ezek 1–2 is so well established, I will not belabor the point. However, Ezekiel's situation has several elements in common with that of the author of Revelation.

In Ezekiel's time, he was in exile. At this period in history, the God of Israel was seen primarily as a territorial god with a temple in which he dwelt. With the destruction of the temple and the removal of God's people to an alien pagan land in which they are subjected to idolatry, how can the true God of Israel be present with them? Ezekiel re-envisions the Glory of YHWH at Sinai who had delivered his people from an evil pagan oppressor. Just as Jacob and his sons left Israel and were in bondage and God delivered them back to their ancestral homeland, so too God would once again deliver Israel from its captivity. The God of Israel is theophanically present in Babylon. A renewed covenant would be established (Ezek 36:24–30). Centuries later, in the midst of the Roman Empire, believers in the True God are once again oppressed by idolaters, but "the One sitting upon the throne" judges the nations. He will vindicate his true followers. Just as Ezekiel re-envisioned the theophany at Sinai and the Exodus tradition, so too the author of Revelation re-envisions the tradition and prophetically applies it to his own situation.[17]

The author cites Dan 4:34 to bring out an important point concerning God: He is the One "who lives forever and ever" (Rev 4:9, 10). "I, Nebuchadnezzar, lifted my eyes to heaven, and my reason returned to me.

> I blessed the Most High,
> and praised and honored the one
> who lives forever.
> For his sovereignty is an
> everlasting sovereignty,
> and his kingdom endures from
> generation to generation." (Dan 4:34)

---

16. For the use of Ezekiel see Vanhoye, "L'utilisation du livre d'Ezéchiel"; Ruiz, *Ezekiel in the Apocalypse*; as well as Vogelgesang, "Interpretation of Ezekiel."

17. In saying this, I am not ruling out any authenticity of an actual vision, but presumably the Seer was a spiritual man and had prayerfully meditated on matters at hand, opening himself up to divine revelation.

Nations rise and fall but the One upon the heavenly throne endures forever. He is the Self-same and will be true to his eternal promises and covenant.

The Sealed Scroll

Dan 12:4 and 9 also figure in with the sealed scroll. "But you, Daniel, keep the words secret and the book sealed until the time of the end" (Dan 12:4). Most commentators are agreed that minimally the scroll represents God's covenantal promise.[18] In fact, it might be the fullness of the Torah that only God's anointed one can properly decipher in its totality. If the scroll is indeed the Torah, this fits in nicely with the Feast of Weeks, the liturgical celebration of God's giving the Torah. As an apocalyptic vision, images in the Book of Revelation (as in other apocalyptic literature) are polyvalent. The scroll might be the Torah as well as a will, a testament. Exod 24:1–8 presents Moses as sealing the Book of the Covenant with the blood of the covenant. A sacrificial offering ratifies the Torah. In Rev 5:5 one of the twenty-four elders declares, "See, the Lion of the tribe of Judah, the Root of David, has conquered, so that he can open the scroll and its seven seals." The imagery immediately shifts to that of "a Lamb standing as if it had been slaughtered" (Rev 5:6).

The Lion and the Lamb are the same character. The imagery is multifaceted. While not a direct quote from Ruth 4:17–22, the common stock phrase is "the root of Jesse" as found in Isa 11:10 and implied in 11:1; there is no biblical phrase "Root of David." It is as if by dissonance that the author of Revelation forces the listener to think of Jesse. The metaphor is not lost of course, but the echo of Jesse causes one to think of Ruth 4:17 referring to Obed who "was the father of David's father, Jesse." In fact, Jesse's name appears three times at the end of Ruth. The scroll of Ruth was read during the Feast of First-Fruits because the drama itself unfolds during the harvest. Furthermore, according to rabbinic tradition, David was born on Pentecost and died on Pentecost.[19] In other words, the Feast of Weeks not only commemorates God's covenant in the giving of the Torah but also God's covenantal promise to David.

---

18. For various interpretations of the Scroll see Caird, *Revelation*, 70–73; as well as Beale, *Book of Revelation*, 339–47.

19. See *Midr. Ruth* 3.2 and 21.12a, as well as Goodman, *Shavuot Anthology*, 2.

It is the descendant of David, the Messiah, who can completely unseal the locked mysteries of God's covenant.[20]

In this regard Sir 45:25 is illuminating: "a covenant was established with David son of Jesse of the tribe of Judah." This is the only text that links David as the Root of Jesse with the tribe of Judah, and it is specifically in the context of covenant. The scroll in the right hand of the One on the throne is the Book of the Covenant in the rich and broad sense of the term. The scroll is the book containing every covenant God has ever decreed. For the author of *Jubilees*, the Feast of Weeks commemorates all of these covenants. It would not be surprising if the author of Revelation holds a similar view.

The Sevenfold Nature of the Lamb

The Lamb alone can open the seven-sealed scroll. For the author of Revelation the Lamb is the embodiment of the fullness of God's sevenfold grace. The Lamb had "seven horns and seven eyes, which are the sevenfold Spirit of God sent out into all the earth" (Rev 5:6 NIV, *following the alternate reading*). The last clause is from Zech 4:10, but the sevenfold nature of the Lamb is to be found elsewhere. Here we have four sets of seven: the seals, the horns, the eyes, and the [seven] spirits (compare NABR). This fourfold pattern of sevens is found in Lev 26, an ancient seder read in preparation for the Feast of Weeks that influences Rev 6. In fact, for the Feast of Weeks, seven unblemished lambs must be offered up (Lev 23:18). The other feasts on which seven lambs are sacrificed are the new moon (Num 28:11), Passover (Num 28:19), New Year (Num 29:2), and the Day of Atonement (Num 29:8). The sevenfold nature of the Lamb in Revelation points to his sacrificial role, but it must be more than just this because he has seven horns and seven eyes; in other words each horn might be covered with seven eyes. The Greek word *kai* presumably carries the underlying Hebrew or Aramaic *we* that can also mean "with." If this is indeed the case, the seven horns covered with seven eyes means that there were forty-nine eyes. Recall that each of the six wings of the four living creatures is covered with eyes. If the Lamb possesses forty-nine eyes this would recall the seven weeks of seven days, the Feast of Weeks.[21] The Lamb is endowed with the fullness

---

20. For various Jewish views of Messiah, see Collins, *Scepter and Star*.

21. Such a multiplication is within the spirit of the Targums. The Palestinian Targum on Ezek 1 calculates that each creature had four faces, and each face had four faces, thus

of power (the horns) and the fullness of insight (the eyes). In short, he is replete with the fullness of the sevenfold Spirit of God.[22]

This sevenfold Spirit of God reflects the text from Isa 11:2, which mentions that upon the promised Davidic king rests the spirit of YHWH, the spirit of wisdom, the spirit of insight, the spirit of counsel, the spirit of power, the spirit of knowledge, the spirit of the fear of the Lord, and the spirit of piety.[23] Significantly, this passage from Isaiah is read on the Sabbath immediately preceding the Feast of Weeks.[24] In other words, the text about the sevenfold Spirit was the previous day's reading. Here the author of Revelation is once again inspired by the Jewish liturgy.

The Spirit-endowed Messianic Ruler is "from the stock of Jesse" (Isa 11:1) and is called "the root of Jesse" (Isa 11:10). This phraseology has influenced the author of Revelation's designation of the one who can open the scroll. The author calls him "the Root of David" (Rev 5:5) and subsequently portrays him as a Lamb (Rev 5:7). He is worthy to open the scroll because he has been sacrificed and with his blood bought people for God from every nation "to be a kingdom and priests serving our God, and they will reign on earth" (Rev 5:10). Here the author crafts a heavenly hymn quoting from Exod 19:6, a verse from the sedarim for Pentecost. The purpose of the Lamb's mission is foremost to create a liturgical people who worthily praise God. The Lamb's victory over evil is secondary. According to the author of the Book of Revelation, redemption does not *primarily* deal with appeasement of God's wrath brought about by sin, i.e., does not address justification by faith; rather

---

each creature really had sixteen faces, and there were four creatures thus totaling sixty-four faces. Furthermore, each face had four wings, meaning each creature had sixty-four wings and all four creatures together had two hundred and fifty-six wings! See Potin, *Fête juive de la Pentecôte*, 184. The Lamb having seven horns covered with seven eyes is not beyond the apocalyptic spirit.

22. The sevenfold character of the Lamb is also reflected in the sevenfold accolade accorded him: "Worthy is the Lamb that was slaughtered to receive power and wealth and wisdom and might and honor and glory and blessing!" (Rev 5:12). It should likewise be noted that sevenfold doxologies were a favorite of the Qumran Community; see Ford, *Revelation*, 119.

23. This is following the LXX reading; however, one must keep in mind that the LXX was a translation done by Jews for Jews based on Hebrew manuscripts (long before Jesus was ever born). Many times the LXX is closer to the version of the Tanakh as found at Qumran than the thirteenth-century Masoretic text.

24. See Goulder, *Evangelists' Calendar*, 181.

the redemption wrought by the Lamb is a liturgical act that creates a liturgical People of God.

Not all sacrifices of a lamb in the temple were for sin. In fact, a lamb was sacrificed with the waving of the sheaf, which marked the count down for the Feast of Weeks. This sacrifice of the lamb was one of thanksgiving and sanctification.

> When you enter the land that I am giving you and you reap its harvest, you shall bring the sheaf of the first fruits of your harvest to the priest. He shall raise the sheaf before the LORD, that you may find acceptance; on the day after the sabbath the priest shall raise it. On the day when you raise the sheaf, you shall offer a lamb a year old, without blemish, as a burnt offering to the LORD. . . . it is a statute forever throughout your generations in all your settlements. And from the day after the sabbath, from the day on which you bring the sheaf of the elevation offering, you shall count off seven weeks. (Lev 23:10–12, 14c–15)

The Book of Revelation is replete with temple imagery and metaphors drawn from Jewish worship. The offering of the lamb at the waving of the sheaf sanctifies the future offerings of the first-fruits and grants God's blessing for a prosperous harvest. The notion of penalty for sin is not operative in this sacrifice of the lamb. Consequently, a sin offering is not necessarily envisaged in the Rev 5:9–10. The quote in verse 10 regarding the "line of kings and priests" is from the Torah reading for the Feast of Weeks. Interpreting the offering of the Lamb in such a context is justifiable.

The Lamb sanctifies the first-fruits and thus sanctifies the people who are offered to God so that they can be a holy priesthood, a sanctified people. I believe this is the primary imagery; any paschal atonement for sin would be secondary—as will be evident in the Book of Revelation, the focus is not on atonement for sin. Only the Lamb is worthy to open the seven-sealed Scroll because he possesses the sevenfold Spirit. This sevenfold Spirit is the Holy Spirit who rests upon "the Root of Jesse," the messianic figure (Isa 11:1–2ff). The Lamb is depicted as possessing the sevenfold Spirit in its fullness and has completed the liturgical action of self-sacrifice. He offers himself up as a first fruit to the Lord. The Messianic Lamb alone has been completely true to the covenant of God and thus he alone can open the sealed Scroll of the Covenant.

The heavenly hymn acknowledging the Lamb is followed by a scene of the immense throng surrounding the throne. Here the author quotes Dan 7:10, "ten thousand times ten thousand of them." Subsequently in Rev 5:13 he presents their giving praise to God in a manner reminiscent of Ps 150:6, "Let everything that breathes praise the LORD," one of the Psalms used during the Feast of Pentecost. "Then I heard every creature in heaven and on earth and under the earth and in the sea, and all that is in them, singing . . ." (Rev 5:13).[25]

The heavenly throng is a priestly people; they chant God's praises and render him worship. The throne vision, as noted earlier, reflects the Sinai event. The author has quoted not only Exod 19:6 in this vision but 19:16 as well: "there were peals of thunder and flashes of lightning" (my translation). The same imagery and wording is found in Rev 4:5, except here the mountain is replaced by God's throne.

Thus, the author of Revelation has skillfully woven texts from every liturgical reading for the Feast of Weeks (from the Law, Prophets, and Writings) into the vision depicted in chapters 4–5. Such a marked concentration of lectionary readings within a mere twenty-five verses betrays the author's theological and liturgical mindset as well as provides the key to unlocking the rest of the book.

The Twenty-four Elders

For centuries the twenty-four elders mentioned in Rev 4:4, 10, and 5:8, 14 have puzzled commentators. Various explanations counted them as the twelve patriarchs plus the twelve Christian apostles, or the twenty-four priestly classes found in 1 Chr 24:1–9. Another explanation obtains without necessarily ruling out these theories. At the Feast of Weeks, Jews from all over Israel were to bring their offerings of first-fruits to Jerusalem. Israel was divided into twenty-four districts, each with its own liturgical elders. The local meeting was called a *ma'amad* and this consisted of reading appropriate liturgical texts for the feast day. Perrot states that this custom was in existence long before the fall of the temple in 70 CE.[26]

---

25. The Jerusalem Bible makes the parallel reference in the column.
26. See Perrot, "Reading of the Bible," 150.

According to the Talmud, the first-fruits (*bikkurim*) are of seven kinds: wheat, barley, grapes, figs, pomegranates, olive oil, and date honey (*Bik.* 1:1–3). They were to be brought to the Feast of Weeks.

> How were the *bikkurim* taken up [to Jerusalem]? All [the inhabitants of] the cities that constituted the *ma'amad* [district] assembled in the city of the *ma'amad* and spent the night in the open place thereof without entering any of the houses. Early in the morning the officer [head of the *ma'amad*] said, "let us arise and go up to Zion, into the house of the Lord our God." Those who lived near [Jerusalem] brought fresh figs and grapes, but those from a distance brought dried figs and raisins [for fresh fruit would rot on the way]. An ox with horns bedecked with gold and with an olive crown on its head led the way. (*Bik.* 1–8)

Each of the twenty-four districts had a liturgical elder who represented the people of the *ma'amad* and who led a procession to the temple for offering the first-fruits. How he was dressed is not explained in the Talmud, however, the ox pulling the cart was covered with gold and wore a crown of olive branches. Interestingly, the twenty-four elders in Revelation are dressed in white robes (presumably liturgical) and are wearing golden crowns. Perhaps their attire reflects a liturgical tradition for the Feast of Weeks besides attributes of glory, honor, power, and closeness to divinity.[27]

Significantly, the twenty-four elders praise God and say,

> "You are worthy, our Lord and God,
> to receive glory and honor and power,
> for you created all things,
> and by your will they were created
> and have their being." (Rev 4:11 NIV)

Note that they praise God because of the fruits of his creation, and not for any other reason. When they sing the new hymn proclaiming the worthiness of the Lamb it is because he has purchased people for God from "every race, language, people and nation" (Rev 5:9 NIV). The wording implies that he has brought people as first-fruits to God. Likewise, when the 144,000 are first introduced in Rev 7, the twenty-four elders along with the heavenly host praise God on account of the 144,000, who in Rev 14:4 are explicitly called those who "have been redeemed from

---

27. For a discussion of crown imagery in Revelation see Stevenson, "Conceptual Background."

humankind as first fruits for God and the Lamb." The elders had just been mentioned in the previous verse. Finally, the twenty-four elders are accorded a rather long doxology in Rev 11:16–18, which appears to presage the final harvest of the world. In *Midr. Tanḥ.* on Exod 29, which predates the fifth century Babylonian Talmud, one reads: "The Holy One, blessed be He, will in the future cause the elders of Israel to stand as in a threshing floor, and he will sit at the head of them all as president, and they will judge the nations of the world."[28] The elders in Revelation do the same.

The liturgical action of the twenty-four elders in the Book of Revelation is always in the context of the first fruits and the harvest. The term "elder" best applies to the leader of the *ma'amad* rather than a priest or prophet or angel or apostle. Nevertheless, given that the whole People of God are to be a lineage of royal priests, the association with the twenty-four priestly classes winsomely applies. The elder is the representative of the priestly people who celebrate the first-fruits of God's harvest.

The mention of "elders" in Rev 4–5 can be accounted for in another fashion correlating with the Feast of Weeks. Immediately after Exod 19:6, in which the "line of kings and priests" is mentioned, comes in the next verse, "So Moses came, summoned the elders of the people ..." The elders played a role in the first Sinai theophany, and hence "elders" play a role here as well. They are connected by the Feast of Weeks lection. Likewise, in Rev 4–5, the elders are mentioned seven times.

Not only are chapters 4–5 a theological tapestry of every type of lectionary reading (Law, Prophets, and Writings) for the Feast of Weeks, but the liturgical practices surrounding Pentecost (sevenfold Lamb and twenty-four elders) are interwoven, as well as the theological festal themes (Torah scroll, first-fruits, and priestly people).

CHAPTERS 6 AND 8: ANALYSIS

The First Four Seals and Lev 26

Not surprisingly, chapter 6 builds off of the same liturgical theme. Verses 1–8 contain the famous scene of the "four horsemen."

> Then I saw the Lamb open one of the seven seals, and I heard one
> of the four living creatures call out, as with a voice of thunder,

---

28. As quoted by Aune, *Revelation*, 290; without, however, making the connection I do.

"Come!" I looked, and there was a white horse! Its rider had a bow; a crown was given to him, and he came out conquering and to conquer.

When he opened the second seal, I heard the second living creature call out, "Come!" And out came another horse, bright red; its rider was permitted to take peace from the earth, so that people would slaughter one another; and he was given a great sword.

When he opened the third seal, I heard the third living creature call out, "Come!" I looked, and there was a black horse! Its rider held a pair of scales in his hand, and I heard what seemed to be a voice in the midst of the four living creatures saying, "A quart of wheat for a day's pay, but do not damage the olive oil and the wine!"

When he opened the fourth seal, I heard the voice of the fourth living creature call out, "Come!" I looked and there was a pale green horse! Its rider's name was Death, and Hades followed with him; they were given authority over a fourth of the earth, to kill with sword, famine, and pestilence, and by the wild animals of the earth.

Scholars have rightly noted the echoing of Lev 26 in this passage, particularly because it mentions God's sevenfold punishment four times. However, what has escaped the scholar and commentator is that Lev 26:14–46 was customarily read right before the Feast of Weeks. According to Rabbi Simeon ben Eleazar (140–165 CE) this was commanded by Ezra himself. Why? Resh Lakish (200–275 CE) explains, "Yea Pentecost is also a New Year's Day, as we have learned in the Tract Rosh Hashana, on Pentecost is decided in Heaven about the fruit of the [next] year" (*Meg.* 31b). Thus rabbis in the mid second century CE and afterwards understood Pentecost as a time of new beginnings; it was like a New Year.

Presuming this tradition was ancient, since R. Simeon b. Eleazar ascribes it to Ezra, the author of the Book of Revelation very well could have interpreted Pentecost as the beginning of a new time period. The Feast of Weeks thus ushers in a new age, the eschatological Year of the Lord, when everything that the Lord has sown comes to fruition. Consequently, when the Lamb, the Root of David, breaks the first four seals he inaugurates the beginning of the Messianic Era, the Day of the Lord, which commences with chastisement in the hopes of converting sinners before the Final Judgment.

The curses of Lev 26 are in light of broken covenantal promises on the part of Israel. God says, "Then will I remember my covenant with Jacob; I will remember also my covenant with Isaac and also my covenant with Abraham, and I will remember the land. For the land shall be deserted by them, and enjoy its sabbath years by lying desolate without them, while they shall make amends for their iniquity, because they dared to spurn my ordinances, and they abhorred by statutes. . . . but I will remember in their favor the covenant with their ancestors whom I brought out of the land of Egypt" (Lev 26:42-43, 45). Given that Lev 26 was read immediately before the Feast of Weeks, this excerpt has particular interest. The idea of God's various covenants is stressed, a theme found in the *Book of Jubilees*—all related as being sealed on the Feast of Weeks. Furthermore, the land of Israel is to have its Sabbaths (note the plural). This idea evokes the notion of the Jubilee Year, seven times seven years, in which the land is given a Sabbath's rest. One can see why Lev 26 was considered an appropriate liturgical reading for the Feast of Harvest. The chapter opens with various blessings that come with obedience, followed by various curses if the people abandoned God. God in turn would abandon the Israelites so that their land would not produce its fruits and so that the land of Israel itself would observe the Sabbath even if its people would not.

The sevenfold punishments in Lev 26 are as follows: famine (vv. 18–20); wild ravenous beasts (21–22); pestilence, sword, and rationing (23–26); and destructive warfare and exile (27–33). These four sevenfold inflictions have inspired the vision in Rev 6:1-8. The author summarizes the four horses and their riders in this fashion: "They were given authority over a fourth of the earth, to kill with sword, famine, and pestilence, and by the wild animals of the earth" (Rev 6:8). The order and expansion in Revelation is different than that found in Leviticus, but the underlying motif is remarkably recognizable. Thus, just like chapters 4–5, the opening of chapter 6 is also demonstrably inspired by the liturgical readings for the Feast of Weeks. The opening of the first four seals reflects the Torah text immediately preceding Pentecost. The author is following the lectionary cycle to the tee.

The Fifth Seal

The fifth seal deals with the souls of those who have been killed for witnessing to the word of God.

> When he opened the fifth seal, I saw under the altar the souls of those who had been slaughtered for the word of God and for the testimony they had given; they cried out with a loud voice, "Sovereign Lord, holy and true, how long will it be before you judge and avenge our blood on the inhabitants of the earth?" They were each given a white robe and told to rest a little longer, until the number would be complete both of their fellow servants and of their brothers and sisters, who were soon to be killed as they themselves had been killed. (Rev 6:9–11)

The souls are underneath the altar, waiting for God to pass judgment against their persecutors. While the text is not explicit, given the liturgical theme running throughout chapters 4–6 one can reasonably see these souls as the first-fruits of martyrdom placed before God's altar. "They were each given a white robe and told to rest a little longer, until the number would be complete both of their fellow servants and of their brothers and sisters, who were soon to be killed as they themselves had been killed" (Rev 6:11). The white robe could be a liturgical garment. Both the Therapeutae and covenanters at Qumran celebrated the Feast of Pentecost, robed in white. The idea of the roll being completed could echo another facet of Pentecost. The Jews also referred to the Feast of Weeks as *Atzereth*, a term meaning "solemn assembly," but also "completion" or "conclusion." Such is the explanation found in *Roš Haš.* 1:2. The Feast of Weeks completed the Passover mystery. Understandably, in an apocalyptic sense the Feast of Weeks was interpreted as the final solemn assembly that concluded Israel's history.

The Sixth Seal

The sixth seal unleashes a cosmic shake-up. Of particular interest is that "the stars of the sky fell to the earth as the fig tree drops its winter fruit when shaken by a gale" (Rev 6:13). Of the seven types of first-fruits that must be offered up on the Feast of Weeks, figs are usually given first place. The heavens are shaken to such an extent that they offer up their first-fruit, the stars. Interestingly, there is a set of seven things that take place: 1) a great earthquake, 2) the sun is darkened, 3) the moon turns blood red, 4) the stars fall like figs, 5) the heavens are rolled up, 6) mountains and islands are dislodged, and 7) all social classes tremble.[29] Since

---

29. See Ford, *Revelation*, 112.

this passage could be chiastic, the middle item—stars falling like figs—would be the main point of the sixth seal.

Furthermore, the figs are dislodged by a strong wind. The Sinai event was depicted with such a driving and tumultuous wind. Ezekiel also mentions the stormy wind blast (Ezek 1:4). The same type of strong wind is prominent in the Pentecost event recounted by Luke (Acts 2:2). The author of Hebrews refers to the Sinai event as "a tempest" (Heb 12:18). When the sixth seal is broken a strong wind is unleashed, and immediately the stars fall like figs and "the sky vanished like a scroll rolling itself up" (Rev 6:14). While this is a quote from Isa 34:4 (not a Pentecost haphtarah), the imagery all the same reflects a visual during the liturgy. Once the lectionary reading is completed, the scroll is rolled up. The text has been concluded.

The Seventh Seal

The seventh seal is not broken until chapter 8; chapter 7 is an aside as it were, though quite important, focusing on the 144,000 who have been sealed. I will analyze this section shortly, but for now wish to address the seventh seal. "When the Lamb opened the seventh seal, there was silence in heaven for about half an hour" (Rev 8:1). Commentators rightly draw a parallel with Hab 2:20:

> "The LORD is in his holy temple;
> let all the earth keep silence before him!"

This verse immediately precedes chapter 3, the other designated prophetic haphtarah for the Feast of Weeks. Hab 3 is an ancient hymn recalling the Exodus and the Sinai theophany. In other words, in the Book of Habakkuk silence precedes God's theophany and judgment against the nations. Once again, the author of Revelation has skillfully utilized a haphtarah from the Feast of Weeks to make his point that the final apocalyptic Harvest is close at hand. It is the silence before the storm.

The breaking of the seventh seal releases another septet. "And I saw the seven angels who stand before God, and seven trumpets were given to them" (Rev 8:2). This image of seven containing seven within itself echoes the Feast of Weeks: seven weeks of seven days. At Shavu'ot, as on any festival, seven trumpets were blown. The seven trumpets themselves do not delimit the liturgical celebration. Nevertheless, a possible clue can be found in the Book of Nehemiah. After the exile, the priests with their seven trumpets were re-instituted (Neh 12:41). The text shortly thereafter specifically mentions "the chambers for the stores, the contributions, the first fruits, and the tithes" (Neh 12:44). Significantly, the priestly blowing of seven trumpets at the restoration of Jerusalem is linked in Nehemiah with the eventual offering of first-fruits. Perhaps this association is at work here in Rev 8:2 as well.

What corroborates such an allusion to the Feast of First-Fruits is the mention of the Seven Angels of the Presence. This phraseology is found in Tob 12:15 and nowhere else in the Hebrew Scriptures.[30] The storyline of Tobit commences on the Feast of Weeks (Tob 2:1), and according to Goulder this religious book was read in preparation for Pentecost.[31] The next two verses in Rev 8 depict the heavenly scene of angelic intercessory prayer joined with that of the saints on earth: "He was given a great quantity of incense to offer with the prayers of all the saints on the golden altar that is before the throne. And the smoke of the incense, with the prayers of the saints, rose before God from the hand of the angel" (Rev 8:3–4). Such an angelology echoes that expressed in Tob 12:12, where the angel Raphael, "one of the seven angels who stand ready and enter before the glory of the Lord" (12:15), tells Tobit, "it was I who brought and read the record of your prayer before the glory of the Lord." Rev 8:2–4 appears to be colored by Tob 12. Significantly, the conclusion of Tobit, chapters 13–14, are apocalyptic portrayals of the restoration of Jerusalem described as a city constructed of jewels with streets paved with gold—a depiction of the New Jerusalem to be found in Rev 21:10–21.[32]

Ergo, the first verse of Rev 8 reflects the prophetic haphtarah from Habakkuk, and verses 2–4 reflect the angelology and concomitant theology of intercessory prayer found in Tobit, a religious text read in preparation for Pentecost. Regarding verse 5, which mentions "peals of thunder and flashes of lightning" and an earthquake, Beale claims Exod 19:16–18 as the background as well as Hab 3.[33] I totally agree.

---

30. Aramaic fragments of Tobit have been found at Qumran, and various rabbis commented on the book.

31. See Goulder, *Evangelists' Calendar*, 132–33.

32. These chapters have been found in Aramaic at Qumran; see Fitzmyer, "Aramaic and Hebrew Fragments." Admittedly, such an image is also found in Isa 54:11–12, but is not as detailed and in congruence with that as in Rev 21:10–21.

33. See Beale, *Book of Revelation*, 458.

Thus, regarding the seven seals of Revelation, the first set of four are rooted in one of the sedarim for the Feast of Weeks, namely Lev 26. The seventh seal itself reflects the prophetic haphtarah from Hab 2:20 in anticipation of Hab 3 wherein God thunders in glory. Seals five and six more likely than not, therefore, are inspired by the liturgical garb worn by some Jewish communities for the Feast of First-Fruits, as well as the offering of figs, here, in an ironic and apocalyptic sense brought on by the theophanic storm wind. Consequently, just as the opening vision in Rev 4–5 is based in the three types of liturgical readings for the Feast, so too the seven seals likewise reflect the appropriate lections from the Law (Leviticus), Prophets (Habakkuk), and Writings (Tobit).

CHAPTER 7: ANALYSIS

The 144,000

We must now return to chapter 7 of Revelation, the sealing of the 144,000, a scene following upon the breaking of the sixth seal. Arguably, this episode must be interpreted within the context of the seven seals themselves and the preceding throne vision, all of which have been demonstrated to be firmly rooted in the liturgical readings for the Feast of Weeks.

> After this I saw four angels stationed at the four corners of the earth, holding back the four winds of the earth so that no wind could blow upon land or sea or against any tree. Then I saw another angel arising from where the sun rises, possessing the seal of the living God. He cried out in a loud voice to the four angels who had been given power to damage the land and the sea, "Do not damage the land or the sea or the trees until we set the seal on the foreheads of the servants of our God." I heard the number of those who had been so sealed: one hundred and forty-four thousand from every tribe of the Sons of Israel: from the tribe of Judah—twelve thousand were sealed, from the tribe of Reuben—twelve thousand, from the tribe of Gad—twelve thousand, from the tribe of Asher—twelve thousand, from the tribe of Naphtali—twelve thousand, from the tribe of Manasseh—twelve thousand, from the tribe of Simeon—twelve thousand, from the tribe of Levi—twelve thousand, from the tribe of Issachar—twelve thousand, from the tribe of Zebulun—twelve thousand, from the tribe of Joseph—twelve thousand, and from the tribe of Benjamin—twelve thousand were sealed.

> After this I looked and beheld an immense multitude, which no one could count, from every nation, tribe, people, and language, standing before the Throne and before the Lamb, wearing white robes and holding palm branches in their hands. They exclaimed in a loud voice, "Salvation to our God who sits upon the throne, and to the Lamb!" And all the angels stood around the Throne in a circle and around the elders and the four living creatures, and they [all] prostrated themselves before the Throne, worshiped God, exclaiming: "Amen. Blessing and glory and wisdom and thanksgiving and honor and power and might belong to our God forever and ever. Amen!"
> Then one of the elders addressed me, asking, "Who are these wearing white robes, and where did they come from?" I answered him, "Sir, you are the one who knows." Then he said to me, "These are the ones who have endured the time of great distress; they have washed their robes and made them white in the blood of the Lamb. For this reason they stand before God's throne and worship him day and night in his temple. The One who sits upon the throne shall shelter them. They shall not hunger or thirst anymore, nor shall the sun or any scorching heat assail them, for the Lamb who is in the midst of the throne shall shepherd them and guide them to springs of life-giving water, and God shall wipe away every tear from their eyes." (Rev 7:1–17, my translation)

Both Ulfgard and Snyder have presented various arguments to tie this scene with the Feast of Tabernacles, also known as the Feast of Booths.[34] In my opinion, the reasons assembled by Ulfgard are not convincing. The imagery used in Rev 7 is quite general. One need not necessarily understand the followers of the Lamb dressed in white robes and holding palms as delimiting the liturgical event to the Feast of Tabernacles. White robes symbolize purity, whether cultic or spiritual. Besides in relation to the Feast of Booths, palms were also used to celebrate victory, such as at the end of the Maccabean Revolt (1 Macc 13:51; 2 Macc 10:7; 14:4). Philo likewise refers to the palm as a symbol of victory.[35] Jesus of Nazareth's entry into Jerusalem (Palm Sunday) is also victorious with messianic overtones of political deliverance

---

34. See Ulfgard, *Feast and Future*; and Snyder, "Combat Myth." Beale (*Book of Revelation*, 141–44) provides a useful synopsis and analysis of Snyder's presentation. Unfortunately I have not been able to acquire a copy of Snyder's dissertation and will have to rely upon Beale's account.

35. See Philo, *Leg.* 3.74.

(John 12:12–16; Matt 21:1–11). In fact, the followers "with palm branches in their hands," "cried out in a loud voice, saying,

> 'Salvation belongs to our God
> who is seated on the throne,
> and to the Lamb!'" (Rev 7:9–10)

There is no need to connect the palm branches with the Feast of Tabernacles. I believe the meaning is *contextually* evident.

The pericope twice mentions trees (Rev 7:1, 3). As in other apocalyptic texts, trees stand for people. A possible connection with Pentecost here is that a tree was cut down in celebration of Pentecost, representing the cutting down of a terebinth. This practice was reflected in King Asa's hewing the terebinths, thus destroying idol worship, at the Feast of Weeks.[36] In Rev 7:1–3, the "trees" are destined for destruction and very well could represent idolaters, since those who are sealed (and thus preserved) stand

> before the throne of God,
> and worship him day and night
> within his temple. (Rev 7:15)

The 144,000 and the trees are in contrast to one another. A liturgical metaphor must obtain in this case, and viewing the trees as the terebinths of Pentecost makes sense.

The 144,000 form an assembly of all Israel. This implies that the liturgical occasion here must be one of the three pilgrimage festivals when all Israel was to assemble in Jerusalem. These elect have a "seal on the forehead." This phrase is a quote from Ezek 9:4. While Ezek 9 is not part of the prophetic haphtarah for the Feast of Weeks, the author's taking the liberty to be influenced by subsequent passages in the prophet is quite understandable.[37] In fact, Rev 7:1 opens with an excerpt from Ezek 7:2 which prophesies God's coming judgment and the End. Furthermore, Rev 7:9—people "from every nation, from all tribes and peoples and languages"—has its closest parallel in Dan 3:4—"peoples, nations, and languages." Thus Rev 7 is riddled with excerpts used in the haphtarot. Commenting on Rev 7:9, Beale observes, "the redeemed from all nations

---

36. See Goulder, *Evangelists' Calendar*, 194–95.

37. Actually the author is at liberty to quote from any passage in the Tanakh to explicate further the theme that he has structured around the liturgical texts from the Feast of Weeks.

fulfill the priestly mission of Israel from Exod 19:6 and the prophesied reign of Israel from Daniel 7."[38] While the reference to Exod 19:6 (a seder for the Feast) is not explicit in this chapter, the theology is nevertheless present.

Regarding the sealing, the members of the Qumran Community applied Ezek 9:4 to themselves as the true remnant of Israel faithful to the covenant (CD 1.12, ms. B, also known as CD 19.12). These covenanters renewed their alliance with God on the Feast of Weeks dressed in white robes.[39] Of course, the sealing likewise recalls the Exodus story with the lintels being sealed with blood. And it is precisely in the context of Exod 19 that whitened robes are mentioned in the Targum rendition. The received Massoretic text simply reads: "So Moses went down from the mountain to the people. He consecrated the people, and they washed their clothes" (Exod 19:14). This was in preparation for reception of the Torah. The Targum, however, makes more explicit the action in this passage: "they whitened their garments."[40] Philo also presents the Israelites as "having washed their garments and being all clothed in the purest white robes, and standing on tiptoe and pricking up their ears, in compliance with the exhortations of Moses, who had forewarned them to prepare for the solemn assembly."[41] While Philo was admittedly writing in Greek, the term *atzereth*, "solemn assembly," also used to denote the Feast of Pentecost, might have been looming in the back of his mind. As previously noted, the Feast of Weeks was the celebration of the giving of the Law, hence the people have their ears pricked up, ready to hear the Torah proclaimed. Ergo, "wearing white robes" (Rev 7:9, 13 NIV) and especially "they have washed their robes and made them white" (Rev 7:14 NIV) is an excerpt from the Targum of Exod 19:14, the designated liturgical lection for the Feast of Weeks.

Tabernacle Imagery

Further proof can be had for the connection with the Feast of First-Fruits when reading the context of the author's allusion to Isa 4:5–6. Having just stated that those who have washed their robes white serve

---

38. See Beale, *Book of Revelation*, 427.
39. See Ford, *Revelation*, 123, who links this with Ezek 9:4.
40. See Potin, *Fête juive de la Pentecôte*, 211.
41. Philo, *Decal*. 45.

God in his sanctuary, the author adds "and he who sits on the throne will spread his tent over them" (Rev 7:15 NIV). Ulfgard sees in this a reference to God's tabernacling with the people due to the Greek verb employed here: *skenoō*, which reflects the Hebrew consonants found in Shekinah—*skn*. Understandably, one would think of the Feast of Tabernacles. However, another association readily applies when looking at the text behind Rev 7:15.

> Whoever is left in Zion and remains in Jerusalem will be called holy, everyone who has been recorded for life in Jerusalem, once the LORD has washed away the filth of the daughters of Zion and cleansed the bloodstains of Jerusalem from its midst by a spirit of judgment and by a spirit of burning. Then the LORD will create over the whole site of Mount Zion and over its places of assembly a cloud by day and smoke and the shining of a flaming fire by night. Indeed over all the glory there will be a canopy. It will serve as a pavilion, a shade by day from the heat, and a refuge and a shelter from the storm and rain. (Isa 4:3–6)

The parallels with Rev 7:15–16 are evident. The theme is the Exodus and reference is made to the Shekinah. The author of Revelation draws attention to this.

Yet when one looks at the preceding verse in Isaiah, one can divine why this text came to mind for the author. "On that day the branch of the LORD shall be beautiful and glorious, and the fruit of the land shall be the pride and glory of the survivors if Israel" (Isa 4:2). The passage opens with a reference to the messianic Branch of God. This is followed by "the fruit of the earth" connected to the faithful remnant of Israel. In short, the People over whom God spreads his tent on Mount Zion are the first-fruits. This is corroborated by the text in Rev 14:1–5 which also speaks of the 144,000. Here they are explicitly called "the first-fruits for God" (Rev 14:4). In fact, the phrase itself is an excerpt from Jer 2:3, where God recounts Israel's journey through the wilderness:

> Israel was holy to the LORD,
> the first fruits of his harvest.

Hence, associating the Twelve Tribes of Israel (144,000) with the first-fruits is itself a biblical metaphor the author of Revelation exploits. In chapter 7 he relates the 144,000 to the text in Isaiah, speaking of Israel as a fruit and a chosen remnant; in chapter 14, where he re-introduces the

144,000, they are related to the passage in Jeremiah where Israel is sacred to God, the "first fruits of his harvest."

Consequently, the whole of Rev 7, which follows the sixth seal and precedes the seventh, is most properly understood in the context of the Feast of Weeks, not the Feast of Tabernacles. While a resemblance to the Feast of Tabernacles is not excluded, this is not the primary motif operative in chapter 7 or in chapters 4–8. Notwithstanding, a nod in the direction of the Feast of Tabernacles can be made because the Feast of Weeks serves as the chiastic point between Passover and Tabernacles. The Feast of Shavu'ot reflects back upon the Feast of Unleavened Bread and looks forward to the Feast of Booths. As Philo remarked, the Harvest Festival "is also in fact anticipatory of another great feast," referring to the Feast of Tabernacles.[42] Just as allusions to Passover should not be ruled out within the corpus of Revelation, so too, comparisons to the Feast of Tabernacles should not necessarily be excluded; but as has been demonstrated so far (and shall further be evinced) the liturgical inspiration for the Book of Revelation is the Feast of Weeks.[43]

CHAPTERS 8–11: ANALYSIS

The Seven Trumpets

We are now in a position to return to chapter 8 and analyze the seven trumpets blown by the Seven Angels of the Presence. The seven angels and trumpets emerged when the seventh seal was broken. The structure itself recalls the seven septets that form the Feast of Weeks. Like the first four seals, the first four trumpets are grouped together, paralleling the format as found in Lev 26, the seder reading in preparation for the Feast of Harvest. The first trumpet brings about hail and fire mixed with blood; the second the sea is destroyed and partially turned into blood due to a fiery mountain; the third contaminates the drinking water; and the fourth affects the heavenly luminaries causing darkness. The parallels between these four trumpets (including the other three) and the plagues

---

42. Philo, *Spec.* 2.30, section 176.

43. It should go without saying that, given the nature of liturgy itself, the three great pilgrimage feasts will indeed have common elements, especially since the theme running throughout all of them is Israel's deliverance from Egypt and entrance into the Promised Land.

of Egypt have long been recognized.[44] The author of Revelation now reflects upon God's judgment against the evil inhabitants of the earth. He utilizes the story found in the chapters of Exodus that precede the designated seder for the Feast. Likewise Rev 8:13, "Woe, woe, woe to the inhabitants of the earth, at the blasts of the other trumpets that the three angels are about to blow!" resonates with Ezek 7:5–6, "Disaster upon disaster! See it comes. An end is coming, the end is coming for you! See it comes!" (my translation). The triplet in Ezekiel is masterfully played out by the author of Revelation who weaves this passage from the book of the appropriate haphtarah into his own apocalyptic midrash.

Chapter 9

The fifth and sixth trumpets also incorporate texts from the liturgical readings for Pentecost. The fifth clarion call signals the opening of the Abyss. "He opened the shaft of the bottomless pit, and from the shaft rose smoke like the smoke of a great furnace" (Rev 9:2). This verse incorporates phrases from Exod 19:18 "Smoke rose from it like the smoke from a gigantic furnace" (NIV). This is part of the seder passage. The seer then weaves in other texts from the prophets, especially Joel. While I have not found any indication that Joel was a reading for the Feast of Weeks, it is curious that Peter quotes from Joel on the Feast of Pentecost as well (Acts 2:17–21). Was there some Jewish tradition outside the mainstream that also utilized Joel? One reason why Joel 1:11–12 could have been used in public worship for Pentecost is this passage speaks about the wheat, barley, figs, grapes, and pomegranates—five out of the seven types of first-fruits one needed to present before the Lord at the Feast of Weeks. In short, the Book of Joel deals with the harvest that has been ruined by locusts, the invading armies. Understandably, one can see how such a prophetic text would fit into the scope of the author of Revelation. Thus, underlying the imagery of locusts and armies in the fifth trumpet is the harvest motif clearly at work in Joel. We are hardly far afield from the Feast of Harvest! Furthermore, as noted above, Resh Lakish associated Pentecost with Rosh Hashanah, and the haphtarah reading for New Year is from Joel. The sixth trumpet continues the same imagery; however, now the reason for God's judgment is specified: the people refused to abandon "idols of gold and silver and bronze and stone

---

44. See Beale, *Book of Revelation*, 465–67; and Aune, *Revelation*, 499–506.

and wood" (Rev 9:20). This is a direct quote from Dan 5:4, a book we have established as part of the Pentecost cycle of readings. In fact, the Feast of Pentecost at one time focused upon the need to uproot idolatry in the land of Israel.

Without even yet analyzing the seventh trumpet, the first six are already based on Pentecost liturgical texts from the Law, Prophets, and Writings. Keep in mind, Daniel was not grouped with the Prophets but with the Writings. This liturgical triadic structure signifies that this portion is complete within itself. The next section, the theophanic angel holding the scroll, forms a complete lectionary unit within itself.

Chapter 10

Chapter 10 is perhaps one of the most enigmatic sections of the Book of Revelation. I do not claim to be able to unravel its mystery but wish to highlight how the Feast of Weeks plays into this vision.[45] The seer relates, "And I saw another mighty angel coming down from heaven, wrapped in a cloud, with a rainbow over his head; his face was like the sun, and his legs like pillars of fire" (10:1). This clearly is a theophany, the Angel of the Lord manifesting the Divine Presence. The imagery immediately recalls the revelation at Sinai and hence the giving of the Torah. The Christian Scriptures presume the Torah was given through angelic mediation (Acts 7:38—wherein the Torah is called the "words of life *logia zōnta*," and Gal 3:19).[46] The verse itself is also deeply impacted by Ezek 1:26–28, part of the haphtarah:

> Above the dome over their heads there was something like a throne, in appearance like sapphire; and seated above the likeness of a throne was something that seemed like a human form. Upward from what appeared like the loins I saw something like

---

45. However, see Appendix E, wherein I show that it functions as a chiastic parallel to Rev 8:1–5.

46. Regarding Gal 3:21 and the Law/Torah not being able to give life (if that is even what *Paul* is arguing in the diatribe), from certain Jewish points of view this can be correct. The Torah on its own cannot impart life if the adherent does not live by faith, that is, in a sincere heartfelt covenantal relationship with God. Each person has free will, and "having" the Torah will not magically save people (no more than baptism will or attending church). There is a fundamental choice that needs to be made (Deut 28 and 30:15–20); faith is a matter of the heart (Deut 6:5 and 10:12). This is echoed throughout the Prophets. Paul himself in the first part of Gal 3:21 emphatically declares that there is no opposition whatsoever between the Torah/Law and God's promises.

gleaming amber, something that looked like fire enclosed all around; and downward from what looked like the loins I saw something that looked like fire, and there was a splendor all around. Like the bow in a cloud on a rainy day, such was the appearance of the splendor all around.

The rainbow, while found in Ezekiel, could also cause the hearer to think of the covenant with Noah as well. Technically, no rainbow was seen at Sinai. If the covenant with Noah is also implied, this would reflect the theology found in the *Book of Jubilees*, namely that the Feast of Weeks is the Feast of Covenants and Noah was the first to observe this feast. In the hand of this angel is a little scroll, unrolled (Rev 10:2).

Given the imagery of the Sinaitic theophany and since the angel has one foot planted in the sea and one on dry land, the scroll appears to be the revelatory Word of God planted firmly between heaven and all the earth. Rabbinic tradition and non-mainstream Judaism all agree that Moses received the Word of God, not just written but oral as well. This is the meaning of Torah. That Sinai is in the author's mind is confirmed by the seven thunderclaps (Rev 10:3–4). God's voice thunders at Sinai (Exod 19:16–19) and the rabbis refer to this as the "seven voices or thunders" (*Midr. Exodus* 15:28; 28:6). Ps 29 also reflects the Sinai event and mentions the "voice of the Lord" seven times, as well as thunder. In fact, Ps 29 is the designated Psalm for the Feast of Weeks in the liturgy of Palestine (*Sop.* 18:3).[47] In Ps 29 God sits enthroned as King, ruling the world.

Curiously, when the seer is about to record what the seven thunderclaps had said, a voice comes from heaven telling him, "Seal up what the seven thunders have said, and do not write it down" (Rev 10:4). This silencing of part of the theophanic revelation reflects the utter ineffable quality of God's word; part of it remains beyond human comprehension.[48] This sealing of the revelation mirrors the angel Michael's directive to the prophet Daniel where he too was charged to "keep the words secret and the book sealed until the time of the end" (Dan 12:4; also see 12:9). Significantly, the angel then "swore by him who lives for ever and ever" (Rev 10:6 NIV). This swearing of an oath bears a remarkable resemblance to the theology found in the *Book of Jubilees*, wherein the Feast

---

47. See Potin, *Fête juive de la Pentecôte*, 193. Also see Thackeray's comments in *Josephus*, 55–57.

48. Also see my comments in Appendix E.

of Shavu'ot is the time of *shevu'ot*, the time of swearing oaths. The angel also swears his oath by the One "who created the heavens and all that is in them, the earth and all that it bears, and the sea and all it contains" (Rev 10:6, my translation). Most of the clause is a direct quote from Exod 20:11, the seder reading for the Feast of Weeks. The midrashic expansion regarding the earth "and all that it bears" probably echoes the idea of bearing first fruits (see JB).

The seer is then commanded to request the scroll from the angel so that he might eat the scroll, just as his predecessor Ezekiel had done centuries before (Ezek 2:9—3:3), thus enabling him "to prophesy again." Ezekiel's eating of the scroll immediately follows his vision of God on the throne carried by the four living creatures.

Once again, the author of Revelation in this section has craftily woven together threads from all three liturgical readings for the Feast of Weeks, from the Torah (Exod 19–20), Nevi'im (Ezek 2), and Ketuvim (Ps 29; Dan 12:4). The author repeatedly remains true to his theological exposition of the Pentecost lectionary.

Chapter 11

The vision now shifts to the seer being given a measuring rod so that he might measure the sanctuary of God. This text is much debated as to its date, whether before the fall of Jerusalem in 70 CE or afterwards.[49] That particular issue does not affect the hypothesis under investigation. This vision, however, signals a marked change in the author's focus: the holy city being beset by pagans. Daniel is utilized extensively, particularly in regard to the three and a half years. The seer's measuring the temple, reflects the commission given to Ezekiel. The two witnesses exhibit the power to work wonders and plagues similar to those wrought against the Egyptians in the book of Exodus. Rev 11 becomes fraught with action and more complex in its subject matter. Nevertheless, the text still attests to the liturgical readings playing a role in the articulation of the prophecy. When the seventh trumpet is finally blown, Ezek 7:5–9 forms part of the backdrop as does Dan 7:14. It is the apocalyptic climax. Beale has pointed out that Rev 11:15–18 captures the ideas and even wording found in the Song of Moses in Exod 15:13–18.[50]

---

49. See Robinson, *Redating the New Testament*, 240–42.
50. See Beale, *Book of Revelation*, 618–19.

The seventh trumpet sounds the grand finale. "Then God's temple in heaven was opened, and the ark of his covenant was seen within his temple; and there were flashes of lightning, rumblings, peals of thunder, an earthquake, and heavy hail" (Rev 11:19). According to some segments of Jewish thought, the Ark of the Covenant would be revealed at the End of Time. One tradition states that the prophet Jeremiah climbed the same mountain Moses did and hid the Ark there, only for it to be revealed at the End when God would re-establish his glory and his cloud would fill the temple (2 Macc 2:4–8). In the apocalyptic work *2 Baruch*, Jeremiah's protogé has a vision in which God conceals the Ark and other sacred liturgical vessels, declaring them to reappear at the End (*2 Bar.* 6).

Apart from the apocalyptic nature of the Ark's appearance here in Rev 11, could there possibly be another significance? The following is mere conjecture, but intriguing nonetheless. The opening apocalyptic vision in Revelation signaled the role to be played by the Lion of the tribe of Judah, the Root of David. This figure is unquestionably messianic. As noted previously, rabbinic tradition states that King David himself was born on Pentecost and died on Pentecost. The appearance of the Root of David at the Feast of Weeks makes liturgical sense.[51] One of the hallmarks of King David's reign was the bringing of the Ark of the Covenant to Jerusalem. This procession of the Ark was accompanied by seven trumpets (1 Chr 15:24). During the procession, the priest Uzziah touched the Ark and died. Interestingly enough, his death occurred at the threshing floor of Nacon (2 Sam 6:6) or of the Javelin (1 Chr 13:9). Here an incident with the Ark is connected to the threshing floor and hence harvest.

The Ark then remained at the house of Obed-Edom for three months (2 Sam 6:11; 1 Chr 13:14) before being carried into Jerusalem. Thus the Ark of the Covenant was processed into Jerusalem on the third month. Was this third month mystagogically interpreted as Sivan and thus the Ark entered at the Feast of Harvest? David feeds the multitudes with a roll of wheat bread, a portion of dates, and a raisin cake. These are all produce offered as first-fruits of the harvest. If there had been a midrashic tradition assigning the entrance of the Ark into Jerusalem at

---

51. The Midrash states that the Messiah would be born on the very day that the Second Temple was destroyed, but this tradition is obviously late and probably supplanted any earlier one. See *y. Ber.* 2, 5a; *Midr. Lam* 1,89–90; *Midr. Panim Aherim*, 78; and *Aggadat Bereshit* 67, 133.

the Feast of Weeks, this would shed further light on why the author of Revelation concludes the seventh trumpet with this scene.[52] By opening the seventh seal, the Root of David re-establishes the Ark of the Covenant on the Feast of Weeks—the seven trumpets have been blown.

Persuaded that something must be going on here with the Ark of the Covenant and the Feast of Weeks, I decided to re-investigate the matter of the Ark itself. Outside of the Torah, the first "appearance" of the Ark is in 1 Sam 4–6 when the Philistines capture it; the Ark in turn overturns the idol Dagon, and then the Philistines return the Ark to Israel. Curiously, the Ark figures in the toppling of idol worship, one of the themes of the Feast of Weeks, but most significantly the Ark returns to Beth-shemesh at the time of harvesting. "Now the people of Beth-shemesh were reaping their wheat harvest in the valley. When they looked up and saw the ark, they went with rejoicing to meet it" (1 Sam 6:13). In other words, the Ark of the Covenant returned to Israel at the Feast of Weeks when the wheat harvest is gathered and offered up. The Ark worked many prodigies that were so fearful that the people there pleaded that the townsfolk of Kiriath-jearim come and take back their Ark (1 Sam 6:20—7:1). There it remained until David brought it up to Jerusalem (2 Sam 6). In short, the history of Israel links the re-appearance of the Ark of the Covenant with the Feast of Weeks.

However, could something even more concrete be operative? Reconstructing the Jewish liturgical readings not only for the Law and Prophets but for some of the Writings as well, Goulder has argued convincingly that the histories found in 1 Samuel through 2 Kings match the Torah readings.[53] Although Goulder draws no special significance to it, he does place the reading of 1 Sam 4–6 at the tenth sidra, in other words immediately before the Feast of Pentecost.[54] This means that liturgically, the author of the Book of Revelation would have just heard during the last Sabbath reading about the return of the Ark of the Covenant. In fact, this would have been the very day before the Feast of Weeks. In the text in 1 Sam 6:13, the Ark reappears at the wheat harvest. Understandably,

---

52. I have searched for the rabbinic teaching as to when the Ark was brought into Jerusalem, but unfortunately have failed to find any text supporting or contradicting my hypothesis. It should be noted that sometimes the rabbis espouse differing traditions, particularly with regard to dating events.

53. See Goulder, *Evangelists' Calendar*, 105–38.

54. See ibid., 143, and his table on 156.

one could easily associate the apocalyptic reappearance of the Ark of the Covenant with the eschatological Feast of Weeks.

Liturgical Summary

To summarize the foregoing analysis, in every section of chapters 4–11, the author has been inspired by the liturgical readings for the Feast of Weeks. The lectionary texts themselves then serve as platforms upon which the seer of the Apocalypse can construct an eschatological midrash. I pause here purposely, because the author records the theophanic angel of Rev 10 as swearing: "There will be no more delay! But in the days when the seventh angel is about to sound his trumpet, the mystery of God will be accomplished, just as he announced to his servants the prophets" (Rev 10:6–7 NIV). The seventh trumpet seems to conclude the apocalyptic revelation and the end of chapter 11 could serve as a fitting conclusion. Some scholars believe Rev 4–11 was originally a separate unit.[55] In these chapters, the name Jesus does not appear whatsoever, nor the term "sign" which occurs seven times in Rev 12:1—22:7. Likewise Babylon and the Beast are only found in Rev 12:1—22:7.[56] As we shall see, the author's marked liturgical pattern of citing or alluding to a passage from the designated Pentecost lection (Law, Prophets, and Writings) is considerably weakened or non-existent in these subsequent chapters. Nevertheless, the Feast of Harvest *motif* continues throughout Rev 12:1—22:7.

CHAPTERS 12–13: ANALYSIS

The Woman

When analyzing the text about the Ark of the Covenant, I suggested that its appearance was linked to the appearance of the Root of David, who liturgically *should be* born on the Feast of Weeks, as was his ancestor King David. Admittedly, I have no external textual evidence to corroborate this theory. However, in the very next scene following the Ark of

---

55. See Boismard, *L'Apocalypse*; Hopkins, "Historical Perspectives"; and Ford, *Revelation*, 3–4, *passim*.

56. Collins (*Crisis and Catharsis*, 57–58) rightly points out that the term Babylon was employed for Rome after 70 CE. She then concludes that the whole of Revelation was written after that date. I disagree; only chs. 12–22 (and 1–3) need be after the destruction of the temple.

the Covenant, the seer has a vision of a woman who "was pregnant and was crying out in birth pangs, in the agony of giving birth" (12:2). "And she gave birth to a son, a male child, who is to rule all the nations with a rod of iron" (12:5). The vision is unquestionably messianic. Mother Israel gives birth to the promised Anointed One of the Lord. Curiously, as soon as the child was born he "was snatched up to God and to his throne" (12:5 NIV).

Potin has pointed out a very interesting parallel to this passage in Rev 12.[57] In his study of the Feast of Pentecost, Potin had reason to analyze the Targum for Exod 24 because this chapter speaks of the ratification of the covenant and God's giving the Torah to Moses. The Targum for verse 10 reads:

> Nadab and Abihu raised their eyes and saw the glory of the God of Israel, and under the footstool of his feet (which had been placed under his throne), like a work of stone of sapphire. It is the memorial of the enslavement by which the Egyptians enslaved the children of Israel, in the clay and in the bricks. The women also trampled underfoot the clay with their husbands. Now there was a young woman there who was weak and who gave birth. She delivered the infant who was trampled into the clay. Gabriel descended and made of him a brick, and caused him to be carried into the highest heavens. He established it as a pavement under the footstool of the Master of the World; its splendor is like a workmanship of precious stone and like the beauty of the heavens when there's not a cloud in the sky.[58]

The child born while Israel is enslaved becomes the footstool for the Holy One and reflects his glory. This theme was popular and recurs throughout Jewish literature. In the Pirqé de Rabbi Eliezer 48, the story is attributed to Rabbi Aqiba. In this recension, the angel is Michael rather than Gabriel. "Michael descended and took the mould of the brick and transported it before the throne of Glory. That night, the Holy One, blessed be he, descended and struck down the first-born of the Egyptians."[59] Echoing in the background is the idea of first-born and first-fruits. In fact, the Targum for Exod 24:5 has changed "young Israelites" to "first-born"; one

---

57. Here I am much indebted to Potin; see *Fête juive de la Pentecôte*, 148–62.
58. Ibid., 149; my translation.
59. Ibid., 156; my translation.

offers up to God their first-born as first-fruits.[60] A similar tale regarding the brick of clay appears in *3 Bar.* 3:5.

Potin demonstrates how the rabbinic literature takes up this theme of the brick serving as the footstool of the Lord. But what is significant for our purposes is that the midrash of Vayikra distinctly associates the brick and pavement of Exod 24:10 with the "sapphire stone" seen in Ezek 1:26 in regard to God's throne. Thus the Sinai event has been merged with the haphtarah text for Shavu'ot in the rabbinic tradition. Without making the connection to a lectionary basis to the Book of Revelation, Potin advances the hypothesis that this Targum on Exod 24:10 lies behind Rev 12.[61] My independent research confirms his theory and supplies the exegetical reason. Potin points out that the woman in Rev 12 symbolizes Israel in the context of the Exodus, and the Dragon represents Egypt, which was often depicted as a monster. In the account of the Apocalypse, here too it is Michael who figures into the scene and combats the Dragon thus protecting the child and its mother.

Not only has the author of Revelation woven into this chapter a midrash on Exod 24:10 merged with Ezek 1:26, but he integrates a motif from Exod 19 from the Harvest seder. "You have seen what I did to the Egyptians, and how I bore you on eagles' wings and brought you to myself" (Exod 19:4). In Rev 12:14, Mother Israel "was given the two wings of the great eagle, so that she could fly from the serpent into the wilderness, to her place where she is nourished for a time, and times, and half a time." Given that she has just birthed the Messiah, a tradition regarding David most probably applies as well. King David died on the Feast of Shavu'ot and his son Solomon "summoned eagles who spread their wings over him that the sun should not beat down upon him," thereby protecting his body from corruption (*Midr. Ruth* 3.2). Thus David was preserved on the Feast of Harvest. In Rev 12 the woman delivers a son who is immediately transported into heaven and preserved from the Dragon and the woman herself is subsequently given eagle's wings and protected in the desert for three and a half years. This preservation in the desert (heat and blazing sun) by eagle's wings and the son being carried to the throne of God (perhaps on eagle's wings as well) strongly suggests a Pentecost motif at work here. The targum and liturgical readings add credence to such an hypothesis.

60. See ibid., 148, 151.
61. See ibid., 159–62.

The Dragon and the Beast

While no text from the prophetic haphtarah appears in Rev 12, the author does utilize images and texts from Dan 7:7, 7:25, 8:10, and 10:13ff. In fact, the image of the Dragon is most probably inspired by Dan 14:23–42, wherein the prophet destroys the Dragon of Babylon immediately before the Harvest Feast. Here the Dragon represents the satanic powers at work in the earthly empire that assaults the true Israel of God. The scene continues to unfold in chapter thirteen which is heavily dependent now upon Daniel. The author applies the prophet's texts to his own historical and religious situation. Of particular note is the theme of idolatry found in the statue of the beast, a Pentecost liturgical theme. "All who refused to worship the statue of the beast were to be put to death" (Rev 13:15, my translation). This verse is a collage of words and images found in Dan 3:5–7. "You are to fall down and worship the golden statue that King Nebuchadnezzar has set up. Whoever does not fall down and worship shall immediately be thrown into a furnace of blazing fire" (Dan 3:5–6).

In the account of Bel and the Dragon (Dan 14), there are two evil gods: a Beast named Bel who is the chief god equated with the Babylonian Empire, as well as a Dragon.[62] Curiously, in Revelation we also have the two evil protagonists.

While the Beast is demonstrably dependent upon texts within Daniel, another passage supports its inclusion here. Ps 68 was one of the hymns used on the Feast of Pentecost because it recounts the Exodus (*b. Meg.* 31a).[63] Referring to Egypt, the psalmist adjures, "Rebuke the Beast dwelling among the reeds" (Ps 68:30, my translation). In Ezek 29:2–5, the prophet likewise depicts the Pharaoh as the Beast of the Nile. In the Book of Revelation, the Beast found in the Pentecost lesson now represents an ungodly empire. Thus, just as chapters 4–11 were firmly situated in the liturgy of the Feast of Weeks, chapters 12–13 bear testimony to this same lectionary inspiration behind the woman, the Dragon, and the Beast.

---

62. For Bel see Jer 50:2; 51:44. Revelation draws from these chapters.
63. Also see Goudoever, *Biblical Calendars*, 201.

CHAPTER 14: ANALYSIS

The 144,000 and the Harvest

The most lucidly graphic presentation of the Feast of Harvest is found in chapter 14. Here the seer re-envisions the 144,000 (the Twelve Tribes assembled for a festal gathering) who have been sealed on the forehead (Ezek 9:4). As previously noted, "They have been redeemed from humankind as first fruits for God and the Lamb" (Rev 14:4). The purpose of their redemption should be connected with that stated in Rev 5:10 to make "them a kingdom and a line of priests to serve our God and to govern the world" (*my translation*). The 144,000 are the priestly people who have given themselves as first-fruits to God and who worship God sacrificially by their very lives.

"It is these who have not defiled themselves with women, for they are virgins" (Rev 14:4). This statement has puzzled commentators for decades, though a few have connected it with the appropriate text—Exod 19:14–15. The Massoretic text reads, "So Moses went down from the mountain to the people. He consecrated the people, and they washed their clothes. And he said to the people, 'Prepare for the third day; do not go near a woman.'" We have already seen that the Targum has expounded on this to "whitened their garments." The matter at hand is cultic purification for reception of the giving of the Torah. Before the first century CE, the Feast of Harvest celebrated this event. Philo draws attention to the necessary sexual purity.

> The people stood by, having kept themselves clean from all connection with women, and having abstained from all pleasures, except those which arise from a participation in necessary food, having been purifying themselves with baths and ablutions for three days, and having washed their garments and being all clothed in the purest white robes, and standing on tiptoe and pricking up their ears, in compliance with the exhortations of Moses, who had forewarned them to prepare for the solemn assembly.[64]

According to Philo, temporary sexual abstinence was part of the liturgical purification for reception of the Law.[65] Josephus makes the same

---

64. Philo, *Decal.* 45.

65. Philo, in *QE* 2.3, 46, recounts how God summoned Moses to the top of Mount Sinai and thereby effected a "second birth" which was a "divine birth." This happened "in

point in his account.⁶⁶ The author of Revelation affirms this tradition.⁶⁷ The 144,000 are cultically pure: "in their mouth no lie was found; they are blameless" (Rev 14:5). This verse is based upon the alternate prophetic haphtarah for the Feast of Harvest, Zeph 3.

> They will do no wrong
> and utter no lies,
> nor shall a deceitful tongue
> be found in their mouths. (Zeph 3:13 NIV)

Thus the author of Revelation presents the Chosen People as purified from all evil, free from all defilement. They are a holy people wholly consecrated to the Holy One of Israel. In short, they are sinless. This point in Revelation is a powerful indication of the liturgical assembly in mind. According to rabbinic tradition, the only time that Israel was totally without sin and did not need any sin offering was at the Feast of Weeks. "In all the other additional sacrifices the sin offering is included, but in connection with Pentecost no sin offering is mentioned, to show that at that time no sin or iniquity attached to them" (*Midr. Cant.* 4.4.1). On every other feast day, a sin offering is made, but on the first Feast of Shavu'ot there was no need, because the people had purified themselves through obedience to God's command through Moses, and the giving of the Torah itself purified them of all defilement. The scene in Rev 14:1–5 perfectly mirrors that in Exod 19.

The Day of Judgment

The subsequent section announces the Day of Judgment. Rev 14:6 is comprised of a snippet from Dan 3:4 and verse 7 is a partial excerpt from Exod 20:11. Verses 8–13 are a tapestry of prophetic threads and colorful images, most, previously woven in earlier chapters. The seer is commanded, "'Write this down: Blessed are those who from now on die in the Lord!' 'Yes,' says the spirit, 'they will find rest from their labors, for their deeds accompany them'" (Rev 14:13, my translation). This benedic-

---

accordance with the Ever-virginal Nature." In other words, the Divine Nature is virginal and those who come in contact with it are virginally transformed by regeneration.

66. See Josephus, *Ant.* 3.5.1.

67. If an underlying Hebrew or Aramaic text is operative here, perhaps the Greek translator confused celibacy with virginity, or the original writer (mis)understood *parthenos* in this broader sense.

tion evokes the image of the Sabbath Rest, here to be understood as the Jubilee Year, the eschatological Feast of Weeks.

The apocalypse now shifts to the final harvest.

> Then I looked, and there was a white cloud, and seated on the cloud was one like the Son of Man, with a golden crown on his head, and a sharp sickle in his hand! Another angel came out of the temple, calling with a loud voice to the one who sat on the cloud, "Use your sickle and reap, for the hour to reap has come, because the harvest of the earth is fully ripe." So the one who sat on the cloud swung his sickle over the earth, and the earth was reaped.
>
> Then another angel came out of the temple in heaven, and he too had a sharp sickle. Then another angel came out from the altar, the angel who has authority over fire, and he called with a loud voice to him who had the sharp sickle, "Use your sharp sickle and gather the clusters of the vine of the earth, for its grapes are ripe." So the angel swung his sickle over the earth and gathered the vintage of the earth, and he threw it into the great wine press of the wrath of God. (Rev 14:14–19)

The author is indebted to both Daniel and Joel. The one like a son of man is definitely an apocalyptic figure encountered in numerous Jewish apocalypses: Daniel, *1 Enoch*, and *4 Ezra* to name the primary ones. He is a representative of God and obeys the heavenly command delivered by another angel. Two harvests are involved here.[68] The first most probably refers to the ingathering of the Elect of God. According to *Midr. Cant.* 8.4.1, the greatness of Israel is compared to a harvest and the verse from Joel 3:13 is used: "Put the sickle in for the harvest is ripe" (my translation). The text is interpreted by the rabbis as referring to standing grain; wheat was one of the first-fruits offered at the Feast of Harvest. The 144,000 were just denominated as "first-fruits" and in Rev 14:12 the seer adjures, "Here is a call for the endurance of the saints, those who keep the commandments of God." This shows that more followers of the Lamb will likewise bear witness by death and must endure. At the final harvest, they will be gathered into God's heavenly storerooms.

The vision then turns to another type of first-fruit offered at the Feast—that of the grape. Here the grape is used in an ironic sense to

---

68. For various views on this harvest see Beale, *Book of Revelation*, 770–79; Ford, *Revelation*, 249–51; Caird, *Revelation*, 188–94; and Feuillet, "Moisson et la vendage de l'Apocalypse."

portray the eschatological reaping of the evildoers and consigning them to the winepress of God's wrath. The author is deeply influenced by the apocalyptic poem found in Isa 63:1–6 merged with Joel 4:13. The harvest is twofold because when Moses delivered the Torah, he set before Israel two choices, life or death. Here the golden grains of wheat presumed within the imagery are a positive symbol of the ingathering of the just, while the red juice of the grape represents the bloodbath of punishment exacted upon the unjust.[69]

CHAPTERS 15–22: ANALYSIS

Exodus Revisited

The eschatological drama now reiterates the Exodus story. Seven angels appear who are given seven bowls filled with seven plagues. But the judgment scene is preceded by the redeemed who sing the Song of Moses (Rev 15:2–3). The seven bowls and seven plagues once again recall the miraculous punishments wrought against the Egyptians but now applied to Babylon the Great. In chapters 12–21 the author now drops the liturgical exegetical pattern of always having the triplet citation or reference to the lections from the Law, Prophets, and Writings regarding the Feast of Weeks. Nevertheless, passages from Exodus and Ezekiel continue to be employed, as well as from Daniel, but not in tightly interwoven patterns as witnessed earlier.[70] Notwithstanding, the theme of harvest is operative. Chapter 14 clearly brings that to the attention of the reader, but subsequent chapters challenge the listener to more attentiveness for the symbolism.

---

69. See Appendix E, wherein the chiastic structure highlights this interpretation.

70. It is my estimation that another hand is at work here—a disciple or school of the author who was behind chs. 4–11. After having formulated my hypothesis, doing the research, and drawing my own conclusions, I came across Goulder's article "The Apocalypse as an Annual Cycle of Prophecies," wherein Goulder theorizes that the Apocalypse is a commentary on Ezekiel. He admits, however, "What I have written is based upon a hypothetical subdivision of the Apocalypse and a hypothetical subdivision of Ezekiel, linked by a hypothetical cyclical reading of the prophet on a hypothetical annual basis" (354). To make his theory work, Goulder drops out numerous chapters from Ezekiel (see 353–54). My liturgical analysis of Revelation led me in a completely different direction and it is based on historically proven liturgical readings. The sedarim and haphtarot serve as theological platforms upon which the author continues to build by quoting relevant texts from the rest of the books in which the lections were selected.

Armageddon

As is well known, the final battle takes place at Armageddon. Most scholars agree that this refers to an area near Megiddo. Many battles had previously been fought in this plain. What correlates Armageddon to my thesis is that this plain was a fertile valley and served as the bread basket of Israel. In other words, most of Israel is desert, and when one thinks of harvesting vast fields of wheat, the agricultural venue for this to take place is in the valley of Megiddo and the surrounding area. The plain naturally served as a corridor for advancing armies, but when one looks at Israel with regard to its ability to produce first-fruits in abundance to offer in the temple, it is precisely this central valley that served as Israel's agricultural center. Here the nations are assembled and hewn down. God summons the birds of the sky to come and feast upon the meal prepared for them (Rev 19:17–18). Armageddon is the sardonic Harvest Feast.

The Fall of Babylon

Earlier the prophet railed against Babylon. The irony is cutting. "The fruit you longed for is gone from you" (Rev 18:14 NIV). God destroys all of Babylon's luxury and produce. The harvest analogy continues, "Then a mighty angel picked up a boulder the size of a large millstone and threw it into the sea, and said,

> 'With such violence
> the great city of Babylon will be
> thrown down,
> never to be found again.'" (Rev 18:21 NIV)

This is followed by a mocking dirge.

> "The sound of the millstone
> will never be heard in you again." (Rev 18:22 NIV)

The symbolism evokes the instruments used at harvest time. Among her produce that is lost are "wine, olive oil, choice flour and wheat" (Rev 18:13), items that for the Jew should have been dedicated to the Lord at the Feast of Weeks. While the author understandably focuses upon the judgment exacted against Babylon and the cosmic conflict at work here, nevertheless, harvest metaphors color the presentation, not to mention the cause for God's wrath: idolatry. It was King Asa centuries earlier who cut down the terebinths and removed the idols and renewed the Mosaic

Revelation as an Apocalyptic Pentecost Commentary

Covenant on the Feast of Shavu'ot. The Whore of Babylon who has prostituted herself with idols and false gods is finally cut down by God.

Victory and the Bride

This is followed by the huge crowd assembled in heaven singing and shouting victorious praise to God. Part of their song of jubilation proclaims:

> "Hallelujah!
>   For our Lord God Almighty reigns.
> Let us rejoice and be glad
>   and give him glory!
> For the wedding of the Lamb has come,
>   and his bride has made herself ready.
> Fine linen, bright and clean,
>   was given her to wear."
> (Fine linen stands for the righteous acts of the saints.)
> (Rev 19:6–8 NIV)

Does rabbinic thought regarding the Feast of Weeks lie behind this scene? The following is attributed to Rabbi Chanina of the first and second centuries CE.

> Moses went forth and came to the camp of the Israelites, and he aroused the Israelites from their sleep, saying to them: Arise ye from your sleep, for behold, your God desires to give the Torah to you. Already the bridegroom wishes to lead the bride and to enter the bridal chamber. The hour has come for giving you the Torah, as it is said, And Moses brought forth the people out of the camp to meet God (Exodus 19:17)..... And the Holy One, blessed be He, went forth to meet them to give them the Torah, as it is said, O God, when thou wentest forth before thy people (Psalm 67:7).[71]

The giving of the Torah is the time when God wed Israel. The Harvest Feast is the Wedding Feast. Note how Rabbi Chanina has woven together the seder (Exod 19) and hagiographical haphtarah (Ps 68) for the Feast of Weeks. The Torah is God's gifts to his bride and she in return offers him her choicest first-fruits. Israel offers the fruits of the earth, as well as

---

71. Pirké de-Rabbi Eliezer 41, Friedlander, trans., *Pirké de-Rabbi Eliezer*, 322. While the tradition reportedly goes back to the first and second centuries CE, the book itself most probably was not edited until the ninth century.

her own sons and daughters, who have been obedient to the commandments and have practiced good works in holiness.

The heavenly Wedding Feast is juxtaposed with another feast. An angel shouts to the birds of the air, "Come, gather for the great supper of God" (Rev 19:17). This is an excerpt from Ezek 39:17, and the prophet's subsequent message matches the presentation given by the seer of the Apocalypse. The feast is the gorging on the flesh of kings and people of every walk of life who have worshipped the Beast. A parody is operative here. The verb "gather" reflects the harvest as well as assembly. This is followed by the golden age of the Messiah's reign, culminating in the Final Judgment and the destruction of Death and Hades itself.

The Heavenly Jerusalem

Once the books have been opened and everyone is judged and assigned their proper place for eternity (Rev 20:4–15), then the seer envisions "a new heaven and a new earth" (Rev 21:1). The centerpiece is the New Jerusalem portrayed as a bride. "And I heard a loud voice from the throne saying, "Now the dwelling of God is with men, and he will live with them. They will be his people, and God himself will be with them and be their God" (Rev 21:3 NIV). This text is woven from Ezek 37:27. However, the wording as well as the previous scene also reflects the seder reading before the Feast of Weeks. "You will still be eating last year's harvest when you will have to move it out to make room for the new. I will put my dwelling place among you, and I will not abhor you. I will walk among you and be your God, and you will be my people" (Lev 26:10–12 NIV). There is perpetual bounty from the harvest that God supplies and a continual renewal. This reflects God's confirming (renewing) his covenant (Lev 26:9) in perpetuity.

The author reiterates the motif later in Rev 22:2. Having spoken of the river of life rising from God's throne and running down the middle of the city, the seer notes: "On either bank of the river grew the trees of life that produce fruit twelve times a year, once each month; and the leaves of the trees are for the healing of the Gentiles" (my translation). The New Jerusalem will celebrate an eternal Feast of Harvest. And just as according to rabbinic tradition, it was on the Feast of Weeks that Israel was without sin, so too, in the Heavenly Jerusalem, the saints are totally consecrated to God and without any sin or blemish. "But nothing unclean will enter it, nor anyone who practices abomination or falsehood, but only those who are written in the Lamb's book of life" (Rev 21:27).

The Construction of the Heavenly City

The description of the New Jerusalem is provided by one of the seven angels that had the seven bowls. This might alert the reader to the Feast of [Seven] Weeks. The very construction of the city itself has a liturgical role. The twelve foundation stones are in almost exact correspondence to the twelve stones on the High Priest's pectoral that represented each of the Twelve Tribes. Above the twelve gates was written the name of each one of the tribes (Rev 21:12).[72] Eight of the twelve stones mentioned in Rev 21:19–20 match with those listed in Exod 39:10–12. The inhabitants of the city are a priestly people. Significantly, Exod 39:14 says that the stones "were engraved as seals are." This image of Jerusalem reflecting the High Priest's breast plate was first developed in Isa 54:11–12. The text in Tob 13:16–18 develops this further and the description of the New Jerusalem as found in Rev 21 is closest to that of Tobit.

> For Jerusalem will be rebuilt as a city to be His dwelling-place for all ages. How blessed shall I be if a remnant of my offspring will see your glory and gratefully acknowledge the King of Heaven! The gates of Jerusalem will be built of sapphire and emerald, and all your walls of precious stone. The tower of Jerusalem will be built of gold and wood, and their embattlements of finest gold. The streets of Jerusalem will be paved with garnet and stone of Ophir. The gates of Jerusalem will sing out with hymns of joy, and all its houses will cry out, "Hallelujah, praised be the God of Israel!" And in you the blessed will praise His holy name for ever and ever.[73]

Beale recognizes that Rev 21 might be dependent on Tob 13, but would rather interpret them as both reflecting a common tradition.[74] But there is no need to discountenance the usage of Tobit, for as we have seen

---

72. One might object that each foundation stone was inscribed with "the name of the one of the twelve apostles of the Lamb" (Rev 21:14), but one must remember that the term apostle means "one who is sent" and that there are twelve Minor Prophets sent to the People of Israel. For 1 Kgs 14:6 both the LXX and Aquila use the noun *apostolos* to refer to the prophet. Matt 23:34 and Luke 11:49 use the verb *apostellō* regarding the prophets. For the term *apostolos* in Jewish usage for prophets, see Rengstorf, "απόστολος." (The four Major Prophets would be represented by the four walls of the city.) A thoroughly Jewish interpretation of the vision can be had without presuming the "apostles" to be those of Jesus Christ. Even in Heb 3:1 Jesus is called "apostle and high priest," clearly a Jewish metaphor.

73. Following Fitzmyer's translation of the Greek and Aramaic in *Tobit*, 303.

74. See Beale, *Book of Revelation*, 1086–87.

this hagiographical book was read right before the Feast of Pentecost and other sections of it have influenced the author of Revelation. In fact, the phrase "Jerusalem, the holy city" (Rev 21:2) is an exact match with Tob 13:9. The Isaiah text does not speak of the streets, whereas Tob 13:17 says they are paved "with the stones of Ophir," i.e., the "gold of Ophir," the author here using a poetic device having just mentioned "embattlements of finest gold."[75] Rev 21:21 likewise has "the street of the city is pure gold." Furthermore, Tob 13–14 has been found at Qumran in both Hebrew and Aramaic.[76] Therefore, the author of the Book of Revelation describes the New Jerusalem according to the liturgical reading used in preparation for the Feast of Weeks. Of course, this is not to dismiss any correlation with Isaiah or any other sacred Jewish text.

The author of Revelation masterfully weaves a tapestry of threads from the Law, Prophets, and Writings, but the warp and woof are the liturgical texts for the Feast of Weeks. Rev 4–11 solidly lays down the pattern and chapters 12–22 develop the artistic design. We are now in a position to survey the prologue, chapters 1–3, and the epilogue, the end of chapter 22.

THE PROLOGUE AND EPILOGUE

Chapters 1–3: A Christian Cover Letter

As mentioned above, the name Jesus does not appear whatsoever in chapters 4–11. Theories of authorship must take this glaring fact into account, especially when a redactor could have easily textually equated the Lamb with Jesus but did not. The name "Jesus" does appear, however, six times in 12:1—22:7, *but always alone*. In 1:1—3:22 the name "Jesus" occurs five times (three of which are "Jesus Christ"), and this amazingly all in 1:1–9. In what most scholars consider the epilogue to the Book of Revelation, 22:6/8–21, "Jesus" appears three times—and that in only the last six verses, where twice he is called "Lord Jesus."

In his analysis of Semitisms operative in the Book of Revelation, Steven Thompson concludes that Rev 2–3 is nearly free from Hebraic constructions et cetera working in the Greek text, whereas the rest of the

---

75. Every single time that Ophir is mentioned in the Hebrew Bible, it is always in reference to gold.

76. See Fitzmyer, "Aramaic and Hebrew Fragments"; and idem, "Tobit," 2:949.

corpus is deeply immersed in grammatical Hebraism.[77] The first chapter is peppered with Semitisms due to citing from the Tanakh eleven times. Something must be going on in Rev 1–3 and 22:8–21 (also the only places where "John" is mentioned) that is not in the rest of the received text. I believe that the majority of the Book of Revelation was originally a Jewish apocalypse that was then appropriated by Jews who espoused faith in Jesus of Nazareth.[78]

The references to "Jesus" in Rev 12:1—22:7 will be dealt with in the following chapter when analyzing the historical context of the writing of the book as we presently have it. Suffice it to say right now, there was another Jewish prophet named Jesus, and he proclaimed the imminent end of Jerusalem during the Jewish War 66–70 CE.

Christology

The first three chapters of Revelation are markedly Christian. Of the five times "Jesus" is mentioned, three of them are the couplet "Jesus Christ." The theology found in Rev 1–3 is decidedly Christian, and chapters 2–3 are in fact introductory cover letters to the Apocalypse that follows (4:1—22:7). In short, one is to read the Apocalypse in the light of faith in Jesus Christ as the promised Messiah. The writer of chapters 1–3 is named John (Rev 1:1-2, 9), and he himself was the recipient of a revelation of the Resurrected Jesus (of Nazareth). For convenience sake, I will refer to the literary producer of these chapters either as the "writer" or simply as John. I distinguish him from the "author," the authoritative source, behind chapters 4–22 (the Apocalypse, henceforth also referred to as the "corpus").

One question specific to this investigation is: Was John aware of the liturgical significance of the corpus? And, did he incorporate readings from the Feast of Weeks into his prologue? If so, he probably was a disciple (i.e., follower) of the "author" to some extent. In other words, he recognized the visions of the seer as authentic and authoritative. John obviously perceived Jesus of Nazareth as the fulfillment of what had been prophetically taught by the seer.

---

77. See Thompson, *Apocalypse and Semitic Syntax*, 107. Also cf. Aune, *Revelation*, clx–ccvii.

78. Here I am indebted to the critique articulated by Ford (*Revelation*, 38–46), which caused me to re-evaluate my own understanding of the book. I do, however, hold a somewhat different view of authorship, as shall be explicated below.

John opens his introduction with: "The revelation of Jesus Christ, which God gave him to show his servants what must soon take place; he made it known by sending his angel to his servant John" (1:1). Here the writer quotes in part Dan 2:28, just as the author of Rev 4:1 did. The literary "disciple" closely links himself with the message of the Apocalypse. John seems to espouse a "low Christology" in that the Resurrected Jesus is in need of a revelation coming from God Almighty; i.e., although in glory, even Jesus does not yet know everything that the Father knows. Furthermore, an angelic mediator is still necessary to communicate this revelation from Jesus to John. John's pneumatology is likewise primitive, in that presumably the Holy Spirit is referred to as "the seven spirits before his [God's] throne" (Rev 1:4 NIV alternate). Note that these "seven spirits" (each?) address one of the seven churches.

Notwithstanding, John categorically views Jesus as the Christ (Messiah of God) and ascribes to him several exalted titles in chapter 1, not to mention 2–3 (and in the epilogue twice calling him "Lord Jesus"). John's view of redemption is in accord with that of the author of the Apocalypse. Jesus Christ "loves us and freed us from our sins by his blood, and made us to be a kingdom, priests serving his God and Father" (1:5–6). However, John now accentuates the washing away of *sin*, something not explicit in 5:9–10. Recall that the sacrificed lamb very well could have been the thanksgiving offering from the waving of the sheaf that inaugurates the countdown to the Feast of Weeks. Here, however, redemption is clearly understood as atonement. This, however, will cause the reader to understand the Lamb as the paschal lamb, something perhaps not intended by the original author of Rev 4–5.

The last clause in 1:6, "made us a kingdom, priests to serve his God," is a direct quote from Exod 19:6, the (by-now celebrated) Pentecost lection. The Greek *kai*, translated as "and," most probably has a Semitic meaning underlying it; thus more properly the verse should be translated: "has washed away our sins with his blood in order to make us a line of kings, priests to serve his God." Significantly, Jesus Christ "has" a God; the theology here is still embedded in Jewish thinking. There is a distinction made between Jesus and God; some sort of "subordination" is operative here, as well as Rev 3:2, 12.[79]

What grants Jesus his exalted status? He is "the faithful witness, the firstborn of the dead, and the ruler of the kings of the earth" (1:5).

---

79. The same is found in John 20:17.

The phrase "firstborn" reflects the idea of first-fruits and is taken from Ps 89:27. Importantly, the Midrash Rabbah for Exod 19:7 ties Ps 89:27 into its excursus and refers this to the "King Messiah."[80] This same Psalm employs the phrase "faithful witness" (Ps 89:37) regarding the moon as a sign of David's throne being everlasting. *Midr. Gen* 97 interprets Ps 89:37 as a messianic prophecy. John sees Jesus as the fulfillment of these prophecies. He is the first-born from the dead, or the first-fruit of the resurrection, and as such can make others "a line of kings, priests to serve his God and Father."

John also utilizes Dan 7:13 in his presentation of Jesus who "is coming with the clouds" (Rev 1:7) and who appears "like the Son of Man" (Rev 1:13). His descriptions of the Son of Man are also based on Daniel. But John also weaves into the portrayal a phrase from Ezek 43:2—"his voice was like the sound of many waters" (Rev 1:15). Christ eventually commands John, "Write down, therefore, what you have seen, and what is presently happening, and what will happen afterwards" (Rev 1:19, my translation). This is heavily influenced by Hab 2:2–3:

> Write down the revelation,
> and make it plain on tablets
> so that a herald may run with it,
> For the revelation awaits an appointed time;
> It speaks of the end
> and will not prove false.
> Though it linger, wait for it;
> it will certainly come and will not delay. (NIV)

Here John alludes to a passage that would readily jump to mind for anyone reading the prophetic haphtarah from Hab 3 for the Feast of Weeks. Hence, in chapter 1 the writer has integrated texts from the liturgical readings for Pentecost from the Law (Exodus), Prophets (Habakkuk and Ezekiel), and Writings (Daniel).

John's vision of the Resurrected Jesus is replete with symbols of seven. In fact, Rev 1–3 contains seven sets of seven: 1) churches (1:4); 2) spirits (1:4); 3) lampstands (1:12); 4) stars (1:16); 5) angels (1:20); 6) descriptions of Christ (chs. 2–3); and 7) "I knows" and concomitant blessings (chs. 2–3). Seven sets of seven thus produce the mystical number 49, so intrinsically linked with the Feast of Weeks. The very first thing John sees in his vision is one like the Son of Man standing in the midst

---

80. See Beale, *Book of Revelation*, 191–92.

of seven golden lampstands (1:12–13). I believe David Aune rightly understands these lampstands to be seven menorahs.[81] Albeit John never explicates that these seven lampstands are each seven-branched, the traditional menorah is alluded to in Zech 4:2, 10b; Philo correlates this to the seven celestial luminaries, and the archaeological find in the synagogue in Peki'in, the coin of Mattathias Antigonus (ca. 40 BCE), as well as the menorah depicted on Titus' Arch of Triumph (81 CE), all have a seven-branched menorah.[82] Seven seven-branched menorahs visually call to mind 7 times 7.

Furthermore, John received his vision on "the Lord's Day" (1:10). Scholars debate whether this means Sunday or Easter. If it were Easter, was John contemplating the liturgical readings for the Feast of Pentecost, one which the apostolic church celebrated?[83] Jesus is dressed in a high priest's linen robe and stands among the seven golden lampstands (1:13).[84] Besides the reference to Pentecost in Acts 2, the Apostle Paul expresses a desire to observe Pentecost in Jerusalem (Acts 20:16). Curiously the only other time the Feast is mentioned in the New Testament is when Paul plans to stay in Ephesus until Pentecost (1 Cor 16:8). He presumably celebrated the Feast of Weeks with the Christian community there. Coincidentally enough (?), the first circular letter that John sends is to the church in Ephesus. The seven epistles, however, bear no noticeable reference to the Feast or the liturgical texts. Each appears personally to address a local situation and each church is a recipient of a blessing that is connected to John's vision of the Resurrected Christ. The one theme in common with the rest of the book and with the Feast of Weeks is that these seven churches to varying degrees dealt with combating idolatry.

Rev 22:8–21: A Redactor's Warning

The next time we encounter John is in Rev 22:8: "I, John, am the one who heard and saw these things." Does this mean that John necessarily saw the whole of the Apocalypse and was its sole author? I do not believe so. It is quite plausible that John did experience an actual vision of the Resurrected Jesus who then recalled to his memory what he, John, had

---

81. See Aune, *Revelation*, 88.

82. See Strauss, "Menorah."

83. Regarding the "day" on which John receives his revelation, see the end of ch. 6 below.

84. See Beale, *Book of Revelation*, 208–9.

previously heard from the seer of the Apocalypse, whether firsthand or through one of his followers. The Resurrected Christ's bringing back to mind things written about him in the Law, Prophets, and Writings was a common Christian occurrence (Luke 24:25-27, 44-45; 1 Pet 1:10-11).[85] Thus I am proposing that John does re-envision in his mind's eye, under the impulse of the Spirit, the prophetic apocalypse as he had received it. John acts as the final redactor and transmitter of the Apocalypse and himself writes the prologue (chs. 1-3) and epilogue (22:8-21). I count 22:7 as the conclusion to the original Apocalypse: "Blessed is the one who keeps the words of the prophecy of this book." This is a fitting ending, closing with a benediction.

The epilogue thus begins with "I, John, am the one who heard and saw these things. And when I heard and saw them, I fell down to worship at the feet of the angel who showed them to me; but he said to me, 'You must not do that! I am a fellow servant with you and your comrades the prophets, and with those who keep the words of this book. Worship God'" (22:8-9). The question is: If John is just now writing down the visions and prophecies, who are "those who keep the words of this book"? The verb *tērountōn* is a present active participle. The angel speaks as if people are presently keeping the words of this book, as if a corpus (whether oral or written) already exists. But if John just finished writing it, no one has read it yet. However, if John saw a vision of the Resurrected Jesus and subsequently re-envisioned through the Spirit what had previously been committed to his "brethren, the prophets," then the angel's statement makes sense.[86] Many commentators either fail to notice this or simply gloss over this presupposition of an already existing corpus. Aune seems to sidestep the issue by translating "words [*logous*] of this book" as "commands."[87] Nothing prevents the theory that John now sees the visions, passed down by the brotherhood of prophets, in a new light, in the light of the revelation of Jesus Christ. Consequently the angel continues, "Do not seal up the words of the prophecy of this book, for the time is near" (22:10). John's new revelation, new insight, is to be publicized because the time of its fulfillment is in fact very soon.

---

85. In short, the ministries of both Peter and Paul were centered around unpacking the Hebrew Scriptures in reference to Jesus, as did the writers of the Gospels.

86. The idea of a brotherhood of prophets is thoroughly Jewish, and in the early Christian communities there were groups of prophets as well.

87. See Aune, *Revelation*, 1186.

But even earlier at the close of what I consider to be the Jewish Apocalypse, in 22:6 one reads, "And he [the angel] said to me, 'These words are trustworthy and true, for the Lord, the God of the spirits of the prophets, has sent his angel to show his servants what must soon take place.'" Note the plural servants. In 10:7 and 11:18 when the text says "servants" it is in the phrase "his servants the prophets," which Aune and others (correctly) take to mean Hebrew prophets.[88] There is no compelling textual reason then to interpret "his servants" in 22:6 in a broader sense to mean the faithful, let alone Christians, which Beale awkwardly tries to justify.[89] It is at least just as plausible that these servants are the recent recipients of the prophetic Spirit who received revelations via an angel. In short, these servants/prophets might be the very authoritative sources of Rev 4–11 and 12:1—22:7. Also note that "Jesus" does not factor into the mediation of the revelation as he does regarding that given to John in 1:1.

Concomitantly, the closing anathema at 22:18-19 likewise suggests that an alteration of the redacted book was a real possibility. "I warn everyone who hears the words of the prophecy of this book: if anyone adds to them, God will add to that person the plagues described in this book; if anyone takes away from the words of the book of this prophecy, God will take away that person's share in the tree of life and in the holy city, which are described in this book." Why is there a need for such a prohibition? If this be a redaction of an already existing body of prophecies, the warning readily makes sense. John's version is to be the normative interpretation of the original author's visions. John's is the correct reading in the light of Jesus Christ.[90]

John's epilogue does not end with any direct Pentecost liturgical text. However, the correct interpretative key to chapters 4–22 is supplied. "It is I, Jesus, who sent my angel to you with this testimony for the churches. I am the root and the descendant of David, the bright morning star" (22:16). This testimony is given in order that the churches may know that Jesus is the one who is the shoot from the Root of David. He is the one to whom the prophecies really refer. The seven churches are

---

88. See ibid., 570, 645; and Beale, *Book of Revelation*, 546.

89. See Beale, *Book of Revelation*, 1124–26.

90. Parallels to Deut 4:1–2 and 29:19–20 do not undermine my thesis. John merely cites a scriptural precedence for his canonical interpretative sanctions. Deuteronomy itself was the "new" authorized version of the oral tradition.

facing assaults from false prophets and pseudo-apostles (2:2; 2:14–15; 2:20–24). These Christian communities have also distinguished themselves from the "orthodox" Jewish teachings delivered in the synagogues (Rev 2:9; 3:9). These Jesus-believing Jews see themselves as the ones who have remained true Jews. "I know your affliction and your poverty, even though you are rich. I know the slander on the part of those who say that they are Jews and are not, but are a synagogue of Satan" (2:9).[91] Thus John has appropriated an originally Jewish apocalypse and interpreted it *correctly* as prophetically speaking about Jesus of Nazareth.[92] This point will be taken up later, as well as the identity of the authoritative source and the redactor named John.

Whatever one's views are regarding the authorship of the Book of Revelation, I believe it is demonstrably clear that the author was steeped not only in the Hebrew Scriptures but also in the Jewish liturgical cycle, and utilized the lectionary for the Feast of Weeks in an inspired fashion. The matter of the author's historical context can now be investigated.

---

91. For a good analysis of this verse see Frankfurter, "Jews or Not?" See also ch. 6 and Appendix E below.

92. I am not arguing that a written text was necessarily existent, though this is possible; rather, I am stating that there was at least an oral prophetic message circulating among some Jews, and that this apocalyptic vision was adopted by a Jewish-Christian network of communities.

5

The Historical, Religious, and Political Contexts

ANTIOCHUS EPIPHANES IV

THE AUTHOR OF THE Book of Revelation creatively re-envisions the salvation history of Israel and under the impulse of the prophetic Spirit applies the theological patterns and promises to his own context. Scholars are generally in agreement that the book in its final form dates from towards the close of the first century CE. The major event in Israel's history during this era was the Jewish War (66–70 CE), at least dating to the destruction of Jerusalem.[1] Some scholars have rightly pointed out that this war lasted three and a half years, just as the seer describes the over-running of Jerusalem (Rev 11:2–3; 12:6, 14; 13:5). The author is quoting Dan 7:25, which refers to the time period when Antiochus Epiphanes IV (167–163 BCE) persecuted the Jews. Antiochus erected a statue of himself in the temple and demanded to be worshiped as a god. In fact, his statute was in the likeness of Zeus! This occasioned the Maccabean Revolt and gave birth to a spate of apocalyptic literature. The conflict with Antiochus and the subsequent Maccabean victory became an archetypal pattern in Jewish thought for fighting idolatry and evil.

Antiochus Epiphanes IV, however, had several successors to his throne, one of them being Antiochus VII (138–129 BCE), a reprehensible figure himself who bedeviled Israel. This Antiochus had been supported by John Hyrcanus, whose political alliances caused many Jews to question John's worthiness to be high priest. Many ancient sources ended up confusing Antiochus VII with his predecessor Antiochus IV because of

---

1. Robinson does date Revelation to c. 68 CE; see his *Redating the New Testament*, 221–53, esp. 248–53. I concur with his analysis.

the similarities.² In some ways, Antiochus VII was a *redivivus*, a re-appearing of Antiochus IV. This is important because Josephus places the death of Antiochus VII right after Pentecost 129 BCE.³ In other words, the "defeat" of the archetypal "Antiochus," re-embodied in his successor, takes place shortly after the Feast of Weeks. The Feast of Seven Weeks witnesses the culmination of Antiochus VII's tyranny.

HASMONEAN AND HERODIAN ERAS

Israel gained independence soon after the Feast of Weeks under John Hyrcanus, and a new kingdom was established. This independent theocratic kingdom was not to last long however. During the reign of John Hyrcanus's grandson the kingdom was lost to Pompey.⁴ The Roman general Pompey arrived at Jericho in the spring of 63 BCE, right at the time of Pentecost, and began a siege of Jerusalem that lasted three months.⁵ This fall of Jerusalem into Roman hands took place exactly seventy years after John Hyrcanus became ethnarch, a vassal to the Seleucid Dynasty. One can only imagine the interpretations given to Daniel and Jeremiah in this context.

Israel was now part of the Roman Empire. From this time period onward, Pentecost became an electrically charged feast. The liturgical readings remark that the people are to be a *kingly* people (Exod 19:6) and that God delivered them from their oppressors (Egypt and Babylon). The Targum for Hab 3 now weaves in Daniel's apocalyptic vision and lists the Roman Empire as another political beast. When providing the context for the Jewish War that erupted in 66 CE, Josephus recounts an episode that had happened nearly a century earlier, but which was still emblazoned on the religious and political consciousness of the Jewish nation. A revolt was waged trying to establish Antigonus back on the throne, he being the great-grandson of John Hyrcanus. Josephus records the following scene.

---

2. See Thackeray, *Josephus*, 355 note b.

3. See Josephus, *Ant.* 13.8.4 sections 251–52.

4. John Hyrcanus' grandson was named after him and thus is distinguished as John Hyrcanus II. For the Hasmonean and Herodian Dynasties see Appendix C.

5. See Josephus, *Ant.* 14.53–54; and *B.J.* 1:149, as well as Solomon, "Pompey," 16:368.

> When the Feast called Pentecost came round, the whole neighborhood of the temple and the entire city were crowded with country-folk, for the most part in arms. Phasael defended the walls; Herod, with a small force, the palace. With this he descended upon the enemy's disordered ranks in the suburb, killed large numbers of them, put the rest to flight and shut them up, some in the city, others in the Temple, others in the entrenched camp outside the walls."[6]

In his *Jewish Antiquities*, Josephus specifies the numbers involved: "tens of thousands of armed and unarmed men gathered round the Temple.[7] This rebellion and blood bath happened in 40 BCE. Once again, the Feast of Weeks became a politically energized event with ideas of religious freedom from one's evil oppressors.

The pattern repeated itself in 4 BCE. In this case Sabinus, the Roman procurator of Syria, advanced into Jerusalem and tried to plunder it of its wealth.

> On the arrival of Pentecost—thus the Jews call a feast which occurs seven weeks after Passover, and takes its name from the number of intervening days—it was not the customary ritual so much as indignation which drew the people in crowds to the capital. A countless multitude flocked in from Galilee, from Idumaea, from Jericho, and from Peraea beyond the Jordan, but it was the native population of Judaea itself which, both in numbers and ardour, was pre-eminent. Distributing themselves into three divisions, they formed three camps, one on the north of the Temple, another on the south, adjoining the hippodrome, and the third near the palace on the west. Thus investing the Romans on all sides, they held them under siege.[8]

Sabinus panicked because the Jews numbered in the tens of thousands; thus fighting erupted between the Roman soldiers and the Jewish populace. Subsequently, the porticoes of the temple were set ablaze and hundreds were burned alive. After the ensuing slaughter, the soldiers plundered the temple treasury. Because of this massive loss of life and desecration of God's temple, the throngs became even more enraged. The whole affair only fueled further uprisings throughout the country.[9]

6. Josephus, *B.J.* 1.13.3 section 253.
7. Josephus, *Ant.* 14.13.4 section 337.
8. Josephus, *B.J.* 2.3.1 sections 42–45.
9. See Josephus, *B.J.* 2.3.2–4.2 sections 46–56, as well as *Ant.* 17.10.2–6.

THE COMMON ERA AND THE JEWISH WAR

Consequently, by the beginning of the Common Era Shavu'ot was a religious feast ablaze with political sentiment and apocalyptic ardor. It is no wonder then that Philo calls Pentecost "the most national of feasts."[10] In addition to the political events, the liturgical readings themselves in the context of harvest and judgment imbue the Feast of Weeks with eschatological import. As Potin writes, "Perhaps it is necessary to suspect that Pentecost had been clothed in a character rather political and patriotic, something which would accord with a Feast of the renewal of the Alliance [with God], given birth to precisely in an atmosphere of violent reaction against the political and religious menacing threats to which Judaism was subjected."[11] In short, is one in alliance with God or with the Romans? One can safely presume that the cultic ceremony and liturgical readings fanned the flames of religious and political independence and that the social climate itself in turn cast an all too apocalyptic feel into the prophetic texts. The Targum on Hab 3 is a vivid example of this.

> For the kingdom of Babel will not endure;
> It will not exercise its power over Israel;
> The kings of the Medes will be killed;
> The powerful rulers of Greece will not prosper;
> The Romans will be destroyed;
> They will not gather the remaining bits of Jerusalem.[12]

The Massoretic text says nothing of the kind, but the Aramaic translator believes he has appropriately captured the spirit of the prophet's message. The liturgy is an embodiment of God's living word to us in our present situation, so says the targumist. In fact, the targumist is justified in his exposition on the text because the prophet Habakkuk, when recalling God's events of old, stated: "Repeat it in our time, reveal it in our time" (Hab 3:2). This liturgical reading and Targum impacted the author of the Book of Revelation. He is a product of his own culture and times. The author of the Apocalypse re-envisions the prophetic message. He believes God has revealed it to him in his own day and age and that God will repeat what he has done in the past. The author's contemporary situation was the conflict with Rome.

---

10. See Philo, *Spec.* 2.176.
11. Potin, *Fête juive de la Pentecôte*, 136.
12. See Potin, *Fête juive de la Pentecôte*, 169; my translation.

Depending upon one's views, as irony, political savvy, or providence would have it, Jerusalem would be assaulted once again at the Feast of Weeks. The Jewish War was a series of battles in various places (see Appendix D). From the vantage point of Jerusalem the war arrived at her doorstep on Pentecost. Vespasian occupied Jericho just a few days before Pentecost in 68 CE.[13] The Qumran Community, which had emphasized the Feast of Weeks as its renewal of the covenant, was destroyed during this very same liturgical season. The members surely interpreted this as an apocalyptic event with eschatological import. General Vespasian's plans to lay siege on Jerusalem promptly followed suit. However, what must have seemed as by divine intervention, Vespasian suspended his siege works on Jerusalem after hearing that Emperor Nero was dead. It was Nero himself who had ordered the campaign against Judaea. Pentecost that year fell late, on June 24 according to the official rabbinic calculation. Vespasian had conquered Jericho, twenty miles away from Jerusalem, four days prior.[14] Nero had committed suicide on June 9; however, the news of the emperor's death did not reach General Vespasian until after he had laid the groundwork for his siege of Jerusalem. By what must have appeared like a miracle, Jerusalem was spared. General Vespasian had other plans of his own; he sought the purple for himself. Vespasian calculated his moves. Three emperors succeeded Nero in the space of one year. Finally, Vespasian was proclaimed emperor on July 1, 69.

The matter of the Jewish Revolt, however, still plagued the Roman Empire, and so Emperor Vespasian assigned his son Titus to finish what he had started. On Passover 70 CE, Titus laid siege to Jerusalem. Josephus recounts the drama in rather lurid detail. Significantly, the Feast of Weeks figures into his account when he relates the "miraculous phenomenon" that presaged the destruction of the temple. Shortly after Passover,

> Throughout all parts of the country chariots were seen in the air and armed battalions hurtling through the clouds and encompassing the cities. Moreover, at the feast which is called Pentecost, the priests on entering the inner court of the temple by night, as their custom was in the discharge of their ministrations, reported that they were conscious, first of a commotion and a din, and after that of a voice as of a host, "We are departing hence."[15]

---

13. See Laperrousaz, "Problèmes d'histoire," 274.
14. For this dating and the historical events see ibid., 271–80.
15. Josephus, *B.J.* 6.5.3 sections 298–300.

The priests of the temple heard the Bat Qol, the Divine Voice, which declared God was abandoning the temple. This event became so well known and repeated that Tacitus refers to it as well.[16]

Given the political history of Jerusalem in relation to the Feast of Weeks, it comes as no surprise that the author of the Book of Revelation would focus on this as an apocalyptic motif for his work, which most probably addressed the fall of Jerusalem and subsequent persecution of God's holy people by the Roman Empire. Pompey had laid siege to Jerusalem at Pentecost in 63 BCE. The same festival witnessed the rebellion and bloodbath concerning Antigonus in 40 BCE. Sabinus wreaked havoc on the Feast of Harvest in 4 BCE. Vespasian began his siege of Jerusalem during Pentecost 68 CE. When his son Titus took up the siege again in the year 70, on the Feast of First-Fruits, the Divine Voice resonated God's intentions. The Feast of Weeks itself is a politically and religiously charged apocalyptic historical event. Pentecost is the logical historical backdrop for the Book of Revelation.

THE BEAST WITH SEVEN HEADS

Scholars have long debated who the seven heads exactly are. The pertinent text says: "This calls for a mind with wisdom. The seven heads are seven hills on which the woman sits. They are also seven kings. Five have fallen, one is, the other has not yet come; but when he does come, he must remain for a little while" (Rev 17:9–10 NIV). Rome, like Babylon, was built upon seven hills. Numerous theories have been proposed, mainly impacted by which date one assigns the book's composition. Those who argue for a late date and presume Domitian is the seventh head are forced into contorted theories to make the description work.

Arguing for an early date (68–70 CE), John A. T. Robinson marshals evidence from early Christian documents that place the Book of Revelation in the time of Emperor Nero. Robinson bolsters these witnesses with arguments from historians such as Bernard Henderson and Arnaldo Momigliano as well as the church historian George Edmundson.[17] Edmundson interprets the "five are fallen" to mean that

> in each of these five cases there was violent death. Augustus and Tiberius could not be described as "fallen," even had their reigns

---

16. See Tacitus, *Hist.* 5.13.
17. See Robinson, *Redating the New Testament*, 221–53.

> come within the seer's purview. The five are Claudius, who adopted Nero as his son and heir, Nero himself, Galba, Otho, and Vitellius. "The one who is" signifies the man for the moment invested with imperial power, Domitian, the acting Emperor, who banished the writer. "The one not yet come" is the real Emperor Vespasian, who had not yet arrived at Rome to take into his hands the reins of government, and "he will continue only a short while," for Nero—"the beast that was, and is not, who is also an eighth, and is one of the seven"—will quickly return from the East whither he had fled, and once more seat himself on the throne.[18]

First, some words of explanation are in order. Domitian is the son of Emperor Vespasian and before Vespasian took the throne while in Alexandria, his son Domitian acted in his stead in Rome.[19] Edmundson presumes that John was indeed exiled by Domitian in early 70. Within the spate of one year, Nero was succeeded by three emperors: Galba was assassinated; Otho committed suicide; and Vitellius also was assassinated. Rumors had circulated that Nero was not in fact dead, but having suffered a major head wound subsequently fled to the East waiting to return one day to reclaim his imperial throne. In fact, an impostor Nero surfaced in 69 and was summarily executed.[20] Duff remarks that Robinson's (and Edmundson's) reading of the text warrants recognition as a viable option.[21] For these commentators, the seven emperors are: Claudius, Nero, Galba, Otho, Vitellius, Vespasian, and Titus.

Robinson himself has some misgivings though, regarding Edmundson's analysis, noting, "to start the count of the emperors with Claudius is strained."[22] But Robinson's discomfort is due in part to his premise that the Book of Revelation is a Christian work, a single whole written by John the Apostle. However, if the corpus of the Book of Revelation were originally a Jewish text, Edmundson's solving of the

---

18. Edmundson, *Church in Rome*, 175–76.
19. See Tacitus, *Hist.* 4.2; and Suetonius, *Dom.* 1
20. See Tacitus, *Hist.* 2.8–9. Bauckham notes that this event might have influenced the *Sibylline Oracles* 4:119 and 123; see Bauckham, *Climax of Prophecy*, 413. Yet because there were subsequent impostors in 80 and 89 CE, and the Oracle mentions the 79 CE eruption of Mt. Vesuvius in lines 130–36, Bauckham concludes that the Revelation must have been written after 80 CE (ibid., 414–16). But copycat occurrences do not negate the earlier event in 69 CE and the already existing myth, however, embryonic in form it might have been. In short, we need not look to the reign of Domitian.
21. See Duff, *Who Rides the Beast?*, 6.
22. Robinson, *Redating the New Testament*, 252.

The Historical, Religious, and Political Contexts 93

riddle makes perfect sense. Why start with Claudius? For at least three good reasons.

(1) According to the contemporaneous Roman historian Suetonius, Emperor Claudius expelled Jews from Rome some time around 50 CE (also see Acts 18:2). While usually favorable to Jews, or at least trying to maintain the peace, Claudius hardly fully sided with the Jews when some might have thought he should have.

(2) Claudius' full name was Tiberius Claudius *Nero* Germanicus. Claudius was the son of Nero Drusus. Claudius' successor was Emperor Nero whom Claudius had adopted as his son, Nero being the biological son of Claudius' fourth wife, Julia Agrippina (who in fact was Claudius' brother's daughter), and thus Nero was Claudius' brother's grandson. In this sense, Claudius inaugurated the Neronian crisis and the Jewish Wars.

In the eyes of both Romans and Jews, Claudius' marriage to Julia Agrippina was incestuous and immoral. She might even serve as another "type" for the Whore of Babylon since Claudius was her third husband.[23] In fact, Julia Agrippina was Emperor Caligula's sister and the two were widely believed to have been incestuous. She eventually plotted to have her brother assassinated through Lepidus, her deceased sister's husband with whom she had had adulterous relations.[24] After the death of her first husband (Gnaeus Domitius Ahenobarbus), Agrippina married her former brother-in-law and was reported to have carried on adulterous affairs. Agrippina's final husband was her uncle Emperor Claudius, whom she allegedly seduced.[25] Due to this marriage she was the first to ever have been granted the title Augusta while her husband was reigning Emperor; she was now herself endowed with imperial status and was to be publicly given homage.[26] When Claudius died, the populace was convinced that she had poisoned him so that her son Nero could more quickly ascend

---

23. To my knowledge, no one else has associated Julia Agrippina with the Whore of Babylon. I definitely do not preclude other imagery concomitantly at work here, namely Israel (the political institution which has "played the whore"—a biblical phrase, by its political alliance with Rome), and Dea Roma.

24. See Suetonius, *Cal.* 24.

25. See Suetonius, *Cl.* 26, 39; and Tacitus, *Ann.* 12.3.

26. See Barrett, *Agrippina*, 108.

to the throne. Eventually Nero had his own conniving mother killed. Suetonius records a popular gematria in Greek about Nero:

> Count the numerical values
> Of the letters in Nero's name,
> And in "murdered his own mother":
> You will find their sum is the same.[27]

Thus, in the popular mind, Nero was closely linked with his mother, the wife of Claudius.

Regarding the description of the Whore of Babylon, Rev 17:4 says, "The woman was clothed in purple and scarlet, and adorned with gold and jewels and pearls." As Augusta, contrary to custom, Julia Agrippina wore the imperial purple as well as gold raiment.[28] Anthony Barrett, a modern Roman historian who has written a comprehensive book on Agrippina, notes that sculpted heads of her "from the Claudian period are sometimes adorned with a diadem. This was an exceptional honour. The diadem was properly the attribute of a goddess, and allowed to mortals only after death. It is likely that Agrippina was the first to receive this distinction during her lifetime—another striking demonstration of her elevated position."[29] Perhaps more importantly regarding the Book of Revelation, an inscription from Aezani in the province of Asia Minor calls her "Divine Agrippina."[30] Likewise, in Asia Minor she sponsored games in which she was hailed as "Divine."[31] In Rev 17:4 the seer also describes the woman as holding a golden cup. Claudius granted Agrippina the right to use the *carpentum*, the ceremonial carriage regularly reserved for priests and statues of deities. Thus this image might be sacral as well. Later, Nero made Agrippina a priestess for her deceased deified husband Claudius; thus she is closely aligned with the imperial cultus.

---

27. Suetonius, *Nero* 39; rendition by Graves, *Twelve Caesars*, 231–32. The translation by J. C. Rolfe in *Suetonius*, 157, is more accurate but less prompting to the modern reader:

> Nero, Orestes, Alcmeon, their mothers slew.
> A calculation new. Nero his mother slew.

Nero's name in Greek adds up to 1005, as does the phrase, "his mother slew."

28. See Tacitus, *Ann.* 12.37, 42, 56; as well as Barrett, *Agrippina*, 129–30, for another occasion.

29. Barrett, *Agrippina*, 109.

30. See ibid., 113. Aezani is not far from the seven churches mentioned in Rev 2–3.

31. See ibid., 124 and 223, for the inscriptions.

Coins show that Nero claimed himself as *Divi Filius*, son of a god.³² In short, Claudius–Agrippina–Nero form a divine dynastic triad.

Besides being tied to Claudius and Nero, Julia Agrippina was previously sexually connected with those who would become Nero's three immediate successors. No sooner had Julia lost her first husband than she made sexual advances on the aristocrat and military commander Galba, hoping to advance herself politically. Galba was married at the time, and his mother-in-law publicly slapped Agrippina in the face for her adulterous wantonness.³³ Otho succeeded Galba as emperor. While emperor, Nero was having an adulterous affair with Poppaea Sabina, the current wife of Otho, a nobleman and friend of Nero's. Poppaea kept pleading with Emperor Nero to divorce Octavia, Claudius' daughter, so that the two of them could marry. Julia Agrippina, it was rumored, was so opposed to this stratagem that she herself bedded her twenty-two-year-old son, hoping he would renounce Otho's wife and choose her as mistress instead!³⁴ Vitellius succeeded Otho as emperor. Emperor Vitellius was the son of consul Lucius Vitellius, who convinced the senate to disregard the ban on a niece marrying an uncle, so that Agrippina could marry Emperor Claudius for the good of the empire.³⁵ In short, all three emperors who followed Nero had some sort of connection with Julia Agrippina and her sexual exploits and machinations.

While Agrippina had no sexual liaison with Emperor Vespasian, it was her son Nero, whom she had made emperor, who assigned General Vespasian to quell the uprising in Judaea in 66. The Jewish Wars could easily be laid at her feet. In fact, another connection can be made: the king of Judaea at the time of the wars was Herod Agrippa II. Agrippa II was raised in Rome in the imperial court of Claudius and Agrippina, and through her intervention, Agrippa II was made king of Judaea.³⁶ Agrippa II later would betray his people to Vespasian. Curiously enough, Herod Agrippa II was the seventh and last king of the Herodian dynasty. The Whore of Babylon sat upon a seven-headed Beast: the primary meaning

---

32. See ibid., 148.
33. See Suetonius, *Gal.* 5.
34. See Dio, *Hist.* 61.12; and Tacitus, *Ann.* 14.2.
35. See Tacitus, *Ann.* 12.5.
36. See Josephus, *Ant.* 20.6.3—7.1; and Barrett, *Agrippina*, 124–27.

is the Roman Empire, but perhaps a secondary veiled irony is at work as well—the Herodian dynasty in liaison with Rome.[37]

(3) Finally, there is another reason to commence the description of the seven-headed Beast with Claudius. Claudius gave Octavia (his biological daughter) in marriage to Nero (his adopted son) at the request of Julia Agrippina. The bloodline of Claudius was literally wed to that of Nero, the son of Claudius' niece, with whom he was in an incestuous marriage. The whole affair was truly "monstrous," and presiding over all of it was Julia Agrippina II.[38] Agrippina embodied the corruption, sexual immorality, and political intrigue associated with Rome, the *mater civitas* of the beastly empire. In the popular mind, she probably came to symbolize the moral decadency of the empire. All of Agrippina's contemporaneous Roman historians were scathing in their report of her.

"JESUS": WHO DO YOU SAY I AM?

Jesus, son of Ananias

Having put the Book of Revelation into the historical context of the Jewish Wars instigated by Nero, and having specifically highlighted the Feast of Weeks in 70 CE, we are now able to analyze the occurrences of "Jesus" in Rev 12:1—22:7. It is highly imperative to note that whenever the name "Jesus" does appear in this latter part of Revelation, *it never appears with any glorified title*. Recall that in 1:1—3:22 the name "Jesus" occurs five times (three of which are "Jesus Christ"), and in what the vast majority of scholars assign to the epilogue, "Jesus" appears three times, and that in the last six verses, 22:16–21, twice in which he is called "Lord Jesus." In other words, in the prologue and epilogue the "Jesus" referred to is definitely the glorified Christ, whereas in 12:1—22:7 he is not demonstrably so by ascription. Textually there is no warrant to presume automatically this Jesus to be the Jesus of Nazareth.

---

37. Herod the Great I was not a Jew and was made king by the Roman Senate. The seven Herodian rulers in succession are: Herod I, Herod II, Herod Archaelaus, Herod Antipas, Philip, Herod Agrippa I, and Herod Agrippa II. Israel had "played the whore" by having non-Jewish kings who were not truly committed to the Jewish religion.

38. Furthermore, Julia Agrippina was the only woman to have an imperial city named after her: *Colonia Claudia Ara Agrippinensium*, modern-day Cologne. This is where Julia Agrippina had been born while her father Germanicus was doing battle. Claudius renamed *oppidum Ubiorum* in her honor. Geographically, this city sits atop the Roman Empire. Could there be a double entendre at work?

The Historical, Religious, and Political Contexts

Josephus remarks that the Voice, the Bat Qol, was heard in the temple at Pentecost. After mentioning this, he continues with an account of a prophet who predicted the fall of Jerusalem. I shall quote the episode in its entirety because the text has great significance for the historical contextual interpretation of the Book of Revelation.

> But a further portent was even more alarming. Four years before the war, when the city was enjoying profound peace and prosperity, there came to the feast at which it is the custom of all the Jews to erect tabernacles to God, one Jesus, son of Ananias, a rude peasant, who, standing in the temple, suddenly began to cry out, "A voice from the east, a voice from the west, a voice from the four winds; a voice against Jerusalem and the sanctuary, a voice against the bridegroom and the bride, a voice against all the people." Day and night he went about all the alleys with this cry on his lips. Some of the leading citizens, incensed at these ill-omened words, arrested the fellow and severely chastised him. But he, without a word on his own behalf or for the private ear of those who smote him, only continued his cries as before. Thereupon, the magistrates, supposing, as was indeed the case, that the man was under some supernatural impulse, brought him before the Roman governor; there, although flayed to the bone with scourges, he neither sued for mercy nor shed a tear, but, merely introducing the most mournful of variations into his ejaculation, responded to each stroke with "Woe to Jerusalem!" When Albinus, the governor, asked him who and whence he was and why he uttered these cries, he answered him never a word, but unceasingly reiterated his dirge over the city, until Albinus pronounced him a maniac and let him go. During the whole period up to the outbreak of the war he neither approached nor was seen talking to any of the citizens, but daily, like a prayer that he had coined, repeated his lament, "Woe to Jerusalem!" He neither cursed any of those who beat him from day to day, nor blessed those who offered him food: to all men that melancholy presage was his one reply. His cries were loudest at the festivals. So for seven years and five months he continued his wail, his voice never flagging nor his strength exhausted, until in the siege, having seen his presage verified, he found his rest. For, while going his round and shouting in piercing tones from the wall, "Woe once more to the city and to the people and to the temple," as he added a last word, "and woe to me also," a stone hurled from the *ballista* struck and killed him on the spot. So with these ominous words still upon his lips he passed away.[39]

---

39. Josephus, *B.J.* 6.5.3 sections 300–309.

Several points need to be made. Josephus directly links the prophet Jesus, son of Ananias, to the voice heard in the temple at the Feast of Pentecost. While this Jesus began his prophetic ministry on the Feast of Tabernacles, he continued his dire predictions unceasingly and was especially vocal on all the feast days. Although Josephus does not say so, one can safely presume that Jesus was particularly inspired on the Feast of Weeks in 70 CE, given that the Bat Qol had thundered in the temple.

The author of the Book of Revelation (and probably the final redactor as well) must have been aware of this prophet Jesus. In fact, it is plausible that this was the original Jesus referred to in the Jewish Apocalypse. Jesus, son of Ananias, commenced his prophetic proclamations, three and a half years before the Jewish Revolt.[40] The Jewish War itself lasted another three and a half years. This Jesus reportedly utilized the bridegroom and bride imagery (perhaps from Jer 7:34) in his eschatological dirges, a motif that is echoed in the Book of Revelation. Likewise, he summoned the four winds as witnesses and was himself unflagging in his witness to the word of God.

In Rev 12:1—22:7 the name "Jesus" appears six times. The name, of course, is the Greek rendition of the common Hebrew name Joshua. The seer of the Book of Revelation, having just spoken of Israel as the bride wed to the bridegroom (19:5–9), relates how he wished to kneel in worship before the angelic mediator. The angel rebuffs him, saying, "You must not do that! I am a fellow servant with you and your comrades who hold the testimony to Jesus. Worship God! For the testimony of Jesus is the spirit of prophecy" (19:10, following alternate). Notably, two out of the six times that the name "Jesus" occurs are in the context of the bride-and-bridegroom motif, and here "Jesus" is explicitly linked with "the spirit of prophecy." This reference could quite easily apply to Jesus, son of Ananias, if it were in the original Apocalypse (as I believe it was). Nevertheless, this passage very well could also be the hand of John, the Christian redactor, who might have inserted this verse (or, for that matter, let it stand, but now to be read in a new light—that of Jesus of Nazareth).

---

40. Josephus rounds this off, saying four years, but given that Josephus says his total time of prophesying lasted seven years and that he died during the siege of Jerusalem, which lasted from April until August of 70 CE, his ministry must have begun three and half years earlier, the Feast of Tabernacles generally occurring in September/October.

The Historical, Religious, and Political Contexts 99

In the context of the three-and-a-half-year period, the Dragon pursues "those who keep the commandments of God and bear testimony to Jesus" (12:17 RSV). Mention of "Jesus" appears again in the context of persecution. "Here is a call for the endurance of the saints, those who keep the commandments of God and hold fast to the faith of Jesus" (14:12). The Greek text does not say "faith *in* Jesus," but rather uses the genitive: "faith *of* Jesus." One could obey God's commandments and have the same faith as Jesus, son of Ananias. Nothing in 12:17 or 14:12 absolutely necessitates that this "Jesus" be the Christian Jesus of Nazareth. The fifth instance is found in 17:6 when speaking of the infamous Whore of Babylon. "I saw that the woman was drunk with the blood of saints, the blood of those who bore testimony to Jesus" (NIV). Some translators naturally render this as "the blood of the martyrs of Jesus" (RSV; see also JB and NJB). The NRSV has "the blood of the witnesses to Jesus." While a Christian understanding is quite plausible, a historical Jewish one is equally viable. The Jewish War caused the martyrdom of hundreds of thousands of Jews in Jerusalem, not to mention the whole nation. Given the seven-year prophetic ministry of Jesus, son of Ananias, and his public exhortations during the pilgrimage festivals, which drew in faithful Jews from all Israel and the Diaspora, this prophet probably had many adherents throughout the countryside, especially because he was "a rude peasant." One of their own was defying the authorities, both Roman as well as religious, those leaders who were seen as in league with the Beast.

The only passage that apparently equates "Jesus" with the Christian figure is 20:4. The theology in this chapter though, is markedly Jewish, speaking of the thousand-year reign of the Messiah, followed by the release of Satan. Contrary to Christian theology, Satan plays a positive role in that he is the Accuser (cf. the Book of Job). God calls him into his court to act as the prosecution against his people. The Holy Spirit serves as Advocate, i.e., defense counsel. The Spirit of Evil makes accusations against God's creatures and the Spirit of Holiness comes to their defense. In this fashion, the Holy One, blessed be He, can pass the Final Judgment. The Messiah acts as Faithful Witness to his followers and he himself supplies testimony that they have obeyed God. In Jewish theology the Messiah does not act as Judge, and this is true in the Book of Revelation; God Almighty is the Arbiter. The "judges" appearing in 20:4 are technically the "jury," the elders who provide counsel and help weigh the evidence. But the verdict is in the hands of God alone. The text says: "Then I saw thrones, and those seated on them were given authority to judge. I also saw the souls of those who had been beheaded for their testimony to Jesus and for the word of God. They had not worshiped the beast or its image and had not received its mark on their foreheads or their hands. They came to life and reigned with Christ a thousand years." Technically the Greek text is "reigned with *the* Christ"; "Christ" is merely the Greek equivalent for the Messiah, the Anointed One.[41] In this text, the title does not necessarily need to refer to Jesus of Nazareth, believed by his followers to be the Christ. "The Christ" in the original apocalypse is more than likely the Lamb whose followers are sealed in contrast to those of the Beast who bear his mark. Jesus, son of Ananias, is a prophet; he is one figure and the Messiah is another. But for the final Christian redactor John, Jesus of Nazareth *is* the Christ; however, whether the writer of chapters 12–22 in their unedited form believed Jesus of Nazareth to be the Christ is difficult to prove. At best, 20:4 would be the only arguable instance compared to the other five. Needless to say, the author (as well as writer/redactor) of chapters 4–11 does not even mention a "Jesus."[42]

The Lord Was Crucified

Likewise there is no absolute need to see Jesus of Nazareth behind the statement found in 11:8—"Their bodies will lie in the street of the great city, which is figuratively called Sodom and Egypt, where also their Lord was crucified" (NIV). The Great City is Jerusalem, castigated by prophets as Sodom (Jer 22:8 coupled with 23:14, Isa 1:9–15 and 3:9, and Amos 4:10–11). Sodom and Egypt were associated together (Ezek 16:23–57; Wis 19:14–17). The Lord being crucified can be explained in a completely Jewish fashion. When giving to the poor, one is lending to the Lord (Prov 19:17). Ancient Babylon's actions against Israel are interpreted as arrogance directed against the Lord (Jer 50:29–34). A similar thought is operative in Ezek 39:7. In poetic parallelism, one of the ten horns of the fourth beast

> "will speak against the Most High
> and torment the holy ones of the Most High."
> (Dan 7:25 *my translation*)

---

41. Cf. Aune, *Revelation*, 1090.

42. Commentators must take this glaring fact into account. If the original writer of the whole work were Christian, and had already mentioned "Jesus Christ" by name in Rev 1, why not mention "Jesus" in 4–11?

Whatever is done against God's holy ones is done against the Holy One himself.⁴³ It was during this Maccabean period described by Daniel that Alexander crucified eight hundred Pharisees in Jerusalem. What was enacted upon the Pharisees for their faithfulness to God can be interpreted as being done to the Lord himself. In this sense, Jerusalem is "where their Lord was crucified" countless times by the Romans who subsequently put God's holy ones to death in this manner, especially during the Jewish Wars. If this clause were not in the original text, then it is the hand of the Christian redactor trying to connect chapters 4–11 with the following ones which do mention a "Jesus" by name, now understood in a Christian appropriation.

The Priestly Clan of Jeshua

But there is yet another reason why the author of the Jewish Apocalypse would have reason to mention "Jesus" in connection with the liturgical motif of the Feast of Weeks which works so prominently within the corpus. The liturgical ministry for the temple was broken down into twenty-four priestly clans. It so happens that the Levitical watch of Jeshua (in Greek, Jesus) commences at the Feast of Pentecost (*Midr. Eccl* 1.3.1).⁴⁴ The priesthood of "Jesus" is responsible for the liturgical duties beginning with the Feast of Weeks. In this sense, it was "Jesus" who bore witness to the commandments of God and the Word of God, the Torah, the giving of which was celebrated on the Feast of Shavu'ot.

Joshua, son of Nun

For the Jew, the giving of the Torah and the Feast had a mystical significance because it was another Jesus (Joshua) who led Israel into the Promised Land and committed the Law of Moses to the people.⁴⁵ According to Pseudo-Philo's *Biblical Antiquities*, written several years after the destruction of the temple in 70 CE, the fifteenth day of the third month was the occasion for the covenant, but in this case the covenant entered into by Joshua, which ratified that of Moses.⁴⁶ The fifteenth of

---

43. The reported words of Jesus of Nazareth, "whatever you do to the least of these you do to me," would have had a blasphemous ring to them.

44. Also see VanderKam, "Shavu'ot," 872.

45. Many Jewish boys bore the name Joshua/Jesus in honor of this Mosaic Joshua, especially during times of occupation when parents longed for deliverance.

46. See Potin, *Fête juive de la Pentecôte*, 126; as well as Goudoever, *Biblical Calendars*, 119, 140.

Sivan was when the Qumran Community as well as others celebrated the Feast of Weeks. In *Midr. Lev* 28:4 the rabbis commented on the phrase "*Ye shall bring the sheaf.*" "It bears on what is written in Scripture: '*Whose harvest the hungry eateth up.*' '*Whose harvest*' applies to Nimrod," the evil founder of the Babylonian Empire. The text goes on to present all sorts of evil oppressors of Israel. The passage finally concludes with Joshua winning the battle against the thirty-one kings.

> By reason of what merit were Israel privileged to possess the Land? You must admit that it was by reason of the merit of following the commandment of the sheaf; for it is written in connection therewith, *When ye are come into the Land.* Accordingly Moses exhorts Israel and says to them: *When ye are come into the land . . . and shall reap the harvest thereof, then ye shall bring the sheaf.*

Thus Joshua's leading the People of God into the Promised Land is integrally connected by rabbinic thought with the Feast of Harvest. It is not difficult to see how some Jews might have thought, in a typological sense, that another Joshua would lead the Chosen People into their final Promised Heritage at the Feast of Pentecost. This being the case, where one reads "Jesus" in chapters 12–19 perhaps the earlier understanding was Joshua as a messianic type, the one who ratified the Law of Moses on the Feast of Shavu'ot and who led the People of God into the Promised Land.

JOHN, THE REDACTOR AND THE AUTHOR OF THE APOCALYPSE

The Christian redactor John, however, assuredly interpreted all of this in a prophetic sense as applying to his Joshua ben Joseph, Jesus of Nazareth. The liturgical priesthood for the Feast of Pentecost is that of Jeshua (now read Jesus Christ). The rabbinic tradition associates the historical Joshua with the ratification of the Law of Moses in connection with the Harvest Feast (here understand Jesus of Nazareth). This Jesus is the true Root of David, the valid Lion of Judah, the Anointed of the Lord.

Who then is the author, the authoritative source, behind the Jewish Apocalypse, known in the New Testament as the Book of Revelation? In her Anchor Bible commentary on Revelation, Josephine Ford advanced an interesting theory. She claimed that the "author" is John the Baptist.[47] He is the oral inspiration behind chapters 4–11; disciples of his composed 12–22, and a Jewish Christian disciple wrote chapters 1–3 and verses 22:16a, 20b, and 21. Ford has since abandoned this theory.

My hypothesis is somewhat similar but not tied down to John the Baptist. The authoritative source of the prophetic message as found in Rev 4–11 was a Palestinian Jew devoted to the liturgical purity of temple worship, someone who understood the Feast of Weeks in an apocalyptic sense. In all likelihood this charismatic seer was deeply influenced by the Qumran Community, and might have been a member. Several scholars have noted similarities between the wording and theology in the Dead Sea Scrolls and the Book of Revelation.[48] If John the Baptist was influenced by Qumran theology, then he would be a likely candidate, but there is no reason to associate the seer of Rev 4–11 with the name "John" as found in 1:1. Nevertheless, John the Baptist was of a priestly family and his prophetic messages included the themes of harvest and ritual purification. As Ford had pointed out, it is John the Baptist who allegedly had some revelation about a messianic Lamb. The Gospels record Jesus as claiming there was no greater prophet than John the Baptist (Matt 11:2–19; Luke 7:18–35). Long after his death, John the Baptist had disciples, even living in Ephesus (Acts 19:1–7). Consequently, one should not rule out of hand the possibility of John the Baptist being the authoritative source behind Rev 4–11. Be that as it may, Rev 4–11 was *possibly* written down by a covenanter from Qumran, or by a disciple of John the Baptist *if* he were the original seer. This text was probably penned shortly before 70 CE.[49] A disciple or school of disciples of the anonymous authoritative source subsequently wrote 12:1—22:7, trying to account for the fall of Jerusalem during the Jewish War and to provide hope for a New Jerusalem. Some solace was found in the destruction

---

47. See Ford, *Revelation*, 3–57 et passim.

48. Beale provides a great service in mustering numerous parallels, as does Ford—two scholars obviously approaching Revelation from divergent poles. Besides their commentaries, see Ulfgard, "L'Apocalypse entre judaïsme et christianisme." Likewise, Aune, throughout his magnum opus, cites correspondences with documents found at Qumran.

49. The title of the Syriac version of Revelation ascribes the vision to the time of Nero; see Gwynn, *Apocalypse of St. John*, 1; or Robinson, *Redating the New Testament*, 224.

of Rome, which burnt during the inter-regnum and as various troops marched on her.

The "John" of chapters 1–3 and 22:8–21 possibly was indeed the Apostle John, or someone bearing his mantle. As is well known, early tradition claims John, son of Zebedee, as the author.[50] John the Apostle, the follower of Jesus of Nazareth, was traditionally known as a disciple of John the Baptist. Thus I believe it plausible that John the Apostle, later in life, re-envisioned an earlier Jewish apocalyptic prophecy (whoever the original seer was) and saw these visions anew in the light of the resurrected Jesus of Nazareth; Jesus was in fact the Lamb of God about whom John the Baptist had received a revelation. Tradition likewise has ascribed the Fourth Gospel to John the Apostle.[51] Curiously, this Gospel is heavily liturgical; in fact, every teaching of Jesus is delivered on a Feast Day. The Gospel of John likewise reflects significant influence from the Qumran Community. Both works emanate from the same theological tradition. Something is going on here. One segment of early Christianity appreciated the richness of the Jewish liturgical calendar and the theology embodied in the feast days. This "school" (elusive as it may be) has been dubbed "Johannine." The Book of Revelation is "Johannine," at least in this broad sense.

DATING OF THE FINAL TEXT

Working with the belief that the seven emperors are Claudius, Nero, Galba, Otho, Vitellius, Vespasian, and Titus (who as general concluded the Jewish Wars at his father's request), I propose the following dating for the distinguished sections of the Book of Revelation: Rev 4–11 before 70 CE; Rev 12:1—22:7 after 81; and Rev 1–3 and 22:8–21 sometime after year 81 and after the completion of 12:1—22:7. Rev 4–11 is a literary unit and in chapter 11 the earthly Jerusalem and temple are presumed to be standing and are under siege. (The heavenly temple in Rev 4 and the earthly one in Rev 11, along with their concomitant twenty-four el-

---

50. See Justin Martyr, *Dial. Trypho* 81 (written around 135 CE); and Irenaeus, *Adv. Haer.*, 5.30 (written about 180 CE). In light of my research and theory, I do not believe that Collins's arguments against the apostle John have any application to my limited ascription of authorship; see Collins, *Crisis and Catharsis*, 25–53.

51. For my analysis that the final redactor of the Gospel of John believed that the Beloved Disciple was the apostle John, see "The Chiastic Key to the Identity of Beloved Disciple."

ders, form bookends.) The thornier question is the dating of 12:1—22:7.[52] This literary unit describes the seven-headed monster several times and equates the seven heads with seven emperors "of whom five have fallen, one is living, and the other has not yet come; and when he comes, he must remain only a little while. As for the beast that was and is not, it is an eighth but it belongs to the seven, and it goes to destruction" (17:10–11). Five of them are "fallen" (the Greek verb implies more than just "gone or deceased"). Claudius was believed to have been poisoned; Nero committed suicide; Galba was assassinated; Otho committed suicide; Vitellius was assassinated. No other consecutive set of five emperors fits this criterion of having "fallen." The "one [who] is living" (more accurately *ho heis estin* = "one is present") would be Vespasian, the sixth. "The other [who] has not yet come" would be Titus who was so instrumental in the Jewish War, the seventh who brought it to completion. Now is "the other has not yet come" truly written temporally, surmising that Vespasian's son Titus will succeed him and will not live long? But Titus, who reigned 79–81 CE, was only forty-two years old when he unexpectedly died of a fever, so it appears this is written after the fact, and in the guise of prediction. But then how is the sixth head, Vespasian, truly still present? He lives on in his son. This then would mean that 12:1—22:7 was written while Domitian was emperor, succeeding his older brother, Titus. *Vespasian lived on in his sons*. It is Vespasian and Titus who as generals attacked Jerusalem on two separate occasions.

Interestingly enough, we have another triad: Vespasian and his two sons Titus and Domitian. In fact, the Greek text more accurately says that the eighth is "from the seven" (*ek tōn hepta*), which Beale takes to mean "descended from the seven."[53] I completely agree. Likewise, historical accounts compare Domitian to Nero.[54] The eighth is descended from one of the seven and is like the Beast himself, Nero. Thus I conclude that Rev 12:1—22:7 was written after 81 CE when Domitian commenced his reign. The prologue and epilogue would have been penned after 12:1—22:7 was completed, thus probably anytime during the reign of Domitian (81–96).

---

52. Rev 12, with Mother Israel/Daughter Zion who gives birth to the Messiah, is paralleled by Israel as God's Bride along with the Messianic Lamb in Rev 21:1—22:7. Just as the Dragon follows the Woman in Rev 12, the Dragon is consigned to eternal punishment in Rev 20. The structure is chiastic; see Appendix E.

53. Beale, *Revelation*, 876.

54. See Juvenal, *Sat.* 4.37ff.; and Martial, *Epigrams* 11.38.

6

Gematria and Some Underlying Hebrew Plays on Words

GIVEN THE THOROUGHLY JEWISH nature of the corpus of Revelation it is not surprising that the book includes the aspect of gematria, the ancient practice of discovering the numerical value of a word by counting the letters. The ancient Hebrews and Greeks had no separate ciphers to indicate numbers; they used the letters of their alphabets. The visual symbol served both as vocalic sound (letter) and numerical value (number). Through habit, the ancient Hebrew's mind (as well as Greek's) had become wired for gematria. For example, what does XLII stand for? Forty-two, but these symbols are actually letters of the Latin alphabet that we have grown accustomed to also reading as numerical symbols.[1] Rev 13:18 is a *locus classicus* as an example of this practice. "There is need for shrewdness here: if anyone is clever enough he may interpret the number of the beast: it is the number of a man, the number 666." Reams have been written about this verse.[2] As early as 180 CE, Irenaeus of Lyons pointed out that many candidates fit the bill and thus it is futile to attempt to crack the code.[3] Nevertheless, innumerable commentators, professional and non-, have not resisted the temptation.

---

1. Roman numerals are also letters but do not follow a sequential value as in Hebrew and Greek. The Roman numerals are I = 1, V = 5, X = 10, L = 50, C = 100, D = 500, and M = 1,000.

2. For a good presentation on the matter see Bauckham, *Climax of Prophecy*, 384–407; Beale, *Book of Revelation*, 718–28; Ford, *Revelation*, 225–27; and Caird, *Revelation*, 174–76.

3. See Irenaeus, *Adv. Haer.* 5.30.

THE FEAST OF WEEKS AND NIMROD AS 666

Significantly, the very matter of gematria arises in a rabbinic passage discussing the Feast of Weeks.[4] Because the Feast is arrived at by multiplying 7 x 7, the Feast of Weeks lends itself to numerical interpretations. The rabbis commented on the phrase:

> "*Ye shall bring the sheaf.*" It bears on what is written in Scripture: "*Whose harvest the hungry eateth up*" (Job v, 5) "*Whose harvest*" applies to Nimrod. "*The hungry eateth up*" applies to Abram our father, peace be upon him, and "*taketh it though without a buckler*" (ib.) neither with weapon but with prayer and supplication, as is proved by the text, "*and when Abram heard that his brother was taken captive, he led forth his trained servants, born in his house, three hundred and eighteen*" (Gen xiv, 14). Resh Lakish explained in the name of Bar Kappara that it was Eliezer alone, for the name Eliezer amounts to three hundred and eighteen. (*Midr. Lev* 28:4)

According to Jewish legend, Nimrod was an enemy of Abraham.[5] When Nimrod heard of Abraham's birth, he ordered the massacre of all male children, thus hoping to annihilate him.[6] This did not succeed, and so when Nimrod encountered Abraham later in life he had him thrown into a blazing furnace because Abraham refused to worship fire.[7] Of course, Abraham was miraculously delivered. Consequently, in rabbinic haggadah, Nimrod becomes the archetype of the idolatrous ruler. This vilification of Nimrod is based upon his name, which in rabbinic literature is interpreted to mean "he who made all the people rebel against God" (*m. Pesaḥ.* 94b). Though Nimrod's name had an original Sumerian root, the Hebrew cognate is מרד (*mrd*), which means to rebel. Jewish teaching holds Nimrod responsible for the building of the Tower of Babel and instigating a rebellion against God. In fact, in rabbinic literature the Tower of Babel is simply known as the "House of Nimrod," which he erected for idol worship so that the whole world would accord him divine homage.[8] Thus Nimrod becomes the prototype of the evil potentate and of rebel-

---

4. Pentecost and the bringing of the sheaf of grain are discussed in *Midr. Lev* 28.3. This continues throughout the next section.

5. For an overview of legends surrounding Nimrod, see Ginzberg, *Legends of the Jews*, 1:178ff.

6. See *Ma'aseh Avraham*, in Jellinek, *Bet ha-Midrash*, 2:118ff.

7. See *Midr. Gen* 38.13.

8. See *b. Abod. Zar.* 53b and *Midr. Hag.* on Gen 11:28; see also Hirschberg, "Nimrod."

lion against God.⁹ Nimrod was also known as Amraphel, king of Shinar (Gen 14:9), and this is why he figures into the rabbinic midrash concerning Abraham and Eliezer.

The numerical value of Nimrod was presumably understood; it comes out to 666 when one follows his name as "Nimrod son of Cush" (Gen 10:8). C. Bruston discovered this in the late 1890s.¹⁰ He arrives at this computation reading the name נמרד בן כש (*nmrd bn csh*).¹¹ נ = 50 + מ = 40 + ר = 200 + ד = 4 + ב = 2 + ן = 50 + כ = 20 + ש = 300 totals to 666. The value of the name Eliezer (אליעזר) is already supplied as 318: א = 1 + ל = 30 + י = 10 + ע = 70 + ז = 7 + ר = 200. The name Abraham (אברהם) adds up to 248: א = 1 + ב = 2 + ר = 200 + ה = 5 + ם = 40. Now when Abraham and Eliezer combined their strength in "steadfastness/ faithfulness" (אמונה, *'emonah*)—by which Abraham was justified—it was enough to defeat Nimrod. א = 1 + מ = 40 + ו = 6 + נ = 50 + ה = 5 totals to 102. 248 + 318 + 102 = 668, thereby outnumbering the force of Nimrod 666. Why 668? Because Abraham and Eliezer each count as one person, thus two more than Nimrod.

Another interesting gematria obtains from the same passage in Gen 14:14. If in Hebrew one literally says "Abraham *and* Eliezer *and* righteousness" (אברהם ואליעזר וצדקה), the phrase adds up to 777. "And" is ו = 6 x 2 = 12 + צ = 90 + ד = 4 + ק = 100 + ה = 5, which adds up to 199. Thus the equation is 248 + 6 + 318 + 6 + 199 = 777. Abraham was justified by his faithfulness and this was *accounted* to him as righteousness (Gen 15:6). The Hebrew verb for "accounted" (חשב, *ḥshb*) also means "to calculate." No matter which way one "calculates" the rabbinic gematria, Nimrod (666) is accounted as outnumbered and defeated, whether by 668 or, more probably, by 777.

Rabbi Eleazar bar Kappara, who pointed out that the name Eliezer equals 318 and spoke of this as significant in reference to Abraham's outnumbering Nimrod, flourished between 180 and 220 CE. Perhaps bar Kappara was repeating an earlier rabbinic tradition. While admittedly

---

9. See *b. Hag.* 13a.

10. See Bruston, Tête égorgée et le chiffre 666."

11. Bruston drops out the "*waw*" in Cush. This is plausible given that the "u" can be represented by the diacritical marks; however there is no textual evidence for this alternate reading. But given the nature of gematria, sometimes rabbis altered things to arrive at the desired meaning. As shall be seen, Nimrod's equaling 666 makes very good sense.

gematria is by its very nature speculative, as perhaps is my own "insight,"[12] nevertheless it is objective fact that Nimrod, whose name comes out to 666, is mentioned in a rabbinic commentary on the Feast of Weeks.

A century ago, Bruston pointed out that Nimrod was the founder of the Babylonian Empire and that he lies behind the imagery in Rev 13:18.[13] Nimrod became apotheosized as the Babylonian war god. This imagery aptly fits into the Book of Revelation, where the Beast is Babylon and its head demands worship.[14] The Targum on Hab 3, read during the Feast of Weeks, makes explicit that the Roman Empire is the heir to the Babylonian Empire. What the author of the Book of Revelation has done is to take a gematria used in connection with the Feast of Weeks, namely the Nimrod motif, the founder of the Babylonian Empire and an idolater who claimed divine status for himself, his name adding up to 666, and to merge it with another name in his own current political situation, namely Caesar Nero.[15]

CAESAR NERO, 666, AND THE FEAST OF HARVEST

In 1831, O. F. Fritsche first proposed that 666 was the name of Caesar Nero according to the Hebrew form of his name, קסר נרון (*Qsr Nrwn*): ק = 100 + ס = 60 + ר = 200 + נ = 50 + ר = 200 + ו = 6 + ן = 50. Three other German scholars independently arrived at this same conclusion.[16] Technically, "Caesar" in Hebrew is spelled קיסר (*Qysr*), but in 1963 D. R. Hillers argued that he found a corroboration of the Aramaic mis-

---

12. To my knowledge, I am the first to make this correlation between the addition of the numerical values of Abraham, Eliezer, and faithfulness and thus outnumbering the "power" of Nimrod. Furthermore, to my knowledge, no one has reckoned "Abraham and Eliezer and righteousness" as equaling 777. The text in the Midrash Rabbah does not make this point. If I am not the first to realize this, my analysis is independent confirmation of another scholar's insight.

13. See Bruston, "Tête égorgée et le chiffre 666"; and Hicks, "Nimrod."

14. Also see Ford, *Revelation*, 227.

15. Charles (*Critical and Exegetical Commentary*, 367) pointed out that the defective spelling of Caesar (*qsr*) had been utilized "because the number 666 is older than the name." He further noted, "The origin of the number is not yet clear." I believe I have solved this age old mystery. While Bruston ("Tête égorgée et le chiffre 666") noted that "Nimrod son of Cush" equals 666, he did not realize the liturgical reason for its usage. Unfortunately, commentators had dismissed Bruston's insight because it was premised upon a Hebrew reading, not a Greek one. Bruston is to be credited with the Babylonian association and "cracking the code."

16. See Bauckham, *Climax of Prophecy*, 387.

spelling *Qsr* in a papyrus dated to the second year of Nero's reign.[17] This identification is further corroborated by the fact that by 180 CE, according to Irenaeus, there was a manuscript variant of 616 instead of 666.[18] When one writes "Caesar Nero" in Hebrew without the final "n" the name adds up to 616. This variant also further substantiates that some were aware of the underlying Hebraic nature of the Book of Revelation. Subsequently, the majority of scholars have accepted this cracking of the code regarding Nero, who, after all, first persecuted the Christians. But given my demonstration that the original version of the Apocalypse was thoroughly Jewish, Nero likewise admirably fits the bill because he initiated the Jewish War.[19] He is the arch-villain. But behind this gematria for Caesar Nero lies another bit of literary wit. The closest homonym in Hebrew to קסר (*qsr*) is קצר (*qtsr*), and the verb *qtsr* means "to harvest." I believe the author of the Book of Revelation is likewise saying that shrewdness is needed to realize that the focus of the Feast of Harvest (*qtsr*) will be Caesar (*qsr*) himself.[20]

Thus I am persuaded that the very theme of the Feast of Harvest is the key to unlocking the gematria of the Beast.[21] Rabbinic tradition regarding the Feast of Weeks links Nimrod (666) to the bringing of the sheaf. Nimrod, the founder of the Babylonian Empire and legendary idolater, demanded to be accorded divine status and his tower rose into the heavens. Caesar Nero, while not explicitly demanding to be worshipped as a god, was nevertheless considered divine like his deified relatives and while alive was widely worshipped as a god in the eastern provinces of the Empire.[22] Nero's great-great-grandfather Emperor Augustus had long been acclaimed divine, and his adoptive father Claudius as well. Caesar

17. See Hillers, "Revelation 13:38," 65; as well as Bauckham, *Climax of Prophecy*, 388.

18. See Irenaeus, *Adv. Haer.* 5.30.1.

19. Understandably, Beale is working out of a Christian bias and thus questions how Greek-speaking Christians would be so familiar with gematria in Hebrew; see Beale, *Book of Revelation*, 719. I, however, espouse an original Jewish audience and even an underlying oral tradition possibly in Aramaic. Admittedly, however, I do agree that the book in its final form was a Christian document for the Greek speaking faithful.

20. Curiously, Revelation uses the term *pantokrator* nine times, whereas it is only found one other time in the NT, in 2 Cor 6:18, which is a conflated quotation from the prophets. *Pantokrator* is heavily Jewish, the Greek term for the Hebrew word Sabaoth meaning hosts. Many clues point to an underlying Hebraic verbage and grammar.

21. Of course, when the Greek word for beast (*thērion*) is transliterated into Hebrew, it happily adds up to 666 as well.

22. See Momigliano, "Nero," 10:732; see also Bauckham, *Climax of Prophecy*, 408–9.

Nero demanded that the Roman gods be worshipped alongside the God of the Jews, and for their defiance of his orders Nero launched the Jewish War. The prophecy in the Book of Revelation was subtle enough that any successor of Nero would fall within his shadow since that successor would bear the mantle of Caesar. The harvest (*qtsr*) was for Caesar (*qsr*), no matter who occupied the throne. The liturgical motif of the Book of Revelation rings true even on the political plane regarding the Roman Emperor.

JULIA AGRIPPINA—THE WHORE OF BABYLON

In the previous chapter I proposed that Julia Agrippina could serve as a symbol for the Whore of Babylon due to her sexual immorality and political exploits, as well as cultic office. Could a gematria be at work here as well? First, one must establish why one could validly suspect a gematria might be at play, before unraveling a hidden meaning. Firstly, Rev 17:5 says "On her forehead was written a name, a mystery." Others translate this as a "cryptic name" (JB and NJB). The mark of the Beast (666) is on the forehead as well (Rev 13:16). Secondly, some scholars see the rider on the white horse in 19:11–16 as in contrast to the Whore of Babylon who rides the Beast.[23] Thirdly, the rider on the white horse has a name inscribed on his thigh: "King of kings and Lord of lords" (19:16). Patrick Skehan has pointed out how in Aramaic this title adds up to 777.[24] The same title (in reverse order) is found in 17:14 referring to the Lamb in contrast to the woman (17:9). Given that gematria is at work in 17:14, suspecting gematria in the cryptic name in 17:5 is justified. But what could it be?

Strikingly enough, "Agrippina the woman" comes out to 666 when written in Hebrew.[25] אגריפינא האשה—א = 1 +ג = 3 + ר = 200 + י = 10 + פ = 80 + י = 10 + נ = 50 + א = 1 + ה = 5 + א = 1 + ש = 300 + ה = 5—totals to 666. The word *ishshah* in Hebrew has several meanings. It can refer to "woman" in general, to a "wife" in particular, as well as to a "concubine or mistress," i.e., the "other woman" in English parlance. Agrippina was

---

23. See for example Beale, *Book of Revelation*, 955.

24. See Skehan, "King of Kings," 398.

25. I am unaware of a Hebrew text spelling her name, thus this is a conjectural reconstruction. As we have seen with Nero, there were variant spellings. Bohak has shown that in some cases gematria works when Greek words are "transliterated into the Hebrew alphabet"; see his article "Greek-Hebrew Gematrias," 119.

all of these and serves as an embodiment of Rome. She was in fact the great granddaughter of the "Divine" Augustus. The grammatical root for *ishshah* is *anash* and means "incurable, grievous, sorrowful." The word *ishsheh,* sounding like *ishshah* and consonantly spelled the same way (אשה), means "offering by fire." Rev 17:18 correlates the Whore of Babylon with "the great city that rules over all the kings of the earth," that is, Rome, and 18:8 says "she will be burned with fire." In 69 CE Rome was seized by Vitellius' foreign mercenaries and they set fire to Rome as they fought off Vespasian's invading troops. Tacitus lamented this destruction and burning of Rome.[26] And yet a striking parallel also exists between Rome being set afire and Agrippina. As previously mentioned, Nero had his mother killed, but few note that he purposely had his mother's corpse burned that very night and not given a proper burial.[27] Nero burned both Rome as well as his mother! The consonantal form אגריפינא האשה, which adds up to 666, serves a double duty: Agrippina the Woman and Agrippina the Burnt Offering.

The burning of Rome in 69 recalls the terrors of the burning of Rome under Nero in 64. There is yet another reason to associate Nero and Agrippina. On Roman coins her image was stamped facing that of Emperor Nero. Barrett underscores, "It is impossible to exaggerate the impact that the numismatic innovations of Nero's reign would have had on his contemporaries. Agrippina became the very first woman during her lifetime to share with a reigning *princeps* the face of an official coin minted in Rome." Barrett highlights the meaning of the inscriptions on the coin: "The legend identifies Agrippina as Agrippina Augusta, the wife of the Deified Claudius, the mother of Caesar, and thus brings together on a single coin the three roles that brought her the greatest pride." [28] The observation made in Rev 13:17 takes on a significant meaning: "No one can buy or sell who does not have the mark, that is, the name of the beast or the number of its name." The Greek word for mark, *charagma*, means "inscription" as well as "stamped money; coin." Besides coins, re-

---

26. See Tacitus, *Hist.* 3.71–73.

27. See Tacitus, *Ann.* 14.9; and Barrett, *Agrippina*, 190. Even I, at first, had overlooked this detail.

28. See Barrett, *Agrippina*, 152. Regarding Agrippina appearing on coins issued under Claudius, see ibid., 109. When Nero became of age, coins were minted depicting Claudius and Agrippina facing each other on one side, and with Nero on the other (116–17). Barrett remarks that this was an innovation.

call that a Greek gematria had already been circulating linking Nero and Agrippina:

> Count the numerical values
> Of the letters in Nero's name,
> And in "murdered his own mother":
> You will find their sum is the same.[29]

Oddly enough, when Nero had his mother killed, her assassins clubbed her on the head while she lay upon a couch.[30] The mark of Nero ironically would have been upon her forehead.

Likewise, in the Mediterranean world, people would place coins on the eyelids of the dead so that they would not pop open and cause fright to those viewing the corpse. This was also done to pay the ferryman to the underworld. Such a practice of placing on the eyes of the dead coins with the image of either Nero or Agrippina on them would bear great theological import. The Greek word used for "forehead" in the texts from Revelation is *metōpon*, which literally means "in the midst of the eyes."

Furthermore with regard to Agrippina being 666 and her face being on a coin, along with her intervention of having Herod Agrippa II installed as king of Judaea, strikingly enough she apparently also had a hand in having Felix appointed as procurator.[31] Barrett remarks, "Felix was a freedman (*libertus*), and the appointment of someone of that rank as a procurator or prefect is almost without parallel. His selection was thus a remarkable one and further evidence of Agrippina's power and influence. Felix certainly felt indebted to her and Judaean coins that appear in 54 . . . honour Agrippina, depicting her name within a wreath on the reverse."[32] Thus Jews (both in Judaea and the Diaspora) were quite familiar with Agrippina and the power she wielded, even through their currency.[33] It is hard not to believe that she at least served as a type of the

---

29. Suetonius, *Nero* 39; rendition by Graves, *Twelve Caesars*, 231–32.

30. See Tacitus, *Ann.* 14.8. She was finally disemboweled.

31. Felix was the brother of Pallas who was one of Agrippina's supporters.

32. See Barrett, *Agrippina*, 126–27. Felix eventually married Drusilla, the sister of Herod Agrippa II.

33. Ignatius of Antioch associates the word "mark" with "coin" in his letter to the *Magnesians* 5. The mark is also on the hand as well (Rev 13:16), but the Greek *epi* translated as "on" can also mean "in." By doing commerce with imperial Rome one supports the "Evil Empire." This recalls the dilemma of paying taxes that Jesus of Nazareth addressed: "Render unto Caesar what is Caesar's and unto God what is God's." From a Jewish point of view, the mark on the hands and the forehead of the followers of the

Whore of Babylon, if she were not indeed the Whore herself envisioned in Rev 17, which concomitantly is Rome. As the great-granddaughter of the "Divine" Augustus, Julia Agrippina II embodied Rome.[34]

The seer unpacks one of the mysterious names on the woman's forehead: "Babylon the Great" (Rev 17:5). Perhaps yet another gematria was at play as well. When one looks to Dan 4:30 (4:27 according to the Hebrew) as inspiration behind the text, the phrase "This Great Babylon the Third" when written in Aramaicized Hebrew comes out to 666. דא היא בביל רבתא = 5 + י = 10 + א = 1 + ב = 2 + ב = 2 + י = 10 + ל = 30 + ר = 200 + ב = 2 + ת = 400 + א = 1 + ג = 3, adding up to 666. According to the Hab 3 Targum, already influencing the author of Revelation, Rome is the third empire to succeed that of the Babylonians and is destined to be destroyed.

Finally, many commentators have pointed out that the Whore of Babylon is in contrast to the woman clothed with the sun in 12:1. The verse opens up, "A great and wondrous sign appeared in heaven" (NIV). This woman then gives birth to the Messiah. As noted before, the woman is Mother Israel, but she also probably alludes to the sign God offered Ahaz as "high as heaven" (Isa 7:11). "The LORD himself will give you a sign. Look, the young woman is with child and shall bear a son, and name him Immanuel" (Isa 7:14). The historical context of the sign was when Judah was being attacked by its enemies who were in league with Assyria, the future Babylon; the son was the future King Hezekiah. Later this verse was given a messianic spin in Jewish history. The writer of Rev 12 aptly applies the sign to the context of oppression by the Roman Empire, the new Babylon. But quite telling is the following gematria: when in Hebrew one says "Behold, the sign: the Woman" (הנה האהא האשה) it adds up to 777.[35] ה = 5 + נ = 50 + ה = 5 + ה = 5 + א

Lamb most probably refers to the tephillin; upon the forehead one wears the phylactery box which contains four excerpts from the Torah. Tephillin are mentioned in Matt 23:5 and Josephus, *Ant.* 4.8.

34. Even Rev 18:7 can be applied to Agrippina: "To the measure of her boasting and wantonness repay her in torment and grief; for she said to herself, 'I sit enthroned as queen; I am no widow, and I will never know grief'" (NABR, compare JB). This verse cites Isa 47:7–8. Agrippina was bent on not being a widow, and when her third husband, Claudius, died he had become an immortal god to whom she was eternally wed, herself being accorded divine status and the title Augusta. She thought she was secure and impervious with her devoted son Nero as reigning Caesar.

35. While Isa 7:14 does not use the defective spelling it is attested to in the Hebrew Scriptures, especially with the definite article; e.g., Exod 4:8, 8:19; and Neh 9:10 in the

= 1 +ת = 400 + ה = 5 + א = 1 + שׁ = 300 + ה = 5 totals to 777. Thus the Whore of Babylon—Agrippina the Woman (666) is in stark contrast to the Woman of the Sign (777).

HEBREW AND ARAMAIC PLAYS ON WORDS

Not surprisingly, the author of the Book of Revelation displays irony in yet another fashion. The true king, the Messianic Lamb, is presented as holding and subsequently unsealing the scroll. The Hebrew word for scroll is מגלה (*mglh*; *megilah*). Later in the Apocalypse, "one like the Son of Man" is depicted as wielding a sickle. The Hebrew word for sickle is מגל (*mgl*; *magal*). The *mglh* contains within itself a *mgl*; the scroll when opened releases the sickle to complete the Feast of Harvest. In the Syriac form of Aramaic, the play on words is even more pronounced. A scroll is ܡܓܠܐ (*mgala*), and a sickle is ܡܓܠܐ (*magla*). Remarkably, the Syriac word ܡܓܠܐ (*magle*) means unveiling, as of the face. It is difficult to know the exact evolution and state of the Aramaic language spoken in Palestine during the first century CE, but if *magle* was already used to mean unveiling, then the play on words is triadic. The Apocalypse (the Greek word itself means unveiling) is the *magle*, the unveiling of the Face of God. This *magle* produces the revelation of the *megala*, the Scroll, and as this is unrolled, the *magla* is revealed, the sickle wielded by the Son of Man. All three words are written the same way consonantally ܡܓܠܐ ; vowel pointing developed later.

Another play on words operates in the throne room scene. The Hebrew word כבש (*kebes*) means a "young ram or lamb." In Rev 5:6 the Lamb is presented as having horns, which a ram possesses. Rev 5:6–7 reads: "Then I saw a Lamb, looking as if it had been slain, standing in the center of the throne, encircled by the four living creatures and the elders.... He came and took the scroll from the right hand of him who sat on the throne" (NIV). The NJB also places the Lamb in the "middle" of the throne. Somehow, the Lamb is in the midst of the throne, which is supported by the four living creatures. When dealing with this text Aune remarks, "An important interpretative issue here is why the Lamb, who has not been seen by John before, suddenly appears on the scene."

---

singular, and for the plural Exod 4:9, 17, 28, and 30. The Greek word *kai* starting Rev 12:1 could be a rendering of the Hebrew *hinneh*, which was translated simply as *kai* in several instances of the LXX; see 1 Sam 13:10, 15:12, 21:10; 1 Kgs 18:7; Isa 29:8; Jer 4:24; Ezek 18:18; and Dan TH 10:20.

He further notes, "The way in which the location of the Lamb is described as 'in the midst of' the throne and the four cherubim and 'in the midst of' the twenty-four elders is problematic."[36] Interestingly, the Hebrew word כבש (*kebesh*) means "footstool."[37] In other words, the Lamb/Ram (*kebes*) is also the footstool (*kebesh*). This explains the peculiar spatial paradox found in Rev 5:6–7 and provides an answer to Aune's questions. Thus the Lamb can be in the middle of the throne while not sitting on the throne, since he, the Lamb, is the footstool.[38]

Now having understood the Lamb as the footstool of YHWH, the midrash on Exod 24 speaking of the child snatched up to the throne of God and becoming his footstool takes on added significance. "And she gave birth to a son, a male child, who is to rule all the nations with a rod of iron. But her child was snatched away and taken to God and to his throne" (Rev 12:5). The messianic figure is the *kebes*, the sacrificial Lamb as well as *kebesh*, the footstool of God. He is precious in the eyes of the Lord.

A further play on words has been suggested by Ford regarding the locusts in Rev 9:1–12. One Hebrew word for locust is *ḥargol*, which appears in Lev 11:22 and sounds like the Southwest Semitic word *ḥarjal* meaning troops. The symbolic context is that of an invading army, historically the Parthians, who shot poisoned arrows while riding on horseback.[39]

THE FEAST OF SHAVU'OT AS 777

Given that the Book of Revelation is steeped in Hebrew plays on words and Jewish symbolism, one naturally might wonder whether a gematria calculation pertains to any of the various terms for the Feast of Weeks. Philo gave a mystical numerological explanation of Pentecost. He pointed out that $50 = 3 \times 3 + 4 \times 4 + 5 \times 5$.[40] Thus trying to find a hidden numerical meaning to the Feast of Weeks is warranted in the

---

36. Aune, *Revelation*, 351.

37. See Holladay, *Concise Hebrew and Aramaic Lexicon*, 151.

38. See Beale, *Book of Revelation*, 350, for "convoluted" attempts to make sense of this spatial impossibility. Knowing the underlying Hebrew play on words solves the conundrum.

39. See Ford, *Revelation*, 150; and Aune, *Revelation*, 891–93, for background on the Parthian army.

40. See Philo, *Spec.* 2.177.

historical context. The logical candidate for a gematria exegesis would be the standard name itself, Shavu'ot. The tri-consonantal root is שבע (shb') which means seven. The plural, shavu'ot, means "sevens, or "seven sets of seven." Transliterating Shavu'ot into English in its consonantal form we have shv'wt. This noun tantalizingly adds up to 778. Is there a way to make it come out to 777? The problem is the consonant ו (waw), which usually is not dropped in verbs and nouns. The regular construct form of the noun (basically equivalent in English to "of weeks") is shv'y; this does not achieve the desired 777. However, if one were to come up with a defective spelling שבעת (shv't, replacing the consonant waw with a vowel sign for the long o) and add the definite article ה (h) in front of it (meaning "the [seven] weeks") we do arrive at 777. Nevertheless, this is a defective form of the noun and the consonant waw really should not be dropped.

There appears to be no basis to force Shavu'ot into adding up to 777, or at least so it seems. But in Jer 5:24 an irregular plural construct of the noun does appear as שבעת (shv't).[41] While the definite article does not precede the noun in this verse, the textual occurrence of shv't verifies that in Hebrew one could say השבעת (hshv't; HaShavu'ot), i.e., "the [seven] weeks of . . ." With this justification of the alternate spelling, the phrase "the [Seven] Weeks of . . ." [YHWH, God, or the Lord—being elliptically understood], one does arrive at the "desired" mystical gematria of 777. ה = 5 + ש = 300 + ב = 2 + ע = 70 + ת = 400 totals to 777. Thus "the [Seven] Weeks of [YHWH]" are the eschatological mystical fulfillment of the covenant. The perfection of God's plan is found in the Feast of Weeks as the author of the *Book of Jubilees* so firmly believed. The Harvest Feast is accounted as 777, while the Beast is enumerated as 666. Significantly enough, in Aramaic the phrase "King of kings, Lord of lords" likewise equals 777.[42] This title is the one borne by the messianic deliverer (Rev 19:16). The Seven Weeks of the King of Kings and Lord of Lords is the penultimate victory over the Beast and the power of the Dragon. The Final Harvest is the cosmic "showdown" during which the Messiah is revealed in all his glory.

41. This irregular variant construct is listed in Holladay, *Concise Hebrew and Aramaic Lexicon*, 358; and in Davidson, *Analytical Hebrew and Chaldee Lexicon*, 699, with note "y" directing the reader to Jer 5:24. Kittel's *Biblia Hebraica*, however, has corrected it to read with the "*waw*."

42. See Skehan, "King of Kings," 398; and Ford, *Revelation*, 323–24, who emphasizes the significance of Skehan's insight.

Liturgically, the Feast of Weeks is commenced with the Levitical priesthood of Joshua/Jesus. As Christian scholars have so aptly pointed out, in Greek Jesus adds up to 888. While this circumstance is fortuitous, I do not believe it was in the mind of the original "author" of the Book of Revelation, who thought in Hebrew/Aramaic; nor does the text of Revelation even mention 888. However, when reference was made to Jesus in the Greek text (from my point of view, originally most probably Jesus, son of Ananias, as well as Jesus, the priestly clan), John the Christian redactor possibly could have interpreted this as yet another prophetic sign pointing to Jesus of Nazareth.[43]

My suspicions concerning an underlying 777 began with an analysis of Shavu'ot and substantiation of the defective spelling in Jer 5:24. The passage from Jer 5 bears quoting. The Lord chastises the people for their infidelity and idolatry (5:21).

> But this people's heart is stubborn and rebellious;
> they turn and go away,
> They do not say in their hearts,
> "Let us fear the YHWH, our God,
> who provides us rain,
> early and late, at its time,
> and keeps for us
> the appointed weeks of harvest."
> Your ill-deeds have upset these things,
> your sins have turned these blessings away from you.
> . . . . .
> What will you do when the end comes? (Jer 5:23–25, 31d, my translation)

Here the prophet Jeremiah associates the later rains and the Feast of Weeks with disobedience and the eschatological end. For those who obey God and are in a relationship with him, there will be eternal blessing and fruitfulness; but for those who break the covenant, there will be an eternal curse and barrenness. This notion of perpetual fruitfulness is borne out in Rev 22:2 where the tree of life bears fruit twelve months out of the year. The author is excerpting from the prophet Ezekiel. "On the banks, on both sides of the river, there will grow all kinds of trees for food. Their leaves will not wither nor their fruit fail, but they will bear fresh

---

43. Bauckham (*Climax of Prophecy*, 397) also expresses doubts as to whether the writer consciously played Jesus in Greek (888) off of the Hebrew 666.

Gematria and Some Underlying Hebrew Plays on Words

fruit every month, because the water for them flows from the sanctuary Their fruit will be for food, and their leaves for healing" (Ezek 47:12). While Rev 22:2 does not delineate how many trees (in fact the Greek employs a singular collective),[44] it is tempting to visualize twelve trees, one for each of the Tribes of Israel, which in the Christian sense parallel the Twelve Apostles. If this imagery obtains, then twelve trees producing fruit twelve times a year brings us back to the mystical number of 144, the number of the followers of the Lamb and the measurement of the New Jerusalem (Rev 21:17).[45] For the faithful, the Harvest Feast is replete with abundance and spiritual blessing.[46] The consummation of the ages is a perpetual Pentecost.

YET ANOTHER MYSTICAL PHRASE EQUALING 777

As has just been pointed out, "The Seven Weeks" and "King of kings, Lord of lords" both add up to 777 respectively. Could another phrase in Hebrew be accounted the same? Limiting the parameters to Rev 4–11, which I have claimed are the core of the original corpus, a phrase can be constructed. Chapter 4 clearly is situated in God's heavenly temple and the Lamb figures prominently. As we have already seen, chapter eleven closes with another scene in the temple, this time of the Ark of God. "Then God's temple in heaven was opened, and the ark of his cov-

---

44. See Beale, *Book of Revelation*, 1104.

45. For the mathematical connection between 666 and 144 see Bauckham, *Climax of Prophecy*, 398–400.

46. It is this theological truth which lies behind the chiliastic presentations of exorbitant produce such as found in Irenaeus, *Adv. Haer.* 5.33.3:

> The days will come, in which vines shall grow, each having ten thousand branches, and in each branch ten thousand twigs, and in each true twig ten thousand shoots, and in each one of the shoots ten thousand clusters, and on every one of the clusters ten thousand grapes, and every grape when pressed will give five and twenty metretes of wine. And when any one of the saints shall lay hold of a cluster, another shall cry out, "I am a better cluster, take me; bless the Lord through me." In like manner [the Lord declared] that a grain of wheat would produce ten thousand ears, and that every ear should have ten thousand grains, and every grain would yield ten pounds of clear, pure, fine flour; and that all other fruit-bearing trees, and seeds and grass, would produce in similar proportions.

I doubt that Irenaeus was a literalist; the symbols are of grapes and wheat, elements of the Eucharistic meal. The imagery is superabundance of "tasting and seeing how good the Lord is." This is nothing less than the Messianic Banquet, the Wedding Feast, the Eschatological Feast of Harvest.

enant was seen within his temple; and there were flashes of lighting, rumblings, peals of thunder, an earthquake, and heavy hail" (11:19). This theophany excerpts phrases from Exod 19:16 which are also quoted in Rev 4:5. Chapter 11 depicts the seventh seal being broken, and hence the fitting climax of the seven-seal scroll introduced in 5:1 that only the Lamb can open.

I have already demonstrated the significance of the Ark of the Covenant in the Feast of Weeks liturgy and apocalyptic speculation. But from a Jewish theological point of view, the Ark contains the Ten Words of God and the manna, as well as Aaron's priestly rod. The Ark was the abode of God, where he dwelt between the cherubim. Thus the Ark of God figured prominently in the early wars of Israel. Therefore the Ark in Rev 11:19 is pregnant with this rich meaning. God comes enthroned to execute judgment and to wage a holy war against the nations, and to re-establish the priestly kingdom. God's throne contains the Word of God and the priestly rod.

Consequently, the author of the Apocalypse confronts the reader with a triadic image: the Ark of God, the Lamb, and the temple. When in Hebrew one says "The Lamb and the Ark of the Lord God and temple," the phrase adds up to 777. First, a brief word about the phrase "Ark of the Lord God." Various epithets appear in Hebrew regarding the Ark. Closest to the phrase that I suggest is "Ark of the Covenant of the Lord your God" found in Josh 3:3, 11. Sometimes it is simply "the ark of God." In 1 Chr 15:12, 14 it is designated as "the ark of YHWH, the God of Israel." Thus there is warrant for the phrase "the ark of YHWH God [or the Lord God]." In Hebrew the phrase "The Lamb and the Ark of the Lord God and temple" (הכבש והארון יהוה אלהים והיכל) adds up to the mystical number 777. ה = 5 + כ = 20 + ב = 2 + ש = 300 + ו = 6 + ה = 5 + א = 1 + ר = 200 + ו = 6 + ן = 50 + י = 10 + ה = 5 + ו = 6 + ה = 5 + א = 1 + ל = 30 + ה = 5 + י = 10 + ם = 40 + ו = 6 + ה = 5 + י = 10 + כ = 20 + ל = 30, totaling to 777. This being the case, when the seventh seal is broken by the Lamb, the Ark of the Lord God appears within the temple. The seventh seal reveals the 777. The gematria and theology of the author of the Apocalypse are profoundly rich and beautiful.[47]

---

47. Another interesting instance is that the phrase in Hebrew "Ark of the Covenant of the Lord your God" as found in Josh 3:3 adds up to 1001. Could this have some connection with the 1,000-year reign of the Messiah? ("Ark of the Covenant" by itself adds up to 869.)

RECOUNTING THE VALUE OF 666

Another instance of gematria might be at work in a Hebrew understanding of the Book of Revelation. Because the following scenario is so strikingly stupendous, I will walk the reader through point by point, in the manner in which I stumbled upon this curiosity. Perhaps here, my divining rod has taken too much of a bent towards divination; nevertheless, I will substantiate each of my assertions. In the *Sibylline Oracles* 5:12–42, the Jewish author practices a bit of gematria by way of the first letter of the Roman emperors' names. Several commentators on the Book of Revelation have noted this, and Giet himself wondered if this might not be the clue to 666. He commenced with Julius Caesar and ended with Vespasian, adding up the numerical value of the first letter of the names in Greek, and arrived at 666. This, however, was achieved by omitting Otho and Vitellius.[48] George Caird and Beale rightly reject such a forced reconstruction that conveniently dismisses two emperors.[49] Nevertheless, the Jewish practice of only adding up beginning letters of names is hereby attested to. I subsequently mused, what is the numerical value in Hebrew of the first letters of the Twelve Tribes enumerated in Rev 7:5–8? Eerily, the sum is 663. I suspected that that was too much of a close coincidence and realized that all I needed to reach the famed 666 was a name or title beginning with the letter *g, gimmel*.

First of all, a word must be said about the list provided by the author of the Book of Revelation. One would rightly expect to find the Twelve Tribes of Israel listed, but this is not the case. The author has purposely deleted the tribe of Dan and replaced it with Manasseh. One poignant reason for this is that rabbis believed the tribe of Dan was associated with idolatry and that an evil one would emerge from this tribe who would attack the Lord's Anointed.[50] Irenaeus also stated that the antichrist would come from Dan, citing Jer 8:16, and claimed this is why the author of the Apocalypse deleted this tribe.[51] Furthermore, the seer commenced the list of tribes with Judah, from which the Messiah was to be born, instead of following the standard pattern of either chrono-

---

48. See Giet, *L'Apocalypse et l'histoire*, 76–79.
49. See Caird, *Revelation*, 174; and Beale, *Book of Revelation*, 720.
50. See *b. Sanh.* 96a; *Midr. Gen* 43:2; *Midr. Num* 2:10; and *Targ. Pal.* Exod 17:8; 22:41–23:1. Also see Beale, *Book of Revelation*, 420–21.
51. See Irenaeus, *Adv. Haer.* 5.30.2.

logical birth order or geographical placement.[52] In short, the author's list of Twelve Tribes would cause the astute Jew to pause and ponder the significance, to find some hidden meaning. The author probably hints at a gematria interpretation because he does not just mention the 144,000 but belabors the point by cataloguing the 12,000 from each tribe.

Thus we are back to the gematria calculation of 663 arrived at by adding up the numerical value of the first letter in Hebrew of each of the Twelve Tribes as enumerated by the author. The list in Rev 7:5–8 is a follows: Judah (י) = 10 + Reuben (ר) = 200 + Gad (ג) = 3 + Asher (א) = 1 + Naphtali (נ) = 50 + Manasseh (מ) = 40 + Simeon (ש) = 300 + Levi (ל) = 30 + Issachar (י) = 10 + Zebulun (ז) = 7 + Joseph (י) = 10 + Benjamin (ב) = 2, totaling to 663. Because the author expects his book to be prayerfully studied and meditated upon, I argue that the dissonance with 666 is marked. Could something be going on here? I suggest that the clue is in the missing tribe of Dan itself. The widespread Jewish understanding was that a false messiah would arise out of the tribe of Dan and lead the people into idolatry. To import a term for ease of discussion, the false messiah is the "antichrist";[53] he is opposed to God and the Lord's true Anointed. Throughout the Book of Revelation, the Beast, the Sea Monster, the False Prophet, etc. all mimic God in a defective manner. The Beast is in opposition to the Lamb. The followers of the Beast bear a mark on the forehead, whereas the Lamb's adherents have a seal instead. The "Antichrist" has a whore for consort, whereas God has a virgin Bride. The Lord God Almighty "was, is, is to come;" whereas the Beast "was, and is not, and is to come" (Rev 17:8). Many commentators have pointed out this mimicry and mockery. The Dragon and his cohorts are a parody of the True God. Accepting this clearly to be the case, is the number of the Beast, 666, itself a mimicry of a divine symbol?

The tribes by themselves equal 663, but they are, in fact, not by themselves—they follow the Lamb. To achieve the required 666, the value of 3 must be added. In Rev 14:3 the author states that the 144,000 are the redeemed. The Lamb is the Redeemer. The Hebrew word for Redeemer is גאל (*Goel*), thus the necessary *g* equaling three is easily arrived at. The Redeemer and the redeemed Twelve Tribes are accounted as 666. Why could this be a positive number? Because God created Adam and Eve

---

52. See Caird, *Revelation*, 98; and Ford, *Revelation*, 124–25.

53. The term "antichrist" does not appear in Revelation; it is only found in 1 John 2:18; 2:22; 4:3; and 2 John 7.

on the sixth day and their divine purpose was to worship God, to be in daily fellowship with the Lord God. The sixth day was God's crowning achievement of creation.

But another worthy candidate for the missing *gimmel* can be found. The tribe of Dan is missing because it gives birth to the false messiah, the archenemy of God. We have already seen that Nimrod was stylized as such. Nimrod was the first potentate upon the earth (Gen 10:8). The noun for potentate is גבור (*gibor*) which some translate as despot.[54] Now the beginning of his kingdom was the famed Babel (Gen 10:10) which produced the tower reaching into the heavens. Nimrod becomes the archetypal despot who claims the heavenly domain for himself. He is a *gibor*. But is there any reason to associate Nimrod with the Messiah?[55] Isaiah 9:5-6 presents a prophecy of the ideal Davidic king. Herein this messianic figure is called "Mighty-God" (*el-gibor*). He is a divine potentate, but in this case a positive figure, a "Prince of Peace" (Isa 9:5). The term *el-gibor* reappears in the next chapter of Isaiah. "On that day the remnant of Israel and the survivors of the house of Jacob will no more lean on the one who struck them, but will lean on the LORD, the Holy One of Israel, in truth. A remnant will return, the remnant of Jacob, to the mighty God [*el gibor*]" (Isa 10:20-21). Interestingly, the *gibor* of God, the *el-gibor*, brings about the ingathering of the Tribes of Jacob. Significantly, Isa 10 was read on the second Sabbath before Pentecost.[56] This text would still be ringing in the author's ears. Thus the Redeemer (*goel*) functions as divine ruler (*gibor*) and leads Israel back to the Holy One. Therefore the holy *gibor* (3) with his followers (663) can be accounted as 666,[57] whereas the evil *gibor*, the ancient evil Nimrod, is a

---

54. See Holladay, *Concise Hebrew and Aramaic Lexicon*, 53.

55. The term "serpent," *nhsh*, was interpreted as representing the Messiah because it has the same numerical value as the Hebrew word *messiah*. Likewise, Moses raised the serpent in the desert and healed the people who gazed upon it with faith; see Num 21:8 and John 3:14. Thus serpent, a symbol for the devil, is also a symbol for the Messiah. Also see Ford, *Revelation*, 225.

56. See Goulder, *Evangelists' Calendar*, 181.

57. Ascribing a positive quality to the One God of Israel in a triadic form is reflected in Isa 6:3, where God is acclaimed as "Holy, holy, holy." In Rev 4:8 this trisagion is combined with the triadic title "he was, he is, and he is to come"—a rabbinic designation for God. The 666 can be a holy assertion of God's creation of humanity that reflects the image and likeness of its Creator. The "antichrist" is a perversion of the priestly vocation of humanity.

perverted 666 who requires of his followers not the divine seal on the forehead, but the mark of the Beast.

There is one final reason to divine a relationship between 666 and the 144,000. "This calls for wisdom: let anyone with understanding calculate the number of the beast, for it is the number of a person. Its number is six hundred sixty-six. Then I looked, and there was the Lamb, standing on Mount Zion! And with him were one hundred forty-four thousand who had his name and his Father's name written on their foreheads" (Rev 13:18—14:1). It is we, in a modern division of the book, who have separated the text into two different chapters. The division by chapter and verse did not come about until the thirteenth century. Thus the early reader and listener could naturally have associated the two different numbers and their representations. Chapter 7 had already supplied the exegetical key.[58] The names of the Twelve Tribes and their Redeemer-King are in direct contrast to the name of the Beast and its head. The Beast and the false messiah are a perversion of the kingdom of God and the Lord's Anointed. Both parties have a sign on their foreheads, whether the seal or the mark of the Beast: 666.

In this interpretation of Revelation, Nimrod, the founder of Babel and the Babylonian Empire, plays a significant role as an archetypal figure who rebels against God and institutes worldwide idolatry. Babylon is in stark contrast to the Israel of God. The thinking is deeply rooted in Jewish thought and gematria. Significantly, Nimrod figured into rabbinic discussions concerning the Feast of Weeks. While my association of the Twelve Tribes and their Redeemer-King to 666 (in a positive sense) might appear "tantalizingly intoxicating," I do believe it is quite probable

---

58. Admittedly, the temptation to find various gematria in the text is beguiling. The 144,000 are the Twelve Tribes (with Manasseh replacing Dan). The high priest's breastplate contained twelve stones, one for each of the tribes. The walls of the New Jerusalem reflect the high priest's ephod. Scholars have pointed out that the order is different in Rev 21 and that the stones are somewhat different, probably due to a translation from Hebrew into Greek. If one merely works off of the Hebrew names for the twelve gems as found in Exod 28:18–20 and adds up the numerical value of the first consonant, one arrives at the number 1244. Did the original author (= authoritative source) purposely change one or more of the Hebrew names to arrive at 1440, the sacred number of the elect and the measurement of the city itself (Rev 21:17)? Unfortunately, we will never know for certain, but my suspicion is that he used an alternate noun for one or two of the rare nouns describing the gems so as to achieve his 1440. Unfortunately, my knowledge of Hebrew and Aramaic names for gems is not proficient enough to make a suggestion! (In Greek, the gems come out to 1872.)

that the original author of Revelation mused upon this very point. As if by poetic justice, there is yet another Hebrew term beginning with *gimmel* that the author might have cast a wry wink at. The word גרן (*goren*) means threshing floor. The 144,000 are the "first-fruits" who have been harvested; the wheat from the chaff has been separated on the threshing floor of God. I believe, however, the author's primary intention was to draw a contrast between Nimrod as *gibor* and the Messiah as *gibor*—between Nimrod as 666, and the 144,000 and their Redeemer-King as the Holy 666.

JEZEBEL

Previously I noted that in Rev 1–3, the prologue to the main apocalyptic drama which unfolds in chapters 4–22, the Christian redactor skillfully employs seven sets of seven, thereby attesting to his awareness of the motif operative in the main corpus based on the Feast of Weeks. John also quotes the relevant seder reading for the Feast: Exod 19:6. Could John also have utilized some gematria? In Rev 2:20 John refers to a woman named Jezebel. Perhaps this is a symbolic epithet based on the biblical Jezebel who led Israel into idolatry, rather than the actual name of a prophetess.[59] Balaam is used figuratively in Rev 2:14. The Jezebel of Rev 2:20 serves as counterpoint to the woman of Rev 12 as well as Jerusalem.[60] But there might be something further going on. In Hebrew, uncannily, "Jezebel" adds up to 49, and this in itself might be an ironic mockery of the Feast of Weeks. The Jezebel of Rev 2:20 lures people "into sexual immorality and the eating of food sacrificed to idols" (NIV). In place of the holy feasting that one would do on the Feast of Weeks (7 x 7), "Jezebel" (7 x 7) leads the beguiled faithful into an idolatrous feasting.

BALAAM SON OF BEOR

Another puzzling character to appear in Rev 2–3 is Balaam. Commentators provide the background to the biblical character and draw allusions to his leading Israel astray through Balak who entices the men to fornicate with foreign women and thereby indulge in idolatry. However, to my knowledge none of the commentators ever explains his sudden appearance other than as a figure of immorality and idolatry. Why

---

59. See Aune, *Revelation*, 203, who seems to posit this without directly saying so.
60. See Duff, *Who Rides the Beast?*, 92–96.

should this obscure figure play such an apparently important role in Rev 2:14? And would Gentile Christians resonate with the metaphor? The resurrected Jesus tells the church at Pergamum, "I have a few things against you: you have some there who hold to the teaching of Balaam, who taught Balak to put a stumbling block before the people of Israel, so that they would eat food sacrificed to idols and practice fornication." Commentators point out that Balaam also appears in Jude 11 as well as 2 Pet 2:15. What is interesting is that 2 Pet 3 deals with the apocalyptic end of the world and mentions the "thousand years." Setting aside the date of 2 Peter and questions regarding possible textual influences, at minimum Balaam appears in two works dealing with the imminent end. Jude likewise deals with impending judgment. So why would Balaam figure into such accounts? Rabbis interpreted Balaam's fifth oracle as a prediction regarding the Messiah:

> "I see him, but not now;
> I behold him, but not near.
> A star will come out of Jacob,
> a sceptre will rise out of Israel." (Num 24:17 NIV)

But more telling is the association made with the seventh oracle. Rabbis understood Asshur to refer to the Assyrian Empire and its successors, and Kittim to the Greek and Roman Empires.[61] Significantly, Balaam had seven oracles and had set up seven altars on which he slew forty-nine animals. The motif of seven is definitely at work and fits in nicely with the Book of Revelation and the "prediction" of a Messiah who destroys the Roman Empire.

But perhaps something more fundamental is concomitantly at work given that Balaam is cast in a negative light by both the rabbis and the writer of Rev 2. For the Christian redactor John, who most probably was a Torah-observant Jew professing faith in Jesus of Nazareth as the Christ, Balaam is the archetypal false prophet who leads some of the Jews astray. Balaam's prophesying for money and attempted cursing of Israel only led to its blessing. The rabbis had pondered much upon Balaam, especially because he appears in the Torah. They reflected upon the etymology of his name, some exegeting it to mean *blʻ ʻm* or *blh ʻm* ("he who

---

61. See the *y. Ta*[insert aleph]*an* 68d; Ginzberg, *Legends of the Jews*, 3:380; and Greene, "Balaam Figure and Type," 212.

consumes the people") or *b 'l 'm* ("rule over the people").[62] According to Charles, the later derivation gives rise to the Greek rendering of his name *nika laon* and hence the mention of Nicolaitans in 2:6, 15.[63] "So you also have some who hold to the teaching of the Nicolaitans. Repent then. If not, I will come to you soon and make war against them with the sword [*rhomphaia*] of my mouth" (2:15–16). The metaphor is blunted unless one notes that Balaam was killed with a sword (*rhomphaia*) (Num 31:8 LXX). Even the first mention of Nicolaitans in Rev 2:6 is followed by an ironic play on words in the next verse: "To everyone who conquers [*nikōnti*]"; the verb *nikaō* means "to conquer or rule" (in English the *k* becomes a *c*). This same battle and victory motif continues with the subsequent six communities.[64]

Balaam son of Beor is the archetypal false Gentile prophet who leads the people of God into apostasy. Here it is important to recall my definition of terms. *In the religious sphere, I am defining a Jew as someone of any ethnic background who espouses monotheism and a belief that God's covenantal love is revealed through the Torah and the Prophets. Such believers adhere to various degrees of Torah observance and utilize a variety of practices. I am defining a Christian as someone of any ethnic background who espouses monotheism and a belief that this One God sent Jesus of Nazareth as Messiah (Anointed One =Christ in Greek) to inaugurate the Messianic Age by his resurrection from the dead. Such believers adhere to various degrees of Torah observance, utilize a variety of practices, and believe in various levels of Jesus' divine status.* Rev 2–3 addresses the issue of religious adherence and practices. The Jewish Jesus-believers need to be on guard against Gentile Jesus-believers who are lax in their observance of ritual purity and who thereby casually participate in pagan idolatry (whether imperial or otherwise) claiming liberty (or spiritual immunity?) through their adherence to faith in Jesus Christ.[65]

62. See *b. Sanh* 105a.

63. See Charles, *Critical and Exegetical Commentary*, 1:52–53; as well as Beale, *Book of Revelation*, 251. Aune (*Revelation*, 149) appears to summarily dismiss such a connection.

64. The seven churches are all joined together in Christ's hand, as well as by a chiastic structure. Embedded in that chiasm are parallel couplets that shed further light on the Nicolaitans; see Appendix E.

65. See Frankfurter, "Jews of Not?" However, while I agree with his analysis I believe the intra-Jewish debate *also* includes non-Jesus-professing Jews. The fact that all types of Jews regarded Balaam as a *Gentile* prophet needs to be taken into account.

At the same time, John's Torah-observant Jews who profess faith in Jesus as Messiah need to explain to their Jewish brethren (whether they believe in Jesus or not) how they (John's group which tries to maintain halakhic purity) are the true Jews (Rev 2:9). The text of chapters 1–3 is fraught with *intra*-Jewish polemics, *not anti-Semitism*.[66] As any Jew knows, when one enters the synagogue and commences morning prayers, the very first words out of one's lips is a quote from Balaam: "How goodly are thy tents, O Jacob! How lovely thy dwellings, O Israel!" (Num 24:5).[67] In short, the argument possibly runs:

> You, our Jewish brothers and sisters, quote Balaam but some of you fail to recognize his prediction as fulfilled in Jesus of Nazareth, and there are some others of you who believe that we think that in the Messianic Age which we claim has started, that there is cause for libertarianism, which is not the case! God forbid! We are true Jews who heed the teaching of Balaam in the true sense (using his blessing in the morning and believing his messianic prophecy is fulfilled), and are most definitely *not* led into idolatry or halakhic impurity.

As such, the opposing Jews (of whatever spectrum and ideology) can be labeled the "synagogue of Satan," for *the term Satan means accuser* (Rev 2:9; 3:9). Unfortunately, the English translation "synagogue" is misleading because the Greek word more properly means "congregation." In short, the appellation is a "congregation of the accuser," or "congregation of accusation." The texts should not be read as John heaping diabolical epithets. It is a matter of Jews hurling *accusations* (slander, 2:9) at one another, a fraternal dispute as well as an internal community argument among Jesus believers.

In fact, "the synagogue of Satan" written in Aramaicized Hebrew (הבית שטנה) adds up to the sacred number 777! Those who belong to "the synagogue of Satan" are not *outside* of the household of God; they are merely taking sides *within* the household of God. Furthermore, the first appearance of the Hebrew term Satan (שטן) in the Torah is precisely in connection with Balaam in Num 22:22, wherein "the angel

---

66. The "bowing at your feet" as found in Rev 3:9 in connection with "synagogue of Satan" can simply be following the type of Joseph's brother's bowing at his feet. The metaphor can be one of fraternal conflict.

67. The earliest witness to this, I believe, is found in *b. Sanh.* 105b coming from R. Johanan of the mid third century, but the practice might have gone back earlier.

of the LORD took his stand in the road as his adversary [*satan*]." The Angel of the Lord is a positive figure doing God's bidding. Those who are making accusations probably sincerely believe they are being led by God.[68] John T. Greene argues that in the Qumran Community the Balaam figure was used "as an example and yardstick for gauging acceptable insider deportment," as well as differentiating between legitimate and illegitimate priesthood.[69] The same is probably happening in Rev 2–3 regarding proper behavior as well as contentions over legitimacy of authentic Jewish identity.[70]

How is my assertion that John and his communities were Jews professing faith in Jesus as Messiah defensible? Rev 1:7 quotes Dan 7:13 and Zech 12:10 and 14 as proof texts. Rev 2:26–28 marshals messianic passages from Ps 2:8–9. Rev 1:12–15 is a collage of texts depicting the Son of Man in a Jewish liturgical setting and role. The Morning Star in Rev 2:28 and especially in the epilogue in 22:16 is an allusion to Balaam's prophecy in Num 24:17 wherein a "star arises" (n.b.: "Morning Star" only appears in the prologue and epilogue).[71] John utilizes figures from Israel's history: Balaam and Jezebel (meaningless to a Gentile audience). The writer employs thoroughly Jewish concepts such as "hidden manna" (the manna was kept in the Ark of the Covenant which was hidden). John presents Jesus as wielding a two-edged sword (*rhomphaia*) when addressing the community at Pergamum and accusing some of them as holding to the teaching of Balaam, who himself was killed by a sword (Num 31:8—the LXX using the same word).

But more importantly, something more remarkable appears to be at work in chapters 1–3. At first glance the appearance of Balaam and Jezebel seems to be a haphazard association based solely on issues of idolatry. Yet if Goulder is correct in his reconstruction of Sabbath readings the connection makes perfect sense. My arguments in chapter 4

---

68. The "deep things of Satan" found in Rev 2:24 could refer to convoluted arguments and accusations which burden the believers.

69. Greene, "Balaam Figure and Type," 198, see also 215. For Greene's cursory treatment of Balaam in Rev 2:14 see the "Balaam Figure and Type," 228–29.

70. For an overview of Jewish communities in Asia Minor see Keener, *Gospel of John* 1:146–49, and his references.

71. For contemporaneous Jewish usage of this imagery see *T. Levi* 18:3 and the note pointing out parallels at Qumran which pre-date the Jewish Wars, as well as *T. Judah* 24:1. According to *y. Ta'an* 4.5 68d, the late-first–to–early-second-century Rabbi Aqiba applied Num 24:17 to the Messiah. Also see Collins, *Scepter and Star*, 63–67.

above were based upon the established readings for the Major Feast Days (in this case Shavu'ot), which scholars accept as being established at least by the first century CE. Regarding regular Sabbath readings there is far less agreement, though Cohen's impressive evidence that Philo followed the regular Sabbath readings cannot be overlooked. Thus if Goulder's reconstruction should be given more weight in light of Cohen's analysis, it has bearing upon Rev 1–3.[72] On the Sabbath when the Torah reading is Num 22–25 (referring to Balaam and Balak) the concomitant reading from the Writings (Ketuvim) is 1 Kgs 19, which mentions Jezebel's seeking revenge (following up on the previous Sabbath's reading of 1 Kgs 18 concerning Elijah, Jezebel, and the prophets of Baal). In other words, the connection between Balaam and Jezebel is due to the *lectionary*![73] The Sabbath readings in question are those for Chislev III. This further explains the mention of Satan in Rev 2–3 since the term first appears in the Torah in Num 22:22, part of the sedar reading (Num 22:2—25:9). Given that we have both the Torah and Ketuvim readings used in Rev 1–3, what is the corresponding one in the Nevi'im according to Goulder? Isa 50–51. The allusions and parallels with Rev 1–3 are striking.

Chapters 50–51 in Isaiah are a continuation of chapter 49 regarding the Servant of the Lord, to which I shall come back (Isa 49 being read on the previous Sabbath along with 1 Kgs 18). Isa 49–51 deals with the destruction and desolation of Jerusalem, and the promise to restore it. One can only imagine how these texts would have been heard after 70 CE. The reading can be understood in an apocalyptic tone because Isa 51:6 says that "the heavens will vanish like smoke." The first striking parallel between Isa 50–51 and Rev 1–3 is Isa 50:4 (LXX): "he has given me an ear to hear." Three times the prophet commands, "Listen" (Isa 51:1, 4, 7). "Let anyone who has an ear to hear, listen," is said to all seven churches. The Isaiah text three times uses the garment metaphor and explicitly focuses on it in 51:8; cf. Rev 3:4–5, 18. Isa 50:11 (especially the LXX, which gives the text a more positive spin) refers to walking in the midst of flames of fire, among the firebrands, an image expounded on in Rev 1:12–13; 2:1, where Christ walks amid the seven burning lampstands. Isa

---

72. See Goulder, *Evangelists' Calendar*, Table 8, insert after p. 306. As will be clearly seen, the congruence between Goulder's proposed readings and Rev 1–3 is too astounding to be merely coincidental, and thus itself corroborates his reconstruction.

73. The zeal of Elijah mentioned in 1 Kgs 19:10, 14 might be behind Christ's wish for ardent fervor in Rev 3:14.

51:3 speaks of Eden and Rev 1:7 recalls the Tree of Life in paradise. Isa 51:9, 17 summon the listener to wake up and rouse from sleep like Rev 3:2–3. Isa 51:13, 16 stress God as the maker of the universe as does Rev 3:14. The same Isaian verse lays the charge that the people have forgotten God (to whom they are wed)—Rev 2:4 rebuffs the people for having forgotten their first love. Isa 51:14 speaks of being thrown in prison as does Rev 2:9; and the same verse mentions being fed with bread paralleled by Rev 2:17 and the hidden manna, bread from heaven. Isa 51:15 depicts God as causing the sound of roaring waves; Rev 1:15 follows suit. Can all of these allusions and parallels be mere coincidence?

Just as the Ketuvim reading of 1 Kgs 19 speaking of Jezebel logically makes the reader reflect back on the previous chapter, in which she is also mentioned, Isa 50–51 cause one to revisit chapter 49. Rev 1:16; 2:12, 16 depict a sharp two-edged sword coming from the mouth of Christ. Aune comments that this image is "bizarre" and that its appearance in 19:11–21 must have been composed 1:9—3:22 for grammatical reasons. Aune does cite Isa 49:2 ("He made my mouth like a sharp sword") as a "possible" basis.[74] While I totally concur that Rev 1–3 was written after the rest of the original text, the appearance of the two-edged sword in 1:16 makes perfect sense based on the Ketuvim reading regarding the Servant of YHWH. In fact, when looking at Isa 49 other parallels emerge. Isa 49:16 portrays God holding her people in the palm of her hand and inscribing their names upon her hands. In Rev 1:16 and 2:1 the Son of Man holds the seven stars, which are equated with the seven churches (1:20), in his hand. Rev 2:17 and 3:12 speak of names being inscribed as memorials. Isa 49 also mentions poverty, riches, and rewards, themes found in Rev 2–3.

JOHN AND THE JEWISH LECTIONARY

Given that nowhere else in the Book of Revelation is either Balaam or Jezebel mentioned, and that they are together in Rev 2, and that they appear in the Torah and Writings readings for the same Sabbath coupled by references to the concomitant Prophets selection, and that the Morning Star from Num 24:17 appears in the prologue and epilogue,

---

74. See Aune, *Revelation*, 98.

I can only conclude that John was influenced by these readings for the Balaq Sabbath—Chislev III.[75] Such congruence cannot be coincidence.

Equally poignant is the fact that this Sabbath is the second one preceding the Feast of Hanukkah, the dedication of the temple. When John wrote the prologue (Rev 1–3) and the epilogue (22:8–21) the temple in Jerusalem had been destroyed. For a Torah-observant Jew professing faith in Jesus of Nazareth as Messiah, how was one to come to grips with the loss of the temple and God's promise to restore the temple? The Son of Man consoles the faithful, telling the community at Philadelphia, "If you conquer, I will make you a pillar in the temple of my God; you will never go out of it. I will write on you the name of my God, and the name of the city of my God, the new Jerusalem that comes down from my God out of heaven, and my own new name" (3:12). The cover letters are clearly influenced by a different set of Jewish lectionary readings than those for 4:1—22:7, especially chapters 4–11. This in itself points to different authors or, at the very least, times of composition.[76] Plausibly, John received his vision on the Lord's Day, a Sunday, immediately after or soon after the Balaq Sabbath preceding the Feast of Hanukkah, and subsequently sent a circular letter to the communities in his care, giving them hope that the temple of God would indeed be restored by Jesus Christ, as an earlier prophet had seen in his vision regarding the Messiah (4:1—22:7). This temple would endure for all eternity and in it the faithful and pure will serve God as a kingdom and priests forever.

But who was this John who was obviously so well-acquainted with the Sabbath lectionary and could amazingly interweave appropriate texts from the Law, Prophets, and Writings? Surely it could not have been a Jew with casual familiarity. In the previous chapter I proposed that John the Apostle, as claimed by tradition, is a viable candidate. Curiously enough, Polycrates, bishop of Ephesus, writing around 190 CE, refers to a "John, who was both a witness and a teacher, who reclined upon the bosom of the Lord, and, being a priest, wore the sacerdotal plate."[77]

---

75. Of course there is the glaring issue that "Jesus Christ" or "Lord Jesus" appear *only* in the prologue and epilogue; "Jesus" does not even appear in Rev 4–11, and when it appears six times in 12:1—22:7 the name stands alone *without any glorified title*.

76. The textual incongruities, lectionary disparities, and theological dissimilarities between Rev 1–3/22:8–21 and 4–22:7 are too great in my mind to warrant the same writer having penned the entire book as we now have it.

77. Polycrates, letter to Victor, bishop of Rome, as quoted in Eusebius, *Hist. Ecc.* 5.24 (McGiffert, 242).

Polycrates obviously associates this John with the "Beloved Disciple" in the Gospel of John. While Polycrates does not call him "apostle" as he did Philip, who textually preceded him, neither does he call him "bishop" as everyone after him in the text is so denominated. Polycrates might presume that everyone knows that this is John the Apostle, though he could be John "the Elder."[78] In the Gospel of John, the Beloved Disciple is always anonymous. Some scholars believe he is the anonymous figure in John 18:15–16: "Simon Peter, and another disciple followed Jesus. Since that disciple was known to the high priest, he went with Jesus into the courtyard of the high priest, but Peter was standing outside at the gate. So the other disciple, who was known to the high priest, went out, spoke to the woman who guarded the gate, and brought Peter in." Curiously, this (beloved) disciple had some connection with the high priest. While R. Alan Culpepper does not believe the Beloved Disciple to be the Apostle John, he does admit that Polycrates as well as his recipient of the letter, Victor, bishop of Rome, would have identified the two.[79] Polycrates could have been conflating John 18:15–16 with what he believed regarding John the Apostle's alleged authorship of the Gospel; but it is also possible that there might have been an authentic independent tradition at work. Hippolytus of Rome (most probably impacted by Polycrates' letter to Victor) accepted this association and called John "a high-priest at Ephesus and prophet."[80] If John the Apostle were the John of Rev 1–3 and 22:8–21, and if he were somehow a priest of enough stature to wear the high priest's breast plate (or mitre depending upon the meaning of the word), then this would account for his in-depth knowledge of the Jewish lectionary.

While none of this can be definitely proven, it is, nevertheless, interesting that such a tradition about the Apostle John's priesthood arose. The prologue to the fifth-century apocryphal *Acts of John by Prochorus* claims that John's father was a priest from Jerusalem who had removed to Capernaum.[81] The Ethiopic translation of an earlier work entitled "The

78. See Culpepper, *John*, 128.

79. See ibid., 61–63, 120, 128. Culpepper thinks it is possible but unlikely that the apostle John was a priest, but he also does not believe he was the Beloved Disciple either. In my article previously referred to, I present the internal literary argument of chiasm as to why the Beloved Disciple most probably is John the son of Zebedee.

80. Hippolytus, "Odes on all the Scriptures," as found in Parisian Codex Coislin 195 and cited in Eisler, *Enigma of the Fourth Gospel*, 55.

81. See Prologue to the *Acts of John by Prochorus* in Vatican Gr. 654, fol. 88v; and

Genealogies of the Twelve Apostles" specifies that John's father was of the tribe of Levi.[82] Ethiopian theology and tradition is itself influenced by the Syrian. Many find it impossible to think that Zebedee was from a priestly clan since he was a fisherman, but who knows—maybe he had been banned from priestly ministry due to some subsequent impurity, defect, or theological point of view. Of course, this is sheer speculation, but we will never have all of the historical evidence before us, and thus to argue conclusively in *either direction* is futile. Nevertheless, is a strand of the tradition trying *to account for something*? Did earlier readers notice not only the liturgical imagery at work in the Book of Revelation, but the *lectionary* foundation as well?

What is equally curious is the very context in which Polycrates makes this assertion. Polycrates is writing to Victor regarding the Asiatic practice of celebrating Pascha on the fourteenth of Nisan, no matter what day of the week it falls on. This is known as the Quartodeciman controversy. Because the issue is of significance much of the text warrants quoting. Polycrates, bishop of Ephesus, catalogues the following people in Asia Minor as having observed the fourteenth of Nisan.

> Among these are Philip, one of the twelve apostles, who fell asleep in Hierapolis; and his two aged virgin daughters, and another daughter, who lived in the Holy Spirit and now rests at Ephesus; and, moreover, John, who was both a witness and teacher, who reclined upon the bosom of the Lord, and, being a priest, wore the sacerdotal plate. He fell asleep at Ephesus. And Polycarp in Smyrna, who was bishop and martyr; and Thraseas, bishop and martyr from Eumenia, who fell asleep in Smyrna. Why need I mention the bishop and martyr Sagaris who fell asleep in Laodicea or the blessed Papirius, or Melito, the Eunuch who lived altogether in the Holy Spirit, and who lies in Sardis, awaiting the episcopate from heaven, when he shall rise from the dead?[83]

Polycrates goes on to mention himself as well as seven of his relatives who also served as bishops, and the many bishops recently assembled with him in council. What is particularly striking is that Polycrates mentions bishops from Ephesus, Smyrna, Sardis, and Laodicea—four out

---

Junod, *Acta Iohannis*, 1:10 and 35. I am indebted to Culpepper (*John*, 66) for this reference.

82. See Budge, *Contendings of the Apostles*, 40.

83. See Eusebius, *Hist. Ecc.* 5.24. The term "episcopate" is an understandable mistranslation of *episkopēn* which means "visitation."

of the seven churches mentioned in Rev 2–3. All of these communities followed a Jewish reckoning of the Passover and a commemoration of the Lord's resurrection. Perhaps the reason was more than just due to what some have interpreted as "Judaizing" tendencies (at worse) or antiquarianism (at best). It may be more than just following a Jewish liturgical calendar and ritual practices; perhaps Asiatic Christ-believing communities also followed a Jewish liturgical *lectionary*, and for *that reason*, did not wish to depart from the tradition and the rule of faith.[84] Changing the date of Pascha throws off the whole lectionary cycle, integral to studying the Scriptures in an oral society, and affects the very homiletic and spiritual life of the community of faith and its practices.[85] To change the scriptural cycle of readings is to change the life of the church and *God's timetable*. The Book of Revelation is a lectionary midrash about God's timetable and the Feast of Seven Weeks. Changing the date of Pascha changes the date of Pentecost. Further studies need to be undertaken regarding ancient lectionaries (Jewish and Christian) as well as the Quartodeciman issue in light of this hypothesis.[86]

CONCLUSION

Demonstrably, a Jewish mindset which utilized gematria and Hebrew plays on words is operative throughout the Book of Revelation. This is

---

84. I would also point out that the list of people emphasizes their devotion to virginity and living in the Holy Spirit (Spirit of holiness?). Frankfurter's observations regarding halakhic purity bear noting.

85. One has only to look at the sad state of affairs between Western and Eastern Christendom, which disagree on the dating of Easter, and how this subsequently impacts the annual lectionary readings and life of the Church. If you are a Protestant reader who belongs to a community that doesn't even follow a lectionary cycle, think of it this way: Would you be reading in public worship from Matt 1–2 or Luke 1–2 in April?

86. For Quartodecimans see Stewart-Sykes, *Lamb's High Feast*, 11–29, 141–206. Discussing the Quartodecimans is beyond the purview of this present study, but I'd make the following preliminary observations: (1) Polycrates connects the saints who have fallen asleep with the Parousia, and (2) there is an emphasis on the Holy Spirit. Pentecost is the coming of the Holy Spirit (even Paul speaks of the *fruit* of the Holy Spirit, a first-fruits Feast of Weeks metaphor), and as I have been demonstrating, the time when some Jews believed the Messiah would come and bring about the end of the world. Furthermore, the whole realm of lectionary studies needs to be researched more vigorously. *Apostolic Constitutions* 8.5.11 evinces that the Syrian churches read from the Law, Prophets, Gospels, and Epistles seemingly reflecting an ancient usage. I wonder how those readings accorded with those of the synagogue.

another clear indication that the thought of the author(s) was so deeply steeped in Hebraic thought that the original authoritative sources could not have been Gentile Christians, but rather were immersed in the vitality of Judaism.[87] The redactor demonstrably was a Torah-observant, Jesus-professing Jew focused on purity and eschatology.[88]

---

87. My overall argumentation provides a response (if not answer) to Thompson's query concerning the grammatical language and authorship of Revelation with regard to chs. 1–3 compared to the rest of the text; see Thompson, *Apocalypse and Semitic Syntax*, 106–8.

88. While not a Jew, as a historical theologian I have tried to be cognizant of, and sensitive to, the first-century Jewish experience.

7

Recapitulation: Re-envisioning Revelation

An ancient Jewish thought was that history repeats itself but at the same time makes advances by summing itself up. The present remembers the past in order to re-envision the collective history and provide a foundation for new beginnings, to see a new vision for the future. In short, this is "prophetic imagination."[1] The Seer of the Apocalypse has done exactly this. He has recapitulated Jewish history, re-envisioned the saving mystery, so as to hear the word of the Lord for his own day and age, as well as his immediate future. The author sincerely believed he was living in the last days, and was on the threshold of the Messianic Era. The liturgical cycle of Jewish worship fueled his faith in God. The festal worship service that spoke deeply to his own situation was the Feast of Weeks.

SUMMARY

My book transpired over the course of a year when I was reading the *Book of Jubilees* and noticed how prominently the Feast of Weeks played in that author's theology. Perhaps this was operative in the Book of Revelation as well? On face value, the Feast of Weeks consists of sevens and surely this is present in Revelation. Furthermore, the harvest motif was particularly clear in chapter 14. My hypothesis led to investigation. Given the rich liturgical background to the Book of Revelation, I posited that perhaps the Feast of Weeks was at work here as well. My bias was that the theology expressed in the Book of Revelation was more thoroughly Jewish than Christian, notwithstanding John's introductory letters to the seven churches. I subsequently, purposely investigated the Book of Revelation as primarily a Jewish work to see if this were plausible.

---

1. See Brueggemann, *Prophetic Imagination*.

Some conclusions to my hypothesis and historical investigation regarding the Book of Revelation can now be drawn.

1. Preceding and contemporaneous Jewish apocalyptic literature utilized the Feast of Weeks. This theological motif served four purposes to varying degrees in Jewish apocalyptic literature. The Feast of Weeks highlights a) God's covenantal promises and faithfulness, b) the giving of the Torah, c) the mystery and reception of divine revelation itself, and d) the apocalyptic harvesting of the world. These four elements are found in the corpus of the Book of Revelation.

2. A liturgical lection of Law, Prophets, and Writings specific to the Feast of Weeks was established before the first century CE, and these influenced the author of the Apocalypse. In fact, in chapters 4–11, the literary format always includes a reference to or a citation from the seder, the prophetic haphtarah, and the hagiographical haphtarah. The subsequent chapters mirror this lectionary influence but not to the same literary extent.

3. The Jewish theology connected to Shavu'ot, such as combating idolatry and keeping the commandments, is also evidenced in the Book of Revelation.

4. Liturgical terminology and customs surrounding Pentecost are also reflected in the corpus, e.g. sevenfoldness, first-fruits, twenty-four elders, whitened robes, sexual abstinence, trumpets, and cutting down trees.

5. Political and religious events in the history of Israel, occurring on or immediately around the Feast of Pentecost, warrant the author's associating his apocalyptic message with this Festival.

6. The Jewish War lasting three and a half years with regard to Jerusalem and the Divine Voice in the temple on Shavu'ot in 70 CE, as well as the prophetic ministry of Jesus, son of Ananias, help to contextualize the author's presentation; as does also the Levitical priesthood of Jeshua ("Jesus").

7. The rabbinic gematria of 666 associated with the Feast of Weeks is found in the Apocalypse, and HaShavu'ot itself adds up to 777. Other gematria in Hebrew probably are at work as well, particularly "King of kings, Lord of lords" and "The Lamb and

Recapitulation: Re-envisioning Revelation

the Ark of the Lord God and temple," which likewise equal 777. Agrippina the Woman/Burnt Offering adds up to 666 as well as do other phrases.

8. Plays on words in Hebrew between Caesar and harvest (*qsr* and *qtsr*) and scroll and sickle (*megilah* and *magal*) lie behind the Greek text. This holds true for the Syriac form of Aramaic as well: scroll (*megala*), sickle, (*magla*) and unveiling (*magle*).

9. The Christian redactor John mildly utilizes the liturgical readings for the Feast of Weeks in chapter 1, but especially those for Chislev III in Rev 1–3.

10. The theme of the Feast of Weeks is not an isolated occurrence, but is integrally operative in chapters 4–11, prominent in 12–14, and recognizable in chapters 15–22.

Based on this evidence, I conclude that the Feast of Weeks is the hermeneutical key to understanding the original theology behind the Book of Revelation.

UNDERLYING APOCALYPSE?

Given the thorough Jewishness of the body of the Book of Revelation, the liturgical theology pulsating within the text, the extent to which Hebrew plays on words are operative, and the richness of the Hebraic gematria, I must seriously postulate the *possibility* of a pre-existing Jewish Apocalypse *in written form* that was taken over by the Christian redactor.[2] This would not be the first occurrence of such an enterprise. Scholars have long pointed out that *4 Ezra* was originally a Jewish work that received a Christian prologue and epilogue, thus "baptizing" it. The apocalypse of *4 Ezra* thus found its way into several copies of the Bible in Latin, Syriac, Ethiopic, and Armenian. Thanks to Christians, the works of Philo and Josephus were preserved. These works were lost to the body of mainstream Judaism and did not enter back into Jewish thought until the sixteenth century.[3] Perhaps it was a Jewish Christian named John who preserved an earlier existing Jewish apocalyptic work—if not in written form, at least arguably in an oral format—and then provided a

---

2. Also note that twice Hebrew words are given first and then translated into Greek; see Rev 9:11; 16:16.

3. See Sandmel, "Foreword for Jews."

prologue and epilogue. The focus on the Feast of Weeks is profoundly Jewish. The last known center emphasizing such a theological tradition was Qumran. Perhaps the original author, the authoritative source, hailed from this community or was deeply influenced by it. Later it was adopted and redacted by a Christian community in Ephesus in Asia Minor that appreciated the liturgical and eschatological theology.

RECOVERING AN EXEGETICAL TRADITION?

Why then, however, was this exegetical breaking of the seals lost? The earliest church father to comment on the Book of Revelation was Irenaeus around 180. He himself hailed from Asia Minor. Irenaeus ascribed the book to the end of the reign of Domitian, who ruled from 81 to 96.[4] This post-apostolic father unquestionably perceives the book as a Christian work. Nevertheless, he is a witness to the underlying Judeo-Christian theology found within the Apocalypse. Irenaeus writes:

> This Spirit did David ask for the human race, saying, "And stablish me with Thine all-governing Spirit"; who also, as Luke says, descended at the day of Pentecost upon the disciples after the Lord's ascension, having power to admit all nations to the entrance of life, and to the opening of the new covenant; from whence also, with one accord in all languages, they uttered praise to God, the Spirit bringing distant tribes to unity, and offering to the Father the first-fruits of all nations.[5]

Three important elements are found in Irenaeus' comments. Irenaeus connects the opening of a new covenant, the gathering of all nations, and the first-fruits to the Feast of Pentecost. While there might be some basis for this in the passage from Acts 2, the wording of "first-fruits" is not found there. His mentioning of all languages, tribes, and nations uttering praise to God is also reminiscent of Rev 5:9–10. It is more likely that he is influenced here by the theology operative in the Book of Revelation.

Later in the mid 200s Origen clearly gives Pentecost an eschatological understanding. He refers to it as "the festal gathering that is preserved for future times."[6] Origen explains that this was foreshadowed in

---

4. See Irenaeus, *Adv. Haer.* 5.30.3.

5. Ibid., 3.17.2.

6. Origen, *On the 150 Psalms* (fragment in Hippolytus, *GCS Hippolitus Werke 1–2*, 138–39), my translation.

the Jubilee year, which contains seven Sabbaths. Origen, like Clement of Alexandria before him, viewed the Book of Revelation as inspired.[7]

Eventually the Book of Revelation was not well received in the Christian East and was not read during the Christian liturgy.[8] Early on, however, it found favor in the West. It is listed among New Testament books in the Muratorian Canon composed in Rome before the end of the second century. The most striking witness to a liturgical understanding of the background on the Book of Revelation is attested to in the *Liber Comicus* dating from the sixth century. The *Liber Comicus* is a lectionary for churches in Spain. Significantly, the Book of Revelation was only read consecutively from Easter Sunday through Pentecost.[9] This Western liturgical cycle of readings suggests that a theological tradition was preserved associating the Apocalypse with the Feast of Pentecost. In fact, on the fourth Sunday after Easter, at the midway point between Pascha and Pentecost, the designated lection is Rev 14:5–16, which in the Vulgate numbering speaks of the Lamb and the followers as first-fruits and concludes with the Son of Man, harvesting the earth. The fourth Sunday serves as the liturgical chiasmus. The last Sunday before Pentecost, observed within the octave of Ascension, necessitates the reading of Rev 4:2–4 and 10–11, the scene of the heavenly throne. Easter Sunday commenced with Rev 1–3. Presumably, the *Liber Comicus* reflects an earlier lectionary tradition. Therefore, one can conclude that in early Western Christianity a theological hermeneutical tradition had been preserved that purposely situated the Book of Revelation within the Fifty Days so that it would culminate with the Feast of Pentecost. This lectionary tradition itself bears testimony to the liturgical theology that inspired the author of the Book of Revelation.

In 1969, the Roman Catholic Church revised its lectionary readings according to the earlier liturgical traditions and produced the *Ordo Lectionum Missae*. Interestingly enough, Year C now recaptures the earlier Western tradition by placing excerpts from the Book of Revelation in the lectionary for the Sundays between Easter and Pentecost. The Revised Common Lectionary 1992, used by a majority of Protestant

---

7. See Origen, *Comm. Joh.* 5.3.

8. For the history of its reception see Boring, *Revelation*, 2–3; and Mounce, *Revelation*, 21–23. Even to this day, the Eastern Christian liturgy does not use Revelation during public worship.

9. See Baudot, *Lectionary*, 47–48.

churches in North America and around the globe who have a lectionary tradition, follows this very pattern, utilizing the same readings as in the Roman Lectionary. Consequently, a vast portion of modern Christendom has re-appropriated a forgotten liturgical understanding of the Book of Revelation.

Lex orandi, lex credendi: The rule of prayer is the rule of faith. The Book of Revelation is the Book of Pentecost. It is the apocalyptic midrash on the Feast of Seven Weeks.

PANORAMIC OVERVIEW

Although it is beyond the purpose and scope of this book to provide a thorough commentary on the Book of Revelation in light of this new insight, a synopsis is required.

When the Jews were first exiled to Babylon (587 BCE) the prophet sustained the people in their faith by his prayer and prophetic ministry. He re-envisioned the saving act of God that delivered the Hebrew people out of bondage to the Egyptian Pharaoh and established for the Jewish people a covenant on Sinai. The theophany at Sinai was re-envisioned on the banks of Chebar.[10] The prophet later envisioned the rebuilding of Jerusalem and the temple. Centuries later, when the Jews were facing Antiochus Epiphanes IV, the prophet re-envisioned the Sinai theophany and Ezekiel's merkabah experience (163 BCE). Daniel saw the Ancient of Days enthroned. He is the One "who lives for ever and ever," never changing (Dan 4:31). Looking back on the Babylonian captivity, Daniel drew inspiration from Jeremiah's prophecy regarding the seventy years and re-interpreted this as seventy weeks of years. Just as the Ancient of Days had delivered Israel from the idolatry of Egypt and the pagan worship of Babylon, so too God was acting in his own day, delivering the Jewish nation from Antiochus who desecrated the temple with a statue of himself.

The author of Revelation draws hope and inspiration from this same salvation history. God is eternal and ever the same (Isa 40:28; 46:4, Bar 4). "He was and he is and he is to come" (Rev 4:8, cf. 11:17). God's saving action shall ever be the same. The author of Revelation re-envisions the crowning vision of Judaism—the merkabah (Rev 4), in particular,

---

10. While the prophet's vision does not occur on the Feast of Shavu'ot, it does happen almost exactly one month afterwards. Perhaps he was reflecting on the Feast and its significance?

the Sinai giving of the Torah. What was previously sealed up by Daniel will be broken by the Lamb. The messianic age is near at hand. God will deliver his people in the face of the Jewish War. Daniel's seventy weeks are now re-interpreted as Seven Weeks. The Feast of Weeks, the Jubilee Year of redemption, is upon us. God will exact from the nations the same punishments he inflicted upon the Egyptians.

The blood of Maccabean martyrs and those who subsequently died for witnessing to the faith will be avenged. God will purify his people and make them a line of kings and priests to serve him. The martyrs are the first-fruits of the coming eschatological harvest. The heavenly liturgy of the Feast of Weeks is nearing its completion. What was celebrated from the beginning by Noah, Abraham, Isaac, Jacob, Moses, and by our ancestors will be consummated by the coming Messiah who will fulfill his kingly and priestly role, leading the Twelve Tribes into the Promised Era.

The temple liturgy of the Feast of Weeks will reach its climax in the New Jerusalem, where the Tree of Life is restored and God's people are refreshed by the River of Life. But for those who obstinately hold onto idolatry despite God's merciful warnings and chastisements, there remains for them only the lake of fire and eternal punishment. The great Dragon, the primeval Serpent, will be destroyed, and all his followers. Victory and salvation belong to God!

This is a précis of the Jewish storyline in the corpus of the Apocalypse.[11] As such it stands as a beautiful piece of Second Temple literature and is worthy of academic study by Jewish scholars.

THE CHRISTIAN VISION

John, the Christian redactor, can give a resounding amen to this theological vision. He himself subsequently is enraptured by the Living One. The prophetic message of the Seer of Revelation is unfolded before John's eyes, and he is commissioned to strengthen his brothers and sisters who likewise suffer for their adherence to God's Word and their faith in Jesus. John now re-envisions the Jewish Apocalypse. He appreciates the liturgi-

---

11. For a Jewish understanding of the text, I encourage the reader to look through the notes and comments made by Ford as well as the wealth of rabbinic texts cited by Beale and Aune. Unfortunately, I cannot at this time present a verse-by-verse Jewish interpretation of the Apocalypse. The intent of the *original* author should be understood in the historical context of the Jewish War.

cal significance of the Feast of Weeks' lectionary and incorporates it into his writing of chapter 1 and is influenced by the lectionary he had just read before receiving his vision. Jesus (of Nazareth) is the fulfillment of the prophecy. John closes his redacted work with a blessing. "The grace of the Lord Jesus be with all the saints. Amen" (22:21). The book closes with a traditional liturgical phrase.[12] This circulated book is now to be read in the Christian liturgy: "Blessed is the one who reads aloud the words of the prophecy, and blessed are those who hear and who keep what is written in it; for the time is near" (1:3). All now is clear in the light of Christ; his radiance illuminates the Law, the Prophets, and the Writings.

"He said to them, 'This is what I told you while I was still with you: Everything must be fulfilled that is written about me in the Law of Moses, the Prophets and the Psalms.' Then he opened their minds so they could understand the Scriptures" (Luke 24:44–45 NIV).

---

12. Compare Rom 16:27; 1 Cor 16:22–23; 2 Cor 13:13; Gal 6:18; Eph 6:23–24; Phil 4:23; Col 4:18; 1 Thess 5:28; 2 Thess 3:18; 1 Tim 6:21; 2 Tim 4:22; Titus 3:15; Phlm 25; Heb 13:25; and 1 Pet 5:14.

Appendix A

Jewish Liturgical Readings for the Feast of Weeks

SEDER: TORAH READINGS

Exod 19:1—20:21

Sinai event: God carried Israel on eagles' wings; kingdom of priests; washing garments (white); trumpet blasts, cloud, lightning, and thunder

Deut 16:9–12 (alternate text)

Seven weeks and harvest with sickle

Torah Reading Immediately before Shavu'ot

Lev 26:1–46

Prohibition against idolatry, blessings and curses; sevenfold chastisement: war, famine, plagues, devouring wild beasts, death by sword, rationing, land laid waste

PROPHETIC HAPHTAROT: READINGS FROM THE PROPHETS

Ezek 1:1—2:3

Theophany of God enthroned upon four living creatures, storm cloud with lightning and rainbow; prophet sent to Israel who has rebelled against God

Hab 2:20—3:19

Theophany of lightning accompanied by pestilence and plague; mention of figs, fruits; Targum mentions Roman Empire

Zeph 3:1–20

> God as judge and witness against unfaithfulness; chastisement is summons for repentance, assembling of the nations for punishment, purification of the people, and restoration of Israel and renewal of (marital) love

Prophetic Readings Immediately before Pentecost

Isa 11:1–16

> Messiah, shoot of Jesse, endowed with (sevenfold, LXX) Spirit, raised as ensign to the nations

HAGIOGRAPHICAL HAPHTAROT: READINGS FROM THE WRITINGS

Ruth

> Time of harvest, Jesse and David

Ps 1

> Righteous and the wicked

Ps 29

> Theophanic seven voices of the Lord

Ps 68

> Exodus theophany, warrior king, rebuke of the beast

Alternate Readings

Tob 13:9–17

> (Book begins at Pentecost) Jerusalem restored and bejeweled, streets paved with gold

Dan 14 (Bel)

> Destruction of the idol Bel and the Dragon; Habakkuk at the Harvest Feast; seven days

Appendix B

The Ancient Empires and Their Major Rulers

ASSYRIAN EMPIRE	746–609 BCE
Tiglath-Pileser III	745–727
Sargon II	721–705
Ashurbanipal	668–621
BABYLONIAN EMPIRE	609–539 BCE
Nebuchadnezzar	605–562
PERSIAN EMPIRE	550–330 BCE
Cyrus the Great	580–529
Darius I	522–486
Xerxes I	486–465
MACEDONIAN EMPIRE	336–323 BCE
Alexander the Great	336–323
SELEUCID EMPIRE	323–64 BCE
Seleucus I	312–280
Antiochus IV Epiphanes	175–164
Antiochus VII Sidetes	138–129
PARTHIAN EMPIRE	250 BCE—225 CE
Mithridates II	128–88
Phraates IV	38–2
Vologases I	51–78 CE

Appendix B

ROMAN EMPIRE 49 BCE—476 CE
    Julius Caesar 49–44 BCE

Julio-Claudian Dynasty
    Augustus 31 BCE—14 CE
    Tiberius 14–37 CE
    Caligula 37–41
    Claudius 41–54
    Nero 54–68

Year of Tumultuous Interlude
    Galba June 68—January 69
    Otho January—April 69
    Vitellius April—December 69

Flavian Dynasty
    Vespasian 69–79
    Titus 79–81
    Domitian 81–96

Appendix C

The Hasmonean and Herodian Dynasties in Israel

HASMONEAN DYNASTY	166–37 BCE	
Mattathias ben Johanan	?–165	
Judah Maccabaeus	165–160	[son of Mattathias]
Jonathan Apphus	160–142	[son of Mattathias]
Simon Thassi	142–134	[son of Mattathias]
Johanan Hyrcanus	134–104	[son of Simon]
Aristobulus I	104–103	[son of Hyrcanus]
Alexander Jannai	103–76	[son of Hyrcanus]
Salome Alexandra	76–67	[wife of Alexander]
Aristobulus II	67–63	[son of Alexander]
Hyrcanus II	63–40	[son of Alexander]
Antigonus	40–37	[son of Aristobulus II]
HERODIAN DYNASTY	37 BCE—93 CE	
Herod the Great	37–4 BCE	[husband of Mariamne I]*
Herod Philip II (tetrarch of Syria)	4 BCE—34 CE	[son of Herod]
Archelaus (ethnarch of Judaea & Samaria)	4 BCE—6 CE	[son of Herod]
Herod Antipas (ethnarch of Galilee & Peraea)	4 BCE—39 CE	[son of Herod]

* Mariamne I was the maternal granddaughter of Hyrcanus II and the paternal granddaughter of Aristobulus II

Herod Agrippa I (tetrarch of Palestine & Syria)	37–44 CE	[grandson of Herod]
Herod of Chalcis	44–48	[grandson of Herod]
Herod Agrippa II	50–93	[son of Herod Agrippa I]

Appendix D

Chronology of the Jewish War (66–70)

Summer 66	Procurator Florus scourges rebels in Jerusalem and has several crucified. Approximate number of deaths, including infants: 3,600.
Aug 66	Eleazar, son of the high priest Hananiah, proposes that no gift from a foreigner be accepted in the Temple. The sacrifices and prayers for Emperor Nero are eliminated.
Aug 66	Jewish revolutionaries take the Roman garrison at Masada.
Aug–Sept 66	Various Jewish factions vie for control of Jerusalem: chaos and riots.
4 Sept 66	Antonia Fortress is seized and Roman soldiers slain; Herod's palace is likewise captured.
17 Oct 66	Cestius Gallus, Roman Governor of Syria, with his Twelfth Legion joins forces with Herod Agrippa's troops; combined they number between 35,000–40,000. They attack Chabulon in the Galilee.
Oct 66	These Roman forces purge the Galilee of resistance.
Nov 66	Cestius advances towards Jerusalem. There are attacks and counter attacks. He eventually gives up his siege of Jerusalem and his retreating armies suffer heavy losses. The rebels have won the day, on 26–27 November.
Dec 66—Mar 67	New revolutionary government is established in Judaea, but chaos reigns while powers vie for control.

Jan–Apr 67	Josephus made commander and fortifications are strengthened.
May 67	General Vespasian secures Galilee.
June 67—June 68	Vespasian's forces systematically move southward and gain control.
Fall 67—Winter 68	Vespasian purposely delays attacking Jerusalem, betting that internal factional fighting will weaken the resistance he will later face. His perception of the situation was accurate.
Spring 68	Vespasian conquers Judaea.
9 June 68	Emperor Nero commits suicide.
10 June 68	Galba becomes Emperor but is assassinated on 15 Jan 69.
20 June 68	Jericho is taken and Vespasian plans his siege of Jerusalem.
24 June 68	Pentecost; Vespasian plans his assault on Jerusalem and cuts the city off.
July 68	Vespasian returns to Caesarea to refresh and strategize, taking some troops with him. Here he learns of Nero's death and awaits further instructions. He breaks off his siege of Jerusalem.
15 Jan 69	Otho assumes the purple, but his rival Vitellius also wishes to claim the throne. After battling, Otho commits suicide on 16 April. Vespasian sits tight and watches the drama unfold, while he himself keeps an eye on the imperial title for himself.
19 Apr 69	Vitellius is proclaimed Emperor.
20 Dec 69	Vitellius is murdered. The same day Rome acclaims Vespasian as Emperor and his son Domitian rules in his absence until Vespasian arrives in Rome. Vespasian then commissions his son Titus to conquer Jerusalem.
Feb–Mar 70	Titus subdues northern Israel and advances on Judaea.

6 April 70	Titus lays siege to Jerusalem on Passover.
26 May 70	On the Feast of Pentecost the Divine Voice declares God's departure from the Temple.
29 Aug 70	The Temple is captured and burned.

Appendix E

Chiastic Structure of the Book of Revelation

REV 2–3

THE LETTERS TO THE seven churches as found in chapters 2–3 form a literary unit. They are organized according to a chiastic structure, in this particular case, punctiliar. The format is **A B C D C' B' A'** highlighting that the central focus of the seven letters is found in the middle, as was the custom of Hebrew and Greek writers.[1]

A Ephesus: Forsaken your first love; Nicolaitans
   B Smyrna: Synagogue of Satan; tribulation
      C Pergamum: Even to the point of death; Nicolaitans
         D Thyatira: Latter works and love exceed the first; all churches will know that I search mind and heart
      C' Sardis: At the point of death; white garments
   B' Philadelphia: Synagogue of Satan; trial
A' Laodicea: Love has grown lukewarm; white garments

The churches collectively are judged by their works, their faithfulness to Christ. At issue is remaining true to one's first love and not getting led astray in the midst of trials and facing accusations. The goal is that one's love and faith, put into action through works, increase and do not wane or grow lukewarm. Christ summons the believers to spiritual fervor and intimacy with him, rather than becoming beguiled by the illusions of Jezebel, or those like her who try to seduce the believers. In the end will be the true *apocalypsis*, the revelation of what is hidden in the mind and heart of each person.

---

1. For punctiliar chiasms in sets of seven in Johannine literature see Stramara, "Chiastic Key."

Along with the chiastic structure we have parallel couplets: **A** & **C** mention Nicolaitans and **A'** & **C'** mention white garments. In **C** the Nicolaitans are linked with idolatry and immorality. In **C'** the white garments are contrasted with not being soiled (Rev 3:4). The Greek verb *molunō* means to soil, stain, defile, contaminate morally, even defile sexually. Suetonius made this telling remark about Nero: "Whenever he rode in a litter with his mother [Agrippina], he had incestuous relations with her, which were betrayed by the stains on his clothing."[2] The writer of Rev 14:4 employs the verb with regard to defilement with women. Apostle Paul uses the verb in 1 Cor 8:7 in connection with defilement due to eating food sacrificed to idols.

The parallel construction of Nicolaitans and white garments evinces that the matter is one of purity and impurity, most probably on a physical level of sexuality that then belies a spiritual infidelity. "Do you not know that your bodies are members of Christ?" (1 Cor 6:15). Safeguarding against sexual immorality is a recurring theme throughout the Christian Scriptures and early church writings. "Yet you have a few persons in Sardis who have not soiled their clothes; they will walk with me dressed in white, for they are worthy. If you conquer, you will be clothed like them in white robes" (Rev 3:4–5). "If you conquer [*nikaō*]" could be a subtle play on words with Nicolaitans, due to the parallel construction. The second part of the couplet makes the sexual association more explicit: "Therefore I counsel you to buy from me . . . white robes to clothe you and to keep the shame of your nakedness from being seen" (Rev 3:18).

Perhaps there is a further play on words operating with the designation Nicolaitans. As mentioned before, *nikaō* means to conquer. If one cannot conquer the desires of the flesh and is in turn ruled by them, then one has become subjected to the "Conqueror of the People," sinful carnal desire that rules the *laos*, the body of people. Corporate identity is demarcated by corporal behavior.

REV 4–11

Chapters 4–11 likewise are a literary unit, as evinced by the following chiastic structure.

---

2. Suetonius, *Nero* 28.

A Heavenly Temple and Throne, 4 Living Creatures, 24 Elders (4:1–11)
  B Seer sees the Scroll and weeps bitterly—Appearance of the Lamb (5:1–14)
    C 1st Seal—Bow and Conquering (6:1–2)
      D 2nd Seal—Civil disturbance (6:3–4)
        E 3rd Seal—Rationing of food (6:5–6)
          F 4th Seal—Death by sword, famine, plague, and wild beasts (6:7–8)
        E' Measuring out the sentence; patient endurance (6:9–11)
      D' Cosmic disturbance (6:12–17)
    C' 144,000 Israel in battle formation (7:1–8)
  B' Appearance of the Lamb—Exchange with the Seer (7:9–14)
A' 24 Elders, 4 Living Creatures, Heavenly Temple and Throne (7:11–17)
    C 7th Seal—Silence, incense, prayers, peals of thunder (8:1–5)
      D 1st Trumpet—Hail and fire; 1/3 of earth burnt (8:6–7)
        E 2nd Trumpet—Blazing mountain; 1/3 seas destroyed (8:8–9)
          F 3rd Trumpet—Huge star fell; 1/3 water poisoned (8:10–11)
            G 4th Trumpet—Cosmic luminaries; 1/3 extinguished (8:12–13)
          F' 5th Trumpet—Star fallen to Abyss; locusts 5 months (9:1–12)
        E' 6th Trumpet—4 angels of Great River; 1/3 human race killed (9:13–16)
      D' 3 plagues of fire, smoke, and sulphur; 1/3 humankind killed (9:17–21)
    C' Theophanic angel with 7 thunderclaps, which are "silenced" (10:1–7)
  B Seer with a scroll that tastes bitter; his ministry and earthly Jerusalem and Temple (11:1–14)
A 7th Trumpet—Messiah reigns, 24 Elders, Heavenly Temple and Ark of the Covenant (11:15–19)

As can be seen from the above, chapters 4–11 form an intricate literary piece. The chiastic structure itself forms an inverted X. Rev 4:1–11 opens with the heavenly Temple and Throne, four living creatures, and twenty-four elders in that order, which appear in reverse order in the middle of the text, at 7:11–17, only to unfold again in a somewhat veiled form in 11:15–19. In 11:15–19 we have the twenty-four elders, the heavenly Temple and the Ark of the Covenant, which architecturally has the six-winged cherubim, recalling the six-winged living creatures. The Ark itself serves as God's Throne. This means that the main central focus of chapters 4–11 is found in 7:11–17—joined now with God and the celestial entourage are those who have washed their robes white in the blood of the Lamb. The heavenly court worships God unceasingly. Those clothed in white robes are protected from the scorching sun (7:16). This chiastic centerpoint in Rev 4–11 will become thunderously important as a counterpoint to the chiastic centerpoint in Rev 12:1—22:7 (see below).

In the first chiastic sequence, in section **B** we meet the seer and then the Lamb appears (5:1–14), and they reappear in reverse order in 7:9–14. The seer from the first sequence, who weeps bitterly that no one can open the Scroll (5:1–14), re-emerges at the end of the second chiastic sequence (11:1–14), this time to eat a scroll that tastes bitter and perform his ministry regarding the earthly Temple in Jerusalem. In both instances, he is the prelude to the denouement.

In the first chiastic sequence, in section **C** the first seal is broken unleashing war (6:1–2); this is paralleled by Israel in battle array, a military census being taken (7:1–8). But the first seal is also mirrored by the seventh seal (8:1–5), the first C in the second sequence. The rest of the parallels in the first chiastic sequence should be self explanatory. They all point to **F**, the fourth seal. Why is this significant? Because in this passage (6:7–8) Death and Hades (= the Grave) are given authority to kill by whatever means necessary. The list recounts the consequences of sin mentioned in Lev 26, the Pentecost lection. This chiastic centerpoint of the first sequence stands as a foil, a counterpoint, to the chiastic centerpoint of the whole literary piece of chapters 4–11—those robed in white who possess eternal life, in contrast to death. In fact, the chiastic centerpoint of the second sequence (8:12–13) likewise stands as a foil to 7:11–17. In 8:12–13 the cosmos is plunged into darkness, whereas the saints dwell in God's glorious presence. Death and Darkness are contrasts to Eternal Light and Life.

The second chiastic sequence (8:1—10:7) blares the seven trumpets emerging from the seventh seal. The sounding of the trumpets is preceded by silence. The seventh seal brings deafening silence followed by peals of thunder (8:1-5). This is coupled with the seven thunderclaps, whose message is kept silent (10:1-7). Note the reverse order. The parallels in the second chiasm are fairly clear. The blazing mountain is coupled with the great river Euphrates because mountains and rivers serve as geographic markers and boundaries. Creatively, the writer has the second sequence roll right into the third set of **B** and **A**, completing the whole chiastic structure. The helix form of the chiasm attests to the writer's creative genius and deeply embedded Hebraic thought patterns. Rev 4-11 is a complete literary unit. Other minor chiasms and overlapping chiasms can be discerned within the above overarching framework.

REV 12:1—22:7

Rev 12:1—22:7 is also a complete literary unit built upon a chiastic structure.

A Heavenly woman Mother Israel (12:1-2)
  B Dragon and War (12:3-17)
    C Beasts (12:18—13:18)
      D Lamb and 144,000 (14:1-5)
        E Angel: hour of judgment has come (14:6-7)
          F Fallen, fallen is Babylon the Great! (14:8-13)
          1a Son of Man on Cloud with sickle (14:14)
            1b Angel from Temple says: Use sickle, harvest is ripe (14:15)
          1a' Son of Man reaps the earth (14:16)
            2a Angel from Temple with sickle (14:17)
              2b Angel from altar says: Use sickle, grapes are ripe (14:18)
            2a Angel gathers grapes into the winepress of God's wrath (14:19-20)
          1c Seven angels with seven plagues (15:1)
            1d Song of the Lamb (15:2-4)
          1c' Seven angels with seven plagues (15:5-8)
            G 1st Bowl: painful sores on idolaters (16:1-2)
              H 2nd Bowl: creatures in the sea die (16:3)

        I 3rd Bowl: drinking water turns to blood (16:4–7)
         J 4th Bowl: sun; people curse the Name of God *and* do not repent (16:8–9)
        I' 5th Bowl: darkness, and people gnaw their tongues (16:10–11)
       H' 6th Bowl: Euphrates dried; up preparations for war (16:12–16)
      G' 7th Bowl: cataclysm and hailstones for those who curse God (16:17–21)
     1a The Great Whore upon the waters (17:1–2)
      1b Beast with blasphemous names (17:3a-c)
       1c Beast with ten horns (17:3d)
        1d Description of the Woman (17:4–6)
         1e Mystery explained (17:7–8)
          1f Mind for wisdom: 7 heads = 7 mountains = 7 emperors (17:9)
        1e' Mystery explained (17:10)
       1d' Description of the Beast (17:11)
      1c' Ten horns (17:12–13)
     1b' Lamb's Holy Name (17:14)
    1a' The Great Whore upon the waters (17:15–18)
    F' Fallen, fallen is Babylon the Great! (18:1–20)
   E' Angel: Babylon is judged (18:21–24)
  b Multitude of heavenly hosts (19:1–5)
   c Marriage Feast/Lamb (19:6–10)
  D' Messiah and White Horse (19:11–16)
 C' Great Supper of God/Beasts (19:17–21)
B' Dragon and War (20:1–15)
A' Heavenly Bride New Jerusalem (21:1—22:7)

This chiastic structure is equally rich and profound. Unlike Rev 4–11, the name Jesus does appear in this section. Unlike Rev 4–11, the term sign (*sēmeion*) is used here, and seven times at that. There are various reasons to argue that Rev 12:1—22:7 is a separate and distinct literary unit, but perhaps most telling is the different chiastic structure from Rev 4–11, which forms a helix, whereas this does not. This apocalyptic "Book of Signs" opens with a very "pregnant" portent. "A great portent appeared in heaven: a woman clothed with the sun, with the moon under her feet, and on her head a crown of twelve stars. She was pregnant and was crying out in birth pangs, in the agony of giving birth" (12:1–2). The next verse declares that "another portent appeared . . ." Much has been written about this woman. I will summarize my position: she is Daughter Zion, Mother Israel, who is ideal, and hence heavenly. The sun, moon, and stars are the means by which time is calculated. Everything has aligned; the time is ripe for the Messiah to appear. She is crowned with twelve stars (*astera*) representing the Twelve Tribes. These tribes were represented on the high priest's ephod as twelve stones and were then correlated with the twelve constellations (*astera*), signs of the Zodiac. Cryptically, as a sign, Mother Israel is a royal and priestly people. She is immediately chased by a Dragon who wages war on her and her child. This motif (ch. 12) is played out in reverse and to a fuller extent in 20:1—22:7. The New Jerusalem is a heavenly Bride to whom God is wed. Her walls are composed of the twelve stones of the high priest's ephod. Israel's chosen child, the Messiah, has now reached maturity, and the messianic age has dawned and will last for all eternity. The pregnant description of Zion found in **A** is unpacked at length in **A'**.

Parts **C-F** and **C'-F'** of the chiasm mirror one another. The Beasts emerge in 12:18—13:18 and appear for the last time in Rev 19:17–21. Next comes the Lamb, with his 144,000 warriors (14:1–5), who is portrayed again as victorious Messiah (19:11–16) charging the battle with his cohort. At this last scene, the writer creatively inserts an overlapping chiasm: **b** and **c**. **C'** the "great supper of God" (19:17–21) wherein the beasts and their minions are devoured by the birds, is in ironic contrast to **c**, the marriage feast of the Lamb (19:6–10). To draw attention to the centrality of the Messianic Figure on the white horse who embodies the Word of God, the Torah, the writer adds **b** (19:1–5), the multitude of heavenly hosts, who parallel **B'**, the Dragon and the final war. Thus **D'** (19:11–16) is given double emphasis by the corresponding **D** (14:1–5) and the mini-chiasm (19:1—20:15). Sections **E–F** and **E'–F'** parallel nicely and bring things to a crescendo: "Fallen, fallen is Babylon the Great" (14:8) echoed verbatim in (18:1). To employ a musical analogy, masterfully the writer creates a "development" to the first "exposition." Rev 12:1—14:13 is an exposition of the theme, using a few keys. Rev 14:14—15:8 is the development wherein the writer plays with the melodic ideas and changes keys. This then leads into what in classical music (which utilizes a chiastic structure) is called the "recapitulation" (16:1–21). The whole is appropriately interspersed with hymns which themselves contain mini-chiasms.

The climax of the entire chiasm (12:1—22:7) is found in 16:8–9: "The fourth angel poured his bowl on the sun, and it was allowed to scorch them with fire; they were scorched by the fierce heat, but they cursed the name of God, who had authority over these plagues, and they did not repent and give him glory" (NRSV). The counterpoint to this is found in 7:16, where the followers of the Lamb praise God and the sun does not scorch them. The writer of 12:1—22:7 has artistically set his "Book of Signs" as a foil to the theological points made in chapters 4–11. The purpose of the plagues and other "evils" is to chastise sinners so that they come into awareness of God and no longer curse him, but repent and praise him; those who will not, suffer the consequences of their allegiance to evil.

The middle chiasm (16:1–21) is devoted to the seven bowls. The first bowl produces painful sores which are paralleled by welts caused by hailstones, the seventh bowl (preceded by the percussion of resonating earthquakes). The second bowl causes creatures in the sea to die, and the sixth dries up another great source of water, the Euphrates, causing death via war from the invading Parthian armies, east of the Great River. The third bowl turns drinking water into blood, and the fifth causes people to gnaw their tongues, thus producing blood in the mouth as well. This leads up to the central focus, that people curse God with their tongues.

The development section of 14:14—15:8 is equally rich. The Son of Man on the cloud reaps the harvest with his sickle. This reaping is a positive harvest, most probably of wheat, the implied produce harvested with a sickle. These are the saints. In contrast, the angel from the altar uses his sickle to gather the grapes which are ripe that are subsequently thrown into the winepress of God's wrath: the sinners. Once again, the punishment of sinners is the focus. Rev 14:14–16 is paralleled by 15:1–8, wherein the seven angels with the seven plagues are introduced by the centerpiece, the Song of the Lamb (15:2–4). Thus **1a–1a'** and **1c–1c'** both portray the messianic Son of Man. The second development (17:1–18) deals with the Great Whore and the Beast she rides. The chiastic format clearly shows the parallel structure. Of note is that the blasphemous names of the Beast, presumably 666, are countered by the Holy Name of the Lamb: "King of kings and Lord of lords," which equals 777. The centerpoint of this mini-chiasm is 17:9, which reads, "This calls for a mind that has wisdom: the seven heads are seven mountains on which the woman is seated; also, they are seven kings," already foreshadowed by Rev 13:18—"This calls for wisdom: let anyone with understanding calculate the number of the beast, for it is the number of a person. Its number is six hundred sixty-six" (NRSV). The mini-chiasm's centerpoint of 7 heads, 7 mountains, and 7 emperors, thus 777, is in mockery of the true King of kings and Lord of lords, 777.

Like a musical composer, the writer of this literary unit has played with the melodic ideas and struck various chords, bringing the opus to several crescendos: Fallen, fallen is Babylon the Great; swing your sickle for the grapes of wrath are ripe, the shrewd mind can understand who is to be harvested (recall the Hebrew play on words between Caesar-*qsr* and harvest-*qtsr*). The unfortunate climax of the whole opus is that some people curse the Name of God and do not repent, failing to render God due praise.

PROLOGUE AND EPILOGUE

As mentioned earlier, Rev 1–3 is the prologue (itself containing the chiastic structure with chapters two through three). Rev 1:1–20, however, stands alone in one sense, and yet is paralleled with the epilogue in 22:8–21. It is only in these two sections that one encounters by name the writer, the final redactor, John. The whole of the Book of Revelation in its final form is a literary masterpiece, resonating with theological inspiration!

Bibliography

ANCIENT PRIMARY SOURCES

Apocalypsis Iohannem (Apocalypse of John). In *The Greek New Testament*, edited by Kurt Aland et al., 832–85. 4th rev. ed. New York: United Bible Societies, 2005.

Babylonian Talmud. Edited and translated by Michael L. Rodkinson. 20 vol. in 10. Boston: Talmud Society, 1918.

Book of Jubilees. Translated by O. S. Wintermute. In *OTP* 2:35–142.

1 Enoch. Translated by E. Isaac. In *OTP* 1:5–89.

2 Enoch. Translated by F. I. Andersen. In *OTP* 1:91–213.

Eusebius of Caesarea. *Historia Ecclesiastica*. Translated by Arthur McGiffert. In *NPNF2*, vol. 1.

4 Ezra. Translated by Bruce M. Metzger. In *OTP* 1:516–59.

Fourth Ezra. Translated by Michael Edward Stone. Hermeneia. Minneapolis: Fortress, 1990.

Irenaeus. *Adversus haereses*. Translated by A. Cleveland Coxe. In *ANF*, vol. 1.

Josephus. Translated by H. St. J. Thackeray et al. 10 vols. LCL. New York: Putnam, 1926–.

Josephus, Flavius. *Antiquitates Judaicae* (Jewish Antiquities). *Josephus*, vols. 4–9.

———. *Bellum Judaicum* (Jewish War). *Josephus*, vols. 2–3.

———. *Contra Apionem* (Against Apion). In *Josephus*, vol. 1.

Midrash Rabbah. Edited by H. Freedman and Maurice Simon. 10 vols. 3rd ed. London: Soncino, 1983.

The Mishnah. Translated by Herbert Danby. Oxford: Oxford University Press, 1987.

Philo Judaeus. *De decalogo*. Translated by F. H. Colson. *Philo*, vol. 10. LCL. Cambridge, MA: Harvard University Press, 1989.

———. *Quaestiones et solutiones in Exodum*. Translated by F. H. Colson. *Philo*, vol. 11. LCL. Cambridge, MA: Harvard University Press, 1989.

———. *De specialibus legibus*. Translated by F. H. Colson. *Philo*, vol. 10. LCL. Cambridge, MA: Harvard University Press, 1989.

Pirké de-Rabbi Eliezer (The Chapters of Rabbi Eliezer). Translated by Gerald Friedlander. London: Kegan Paul, 1916.

Pseudo-Philo (*Liber antiquitatum biblicarum*). Translated by D. J. Harrington. In *OTP* 2:297–377.

Sibylline Oracles. Translated by John J. Collins. In *OTP* 1:317–472.

Suetonius. Translated by John C. Rolfe. 2 vols. LCL. New York: Macmillan, 1924.

Suetonius, Gaius. *De vita Caesarum* (The Lives of the Caesars). *The Twelve Caesars*. Translated by Robert Graves. Baltimore: Penguin, 1957.

MODERN SOURCES

Afzal, Cameron. "Wheels of Time: *Merkavah* Exegesis in Revelation 4." *Society of Biblical Literature Seminar Papers* 37 (1998) 465–82.

Aune, David. *Revelation.* 3 vols. WBC 52A–C. Nashville: Nelson, 1997–98.

Barrett, Anthony. *Agrippina: Sex, Power, and Politics in the Early Empire.* New Haven, CT: Yale University Press, 1996.

Bauckham, Richard. *The Climax of Prophecy: Studies on the Book of Revelation.* Edinburgh: T. & T. Clark, 1993.

Baudot, Jules. *The Lectionary: Its Sources and History.* Translated by Ambrose Cator. St. Louis: Herder, 1910.

Beale, Gregory K. *The Book of Revelation: A Commentary on the Greek Text.* NIGTC. Grand Rapids: Eerdmans, 1999.

———. "The Influence of Daniel upon the Structure and Theology of John's Apocalypse." *Journal of the Evangelical Theological Society* 27 (1984) 413–23.

———. *The Use of Daniel in Jewish Apocalyptic Literature and in the Revelation of St. John.* Lanham, MD: University Press of America, 1984.

Bohak, Gideon. "Greek-Hebrew Gematrias in *3 Baruch* and in Revelation." *Journal for the Study of the Pseudepigrapha* 7 (1990) 119–21.

Boismard, M. E. *L'Apocalypse. La Sainte Bible.* Paris: Cerf, 1959.

———. "Notes sur l'Apocalypse." *Revue biblique* 59 (1952) 161–81.

Boring, M. Eugene. *Revelation.* Interpretation. Louisville: John Knox, 1989.

Brueggemann, Walter. *The Prophetic Imagination.* Rev. ed. Minneapolis: Fortress, 2001.

Bruston, C. "La tête égorgée et le chiffre 666." *Zietschrift für die neutestestamentliche Wissenschaft und die Kunde des Urchristentums* 5 (1904) 258–61.

Budge, E. A. Wallis. *The Contendings of the Apostles.* Oxford: Oxford University Press, 1935.

Caird, George Bradford. *A Commentary on the Revelation of St. John the Divine.* 2nd ed. London: A. & C. Black, 1984.

Charles, Robert H. *A Critical and Exegetical Commentary on the Revelation of St. John.* 2 vols. ICC. New York: Scribner, 1920.

Cohen, Naomi G. *Philo's Scriptures: Citations from the Prophets and Writings—Evidence for a Haphtarah Cycle in Second Temple Judaism.* Supplements to the Journal for the study of Judaism 123. Leiden: Brill, 2007.

Collins, Adela Yarbro. *Crisis and Catharsis: The Power of the Apocalypse.* Philadelphia: Westminster, 1984.

Collins, John J. *Apocalypticism in the Dead Sea Scrolls.* Literature of the Dead Sea Scrolls. New York: Routledge, 1997.

———. "Introduction: Towards the Morphology of a Genre." *Semeia* 14 (1979) 1–20.

———. *The Scepter and the Star: The Messiahs of the Dead Sea Scrolls and Other Ancient Literature.* Anchor Bible Reference Library. New York: Doubleday, 1995.

Culpepper, R. Alan. *John, the Son of Zebedee: The Life of a Legend.* Minneapolis: Fortress, 2000.

Davidson, Benjamin. *The Analytical Hebrew and Chaldee Lexicon.* Grand Rapids: Zondervan, 1979.

Davila, James R. "The Dead Sea Scrolls and Merkavah Mysticism." In *The Dead Sea Scrolls in Their Historical Context*, edited by Timothy Lim, 249–66. Edinburgh: T. & T. Clark, 2000.

Duff, Paul B. *Who Rides the Beast?: Prophetic Rivalry and the Rhetoric of Crisis in the Churches of the Apocalypse.* Oxford: Oxford University Press, 2001.

Edmundson, George. *The Church in Rome in the First Century: An Examination of Various Controverted Questions Relating to Its History, Chronology, Literature and Traditions.* Bampton Lectures, 1913. London: Longmans, Green, 1913.

Eisler, Robert. *The Enigma of the Fourth Gospel: Its Author and Its Writer.* London: Methuen, 1938.

Fekkes, Jan. *Isaiah and Prophetic Traditions in the Book of Revelation: Visionary Antecedents and Their Development.* Journal for the Study of the New Testament, Supplement Series 93. Sheffield: JSOT. 1994.

Feuillet, André. "Essai d'interprétation du chapître XI de l'Apocalypse." *New Testament Studies* 4 (1958) 183–200.

———. "La moisson et la vendage de l'Apocalypse (14, 14–20)." *Nouvelle Revue Théologique* 94 (1972) 113–32.

Finch, R. G. *The Synagogue Lectionary and the New Testament: A Study of the Three-Year Cycle of Readings from the Law and the Prophets as a Contribution to New Testament Chronology.* London: SPCK, 1939.

Fishbane, Michael. *Haftarot.* JPS Bible Commentary. Philadelphia: Jewish Publication Society, 2002.

Fitzmyer, Joseph A. "The Aramaic and Hebrew Fragments of Tobit from Qumran Cave 4." *Catholic Biblical Quarterly* 57.4 (1995) 655–75.

———. "The Significance of the Hebrew and Aramaic Texts of Tobit from Qumran for the Study of Tobit." In *The Dead Sea Scrolls Fifty Years after Their Discovery: Proceedings of the Jerusalem Congress, July 20–25, 1997*, edited by Lawrence H. Schiffman et al., 418–25. Jerusalem: Israel Exploration Society, 2000.

———. *Tobit.* Commentaries on Early Jewish Literature. New York: de Gruyter, 2003.

———. "Tobit, Book of." In *Encyclopedia of the Dead Sea Scrolls*, 2:948–50. New York: Oxford University Press, 2000.

Ford, Josephine Massyngberde. *Revelation.* AB 38. Garden City, NY: Doubleday, 1975.

Frankfurter, David. "Jews or Not? Reconstructing the 'Other' in Rev 2:9 and 3:9." *Harvard Theological Review* 94.4 (2001) 403–25.

Giet, Stanilas. *L'Apocalypse et l'histoire: étude historique sur l'Apocalypse johannique.* Paris: Presses Universitaires, 1957.

Ginzberg, Louis. *The Legends of the Jews.* Translated by Henrietta Szold. 7 vols. Philadelphia: Jewish Publication Society of America, 1967.

Goodman, Philip. *The Shavuot Anthology.* Philadelphia: Jewish Publication Society of America, 1974.

Goudoever, J. van. *Biblical Calendars.* Leiden: Brill, 1961.

Goulder, M. D. "The Apocalypse as an Annual Cycle of Prophecies." *New Testament Studies* 27.3 (1981) 342–67.

———. *The Evangelists' Calendar: A Lectionary Explanation of the Development of Scripture.* London: SPCK, 1978.

Guilding, Aileen. *The Fourth Gospel and Jewish Worship: A Study of the Relation of St. John's Gospel to the Ancient Jewish Lectionary System.* Oxford: Clarendon, 1960.

Greene, John T. "The Balaam Figure and Type before, during, and after the Period of the Pseudepigrapha: Hebrew Bible, Deir 'Alla, and Qumran." In *Probing the Frontiers of Biblical Studies*, edited by. J. Harold Ellens and John T. Greene, 193–222. Princeton Theological Monograph Series 111. Eugene, OR: Pickwick, 2009.

———. The Balaam Figure and Type before, during, and after the Period of the Pseudepigrapha: 1 Enoch, Philo, NT, Josephus, Rabbinics, Islamics, and Modern

Literature." In *Probing the Frontiers of Biblical Studies*, edited by. J. Harold Ellens and John T. Greene, 223–38. Princeton Theological Monograph Series 111. Eugene, OR: Pickwick, 2009.

Gwynn, John, editor. *The Apocalypse of St. John in a Syriac Version Hitherto Unknown*. Dublin, 1897.

Hayward, C. T. R. "Therapeutae." In *Encyclopedia of the Dead Sea Scrolls*, 2:943. New York: Oxford University Press, 2000.

Heinemann, Joseph. "The Triennial Lectionary Cycle." *Journal of Jewish Studies* 19 (1968) 41–48.

Hempel, Charlotte. "Qumran Community." In *Encyclopedia of the Dead Sea Scrolls*, 2:746–51. New York: Oxford University Press, 2000.

Hicks, L. "Nimrod." In *The Interpreter's Dictionary of the Bible*, edited by George Arthur Buttrick et al., 3:551. New York: Abingdon, 1962.

Hillers, D. R. "Rev 13:38 and a Scroll from Murabba'at." *Bulletin of the American Schools of Oriental Research* 170 (1963) 65.

Hirschberg, Haïm Z'ew. "Nimrod," In *Encyclopedia Judaica*, edited by Fred Skolink et al., 15:269–70. 2nd ed. New York: Thompson-Gale, 2007.

Holladay, William L. *A Concise Hebrew and Aramaic Lexicon of the Old Testament*. Grand Rapids: Eerdmans, 1971.

Hopkins, M. "The Historical Perspectives of Apoc 1–11." *Catholic Biblical Quarterly* 27 (1965) 42–47.

Jacobs, Louis. "Shavuot." In *Encyclopedia Judaica*, edited by Fred Skolink et al., 18:422–23. 2nd ed. New York: Thompson-Gale, 2007.

Jellinek, Adolph. *Bet ha-Midrash*. 6 vols. Jerusalem: Sifre Vahrmann, 1967.

Junod, Eric, and Jean-Daniel Kaestli. *Acta Iohannis*. 2 vols. Corpus Christianorum, Series Apocryphorum 1–2. Turnhout: Brepols, 1983.

Keener, Craig S. *The Gospel of John: A Commentary*. 2 vols. Peabody, MA: Hendrickson, 2003.

Kretschmar, Georg. "Himmelfahrt und Pfingsten." *Zeitschrift für Kirchengeschichte* 66 (1954–55) 209–53.

Laperrousaz, E-M. "Problèmes d'histoire et d'archéologie qoumrâniennes: à propos d'un souhait de précisions." *Revue de Qumrân* 10.2 (1980) 269–91.

Lupieri, Edmondo F. *A Commentary on the Apocalypse of John*. Translated by Maria Poggi Johnson and Adam Kamesar. Grand Rapids: Eerdmans, 1999.

Mann, Jacob. *The Bible as Read and Preached in the Old Synagogue: A Study in the Cycles of the Readings from Torah and Prophets*. Library of Biblical Studies. New York: KTAV, 1971.

Marshall, John W. *Parables of War: Reading John's Jewish Apocalypse*. Studies in Christianity and Judaism 10. Waterloo, ON: Wilfrid Laurier University Press, 2001.

Martínez, Florentino García, editor. *The Dead Sea Scrolls Translated: The Qumran Texts in English*. Translated by Wilfred G. E. Watson. 2nd ed. New York: Brill, 1996.

Momigliano, A. "Nero." In *The Cambridge Ancient History*, edited by. S. A. Cook et al., 10:702–42. Cambridge: Cambridge University Press, 1934.

Moore, Carey A., translator. *Daniel, Esther, and Jeremiah: The Additions*. AB 44. Garden City, NY: Doubleday, 1977.

Morris, Leon. *The New Testament and the Jewish Lectionaries*. London: Tyndale, 1964.

Mounce, Robert H. *The Book of Revelation*. Rev. ed. New International Commentary on the New Testament. Grand Rapids: Eerdmans, 1998.

Mulder, Martin Jan, editor. *Mikra: Text, Translation, Reading and Interpretation of the Hebrew Bible in Ancient Judaism and Early Christianity*. Compendia rerum Iudaicarum ad Novum Testamentum. Philadelphia: Fortress, 1988.

Murphy, Frederick J. *Fallen Is Babylon: The Revelation to John*. The New Testament in Context. Harrisburg, PA: Trinity, 1998.

Na'eh, Shelomoh. "Sidrei Keri'at ha-Torah be-'Eritez-Yisra'el: 'Iyyun Mehudash." *Tarbiz* 67 (1998) 167–87.

Nanos, Mark D. *The Irony of Galatians: Paul's Letter in First-Century Context*. Minneapolis: Fortress, 2002.

———. *The Mystery of Romans: The Jewish Context of Paul's Letters*. Minneapolis: Fortress, 1996.

———. "The Myth of the 'Law-Free' Paul Standing between Christians and Jews." *Studies in Christian-Jewish Relations* 4 (2009) 1–21.

———. "Paul and Judaism: Why Not Paul's Judaism?" In *Paul Unbound: Other Perspectives on the Apostle*, edited by Mark D. Given, 117–60. Peabody, MA: Hendrickson, 2009.

———. "What Was at Stake in Peter's 'Eating with Gentiles' at Antioch?" In *The Galatians Debate: Contemporary Issues in Rhetorical and Historical Interpretation*, edited by Mark D. Nanos, 282–318. Peabody, MA: Hendrickson, 2002.

Noack, Bent. "The Day of Pentecost in Jubilees, Qumran, and Acts." *Annual of the Swedish Theological Institute* 1 (1962) 73–95.

O'Rourke, John J. "The Hymns of the Apocalypse." *Catholic Biblical Quarterly* 30.3 (1968) 399–409.

Ozanne, C. G. "The Language of the Apocalypse." *Tyndale House Bulletin* 16 (1965) 3–9.

Perrot, Charles. "The Reading of the Bible in the Ancient Synagogue." In *Mikra: Text, Translation, Reading and Interpretation of the Hebrew Bible in Ancient Judaism and Early Christianity*, edited by Martin Jan Mulder, 137–59. Compendia rerum Iudaicarum ad Novum Testamentum. Philadelphia: Fortress, 1988.

Potin, Jean. *Le fête juive de la Pentecôte: études des textes liturgiques*. Vol. 1. Lectio divina 65. Paris: Cerf, 1971.

Prigent, P. *L'Apocalypse et liturgie*. Cahiers théologiques 52. Paris: Delachaux et Niestle, 1964.

Rengstorf, Karl. "ἀπόστολος." In *Theological Dictionary of the New Testament*, edited by Geoffrey W. Bromiley, 1:413–20. Grand Rapids: Eerdmans, 1976.

Robinson, John A. T. *Redating the New Testament*. Philadelphia: Westminster, 1976.

Ruiz, J.-P. *Ezekiel in the Apocalypse: The Transformation of Prophetic Language in Revelation 16,17—19,10*. European University Studies 23/376. Frankfurt: P. Lang, 1989.

Sandmel, Samuel. "Foreword for Jews." In *OTP* 1:xi–xiii.

Skehan, Patrick W. "King of Kings, Lord of Lords (Apoc 19:16)." *Catholic Biblical Quarterly* 10 (1948) 398.

Smith, Payne. *A Compendious Syriac Dictionary*. Oxford: Clarendon, 1976.

Snyder, Barbara W. "Combat Myth in the Apocalypse: The Liturgy of the Day of the Lord and the Dedication of the Heavenly Temple." PhD diss., Graduate Theological Union and University of California, Berkeley, 1991.

Solomon, David. "Pompey." In *Encyclopedia Judaica*, edited by Fred Skolink et al., 16:368. 2nd ed. New York: Thompson-Gale, 2007.

Stevenson, Gregory M. "Conceptual Background to Golden Crown Imagery in the Apocalypse of John." *Journal of Biblical Literature* 114.2 (1995) 257–72.

Stewart-Sykes, Alistair. *The Lamb's High Feast: Melito, Peri Pascha, and the Quartodeciman Paschal Liturgy at Sardis.* Supplements to Vigiliae Christianae 42. Leiden: Brill, 1998.

Stone, Michael Edward. *Fourth Ezra.* Hermeneia. Minneapolis: Fortress, 1990.

Stramara, Daniel F., Jr. "The Chiastic Key to the Identity of Beloved Disciple." *St. Vladimir's Theological Quarterly* 53.1 (2009) 5–27.

Strauss, Heinrich. "Menorah—Menorah on the Arch of Titus." In *Encyclopedia Judaica*, edited by Fred Skolink et al., 14:51–52. 2nd ed. New York: Thompson-Gale, 2007.

Thompson, Steven. *The Apocalypse and Semitic Syntax.* Society for the New Testament Studies Monograph Series 52. Cambridge, MA: Cambridge University Press, 1985.

Trudinger, L. P. "'O AMHN' (Rev. III:14) and the Case for a Semitic Original of the Apocalypse." *Novum Testamentum* 14 (1972) 277–79.

———. "Some Observations Concerning the Text of the Old Testament in the Book of Revelation." *Journal of Theological Studies* 17 (1966) 82–88.

Ulfgard, Håkan. "L'Apocalypse entre judaïsme et christianisme: précisions sur le monde spirituel et intellectuel de Jean de Patmos." *Revue d'histoire et de philosophie religieuses* 79 (1999) 31–50.

———. *Feast and Future: Revelation 7:9-17 and the Feast of Tabernacles.* Coniectanea biblica, New Testament Series 22. Stockholm: Almqvist & Wiksell, 1989.

VanderKam, James C. *Enoch: A Man for All Generations.* Studies on Personalities of the Old Testament. Columbia, SC: University of South Carolina Press, 1995.

———. "Shavu'ot." In *Encyclopedia of the Dead Sea Scrolls*, 2:871–72. New York: Oxford University Press, 2000.

———. *Textual and Historical Studies in the Book of Jubilees.* Harvard Semitic Monographs 14. Missoula, MT: Scholars, 1977.

Vanhoye, A. "L'utilisation du livre d'Ezéchiel dans l'Apocalypse." *Biblica* 43 (1962) 436–76.

Vogelgesang, J. M. "The Interpretation of Ezekiel in the Book of Revelation." PhD diss., Harvard University, 1985.

Wacholder, Ben Zion. "Prolegomenon." In *The Bible as Read and Preached in the Old Synagogue: A Study in the Cycles of the Readings from Torah and Prophets*, by Jacob Mann, xi–l. Library of Biblical Studies. New York: KTAV, 1971.

Webb, Robert L. "John the Baptist." In *Encyclopedia of the Dead Sea Scrolls*, 1:418–21. New York: Oxford University Press, 2000.

Weinfeld, Moshe. "Pentecost as Festival of the Giving of the Law." *Ecumenical Theological Research Fraternity in Israel* 8 (1978) 7–18.

Witherington, Ben. *Revelation.* New Cambridge Bible Commentary. Cambridge: Cambridge University Press, 2003.

Subject Index

2 Baruch, 20, 64
2 Esdras. See 4 Ezra.
4 Ezra, 3, 16–17, 20, 72, 139
144, 119
318, 108
666, 5, 106–15, 117, 121–25, 138–39, 161
777, 108–9, 111, 114–20, 128, 138–39, 162
888, 118
144,000, 47, 52, 54, 56, 58–59, 70–72, 122, 124–25, 156, 158, 160

Abraham, 11–12, 14, 19, 34, 50, 107–9, 143
Adam, 11–12, 122
Aezani, 94
affliction, 23–24, 85
Agrippa II, Herod, 95, 113, 150–51
Agrippina, Julia, 93–96, 111–15, 139, 155
Ahaz, 114
Akibah, R., 25, 67
Albinus, 97
Alexandria, 92, 141
altar, 2, 51, 53, 72, 126, 158, 161
Amraphel, 108
Andersen, F. I., 20, 163
angels, 2, 8, 13, 36, 48, 52–55, 59–63, 66–67, 72–74, 76–77, 80–81, 83–84, 98, 116, 120, 128–29, 156–59, 161
animals, 9, 13, 49–50, 68, 87, 126, 145, 156
Antichrist, 121–23
Antigonus, Mattathias, 82, 87, 91
Antiochus VII, 86– 87
Antiochus Epiphanes IV, 86–87, 142
apocalypses, Jewish, 1–4, 16, 20–21, 56, 72, 79, 84–85, 98, 104, 110, 138–39
apocalypticism, 1, 4, 7–10, 14–15, 24, 28, 33, 37, 42, 52, 54, 86, 126
apostles, 18, 46, 48, 77, 82, 85, 92, 104, 119, 132–34, 155
Ark of the Covenant, 2, 64–66, 119–20, 129, 139, 156–57
Armageddon, 74
Asa, king, 24–25, 56, 74
Ascension, Feast of, 140–41
Asia Minor, 94, 134, 140
Assyrian Empire, 114, 126, 147
atonement, 45, 80
Atonement, Day of, 43
Atzereth, 51, 57
Augusta, 93–94, 112, 114
Augustus, 91, 110, 112, 114, 148
Aune, David, 82–84, 115–16, 131
Azariah, 24

Baal, 130
Babel, 38, 89, 107, 123–24
Babylon, the Great, 66, 69, 73–75, 114, 158–60, 162
Babylonian Empire, 39–41, 69, 87, 91, 100, 102, 109–10, 114, 124, 142, 147
Balaam, 125–31, 165
Balak, 125–26, 130
Barrett, Anthony, 94, 112–13
Bat Qol. *See* voice, divine.
Beale, Gregory K., 30, 40, 53, 56, 63, 77, 84, 105, 121
Beast, 5, 9, 50, 66, 69, 76, 87, 91–92, 95–96, 99–100, 105–6, 109–12, 117, 122, 124, 146, 158–62
Bel and the Dragon, 39–40, 69, 146
Beliar, 11
Beloved Disciple, 104, 133
Beth-shemesh, 65
blood, 36, 42, 44, 51, 55, 57–59, 73, 80, 88, 91, 96, 99, 143, 157, 159, 161
bowls, 2, 36, 73, 77, 161
branch, 47, 55–56, 58, 119
breast plate, 77, 124, 133, 160
brick, 67–68
bride, 75–76, 97–98, 122, 159–60
Bruston, C., 108–9
burning, 17, 35, 58, 104, 112, 130, 153, 156
burnt offering, 45, 88, 112, 139

Caesar, emperor, 109–12, 139, 162
Caird, George, 121
calendar, 10, 16, 21, 38, 104, 135
Caligula, 93, 148
canon, 2, 20, 141
carpentum, 94
Chalaphta, R. ben, 25

Chanina, R., 75,
charagma, 112
chariot, 29, 37, 90, 142
Charles, R. H., 33, 127
chiasms, 6, 52, 59, 141, 154–62
Chosen People, 33–34, 58, 71, 102
Christian, definition, 3, 79, 85, 127
christology, 20, 79–82
churches, seven, 80–85, 130–31, 134–35, 137, 154
Claudius, 92–96, 104–5, 110, 112, 114, 148
Clement of Alexandria, 141
cloud, 58, 61–62, 64, 67, 72, 81, 90, 145, 158, 161
Cohen, Naomi, 27, 31, 130
coins, 82, 95, 112–13
cosmic battle, 9, 51, 74, 117, 156
Covenant, 3, 10–14, 19, 23–26, 31, 34, 41–43, 45, 50, 62, 67, 74–76, 90, 101, 118, 127, 138, 140, 142
creation, 11, 13–14, 19–20, 47, 123
crown, 35, 47, 49, 72, 94, 160
crucifixion, 100–101, 151
Culpepper, R. Alan, 133
cultic ceremony, 28, 55, 70–71, 89, 94, 111

Dagon, 65
Damascus Document, 15
Dan, tribe of, 121–23
Daniel, Book of, 15, 30, 37–40, 61, 63, 69, 72–73, 81, 87, 101, 143
Daniel, the prophet, 39–40, 42, 62, 142
David, king, 11, 42–44, 64–66, 68, 81, 84, 123, 140, 146
Dead Sea Community. *See* Qumran.

Dead Sea Scrolls, 103
defilement, 12, 70–71, 155
Divi Filius, 95
Domitian, 91–92, 105, 140, 148, 152
dragon, 39–40, 68–69, 99, 117, 122, 143, 146, 158–60
Drusus, Nero, 93
Duff, Paul, 92

eagles, 35, 68, 145
earthquake, 51, 53, 64, 120, 177
Easter. *See* Pascha.
Edmundson, George, 91–92
Egypt, 12, 19, 22–24, 50, 60, 63, 67–69, 73, 87, 100, 142–43
el-gibor, 123
El'azar, R., 25
elders, 35–37, 42, 46–48, 55, 99, 115–16, 138, 156–57
Eleazar, R. Simeon ben, 28–29, 49
Eliezer, 107–9
Elijah, 130
End of Time, 4, 7, 9, 13–14, 16–19, 31, 38, 40, 48–52, 64, 72, 76, 99, 102, 117, 126, 137
Enoch, Book(s) of, 15–16, 20–21, 72
Enoch, the figure, 20–21
Ephesus, 82, 103, 132–34, 140, 154
ephod. *See* breast plate.
eschatology. *See* End of Time.
Eumenia, 134
Exile, 23, 41, 50, 52, 142
Exodus event, 15–16, 22–23, 33–34, 38, 41, 46, 52, 57–58, 60, 63, 68–69, 73, 146
eyes, 35–36, 43–44, 55

Ezekiel, the prophet, 37, 41, 52, 63, 118, 142
Ezra, the prophet, 28–29, 49

Felix, 113
figs, 47, 51–52, 54, 60, 145
first-fruits, 3–4, 11, 13–14, 17–19, 22–23, 26, 34, 42, 45–51, 53–54, 57–60, 63–64, 67–70, 72, 74–75, 81, 91, 125, 138, 140–41, 143, 145
Fishbane, Michael, 27
footstool, 67–68, 116
Ford, Josephine, 102–3, 116
forehead, 54, 56, 70, 100, 111, 113–14, 122, 124
forty-nine, 12, 43, 81, 125–26
four living creatures, 35–37, 43, 48–49, 55, 63, 115, 145, 157
Fritsche, O. F., 109

Gabriel, 67
Galba, 95, 104–5, 148, 152
Galilee, 88, 149, 151–52
gematria, 2, 5, 9, 13, 106–25, 128
gibor, 123, 125
Giet, Stanilas, 121
Glory, divine, 9, 34, 41, 53–54, 58, 64, 67, 77, 80
gods, 69, 75, 94, 111
goel, 122–23
gold, 35, 36, 47, 53, 60, 69, 72–73, 77–78, 82, 94, 146
goren, 125
Goudoever, J. van, 16, 20–21, 30
Goulder, Michael, 25, 29–30, 38, 40, 53, 65, 129–30
grapes, 47, 60, 72, 119, 158, 161–62
Greece, 38, 89

Greene, John T., 129
grinding stone, 18–19, 74
Habakkuk, Book of, 29–30, 38–40, 52–53, 81
Habakkuk, the prophet, 39–40, 89, 149
harvest, 1–4, 11–19, 22–23, 26, 28–31, 34, 37, 39–40, 42, 45, 48, 50, 52, 58–60, 64–76, 89, 91, 102–3, 107, 109–11, 115, 117–19, 125, 137–41, 143, 145–46, 158, 161–62
Hasmonean Dynasty, 5, 87, 149
Heinemann, Joseph, 27
Henderson, Bernard, 91
Herodian Dynasty, 6, 87–88, 95–96, 149
Hezekiah, 114
Hierapolis, 134
high priest, 14, 77, 82, 86, 133, 151, 160
Hillers, D. R., 109, 133
Hippolytus, 133
history, Jewish, 4–5, 7, 10–15, 18, 21, 23–24, 30, 41, 51, 65, 69, 79, 85–105, 114, 116–17, 129, 134, 137–38, 142
Holy Spirit. *See* Spirit(s) of God.
horns, 36, 43–44, 47, 100, 115, 159
horsemen, 48–50
hymns, 2, 15, 36, 44, 46–47, 52, 63, 69, 73, 75, 77, 158, 161
Hyrcanus, John. *See* John Hyrcanus.

idolatry, 24, 39–41, 56, 60–61, 65, 69, 74, 75, 82, 86, 107, 109–10, 118, 121–29, 138, 142–46, 155, 158
Immanuel, 114
incense, 2, 36, 53, 97, 156

inscribed, 77, 94, 111–12, 131
Irenaeus, 104, 106, 110, 119, 121, 140
Isaac, 11–12, 14, 19, 34, 50, 143
Isaiah, Book of, 26, 44, 58, 78, 123, 130
ishshah, 111–12

Jacob, 11–12, 14, 19, 41, 50, 123, 126, 128, 143
Jeremiah, Book of, 59, 87, 142
Jeremiah, the prophet, 64, 118, 142
Jericho, 87–88, 90, 152
Jerusalem, fall of, 2, 5, 38, 63, 86–88, 90–91, 97, 103–5, 138, 151–53
Jeshua, 101, 118, 138
Jesse, 42–45, 146
Jesus, the name, 66, 78–79, 84, 96, 98–102, 118, 159
Jesus, son of Ananias, 79, 96–100, 118, 138
Jesus of Nazareth, 3, 17–19, 26, 55, 79–85, 96, 98–100, 102–4, 118, 126–29, 132–33, 136, 143–44
Jew, definition, 3, 127
jewels, 30, 35, 53, 77, 94, 146
Jewish War, 2, 5–6, 79, 86–90, 93, 95–105, 110–11, 138, 143, 151–53
Jezebel, 125, 129–31, 154
Joel, Book of, 19–20, 60, 72
Johanan b. Suri, 19
Johannine School, 104, 154
John, apocalyptic seer, 79–85, 92, 98, 100, 102–4, 115, 118, 125–26, 128–29, 131–32, 137, 139, 143–44, 162
John, the apostle, 92, 104, 132–34
John the Baptist, 17, 103–4
John Hyrcanus, 14, 86–87, 149

Subject Index

Jose, R., 25
Joseph, 12, 54, 122
Josephus, 3, 27, 70, 87–88, 90, 97–98, 139, 152
Joshua, figure, 21, 25, 101–2
Jubilee, Year of, 10–13, 50
Jubilees, Book of, 1, 4, 10–15, 18–21, 23, 25, 34, 43, 50, 62, 117, 137
Juda ha-Nasi, R., 29
Judaea, 39, 88, 90, 95, 113, 149, 151–52
Judah, 11, 24, 36, 42–43, 64, 102, 114, 121–22
Judah, R., 29
Judas Maccabeus, 14
judgment, 9, 16–19, 49, 51–52, 56, 58, 60, 71, 73–76, 89, 99, 120, 126, 158
Julius Caesar, 121, 148

Kappara, Eleazar bar, 107–8
kebes, 115–16
kebesh, 116
kingdom of priests, 11, 34, 36–37, 44–46, 48, 57, 70, 77, 80–81, 120, 132, 143, 145, 160
Kiriath-jearim, 65
Kittim, 126

Lamb, 36–37, 42–49, 52, 55–56, 70, 72, 75–78, 80, 100, 103–4, 111, 115–16, 119–124, 138, 141, 143, 156–62
lampstand, 35, 81–82, 130
Laodicea, 134, 154
Law. *See* Torah.
Leah, 11
lectionary, 4–5, 22–31, 37–38, 46, 48, 50, 52, 61, 63, 66, 68–69, 85, 130–36, 138, 141–42, 144

Lepidus, 93
Levi, 34, 54, 122, 134
Liber Comicus, 141
lightning and thunder, 35, 46, 48, 53–54, 62, 64, 98, 120, 145, 156, 158
Lion of Judah, 36, 42, 64, 102
locusts, 60, 116, 156

ma'amad, 46–48
Maccabean Period, 14, 55, 86, 101, 143
Maccabeus, Judas. *See* Judas Maccabeus.
magal, 115, 139
magla, 115, 139
magle, 115, 139
Mann, Jacob, 26
manna, 120, 129, 131
martyrdom, 51, 99–100, 134, 143
mater civitas, 96
Medes, 38, 89
megala, 115, 139
Megiddo, 74
megilah, 115, 139
Melito, 134
menorah. *See* lampstand.
merkabah. *See* chariot.
Messiah, 3, 20, 42–45, 49, 55, 58, 64, 67–68, 76, 79–81, 99–103, 114–17, 121–29, 132, 137, 143, 146, 156, 159–61
mgala, 115
Michael, archangel, 62, 67–68
Miriam, 15
Mishnah, 19, 25–26, 28
Momigliano, Arnaldo, 91
Moses, 4, 10, 12–14, 19, 21, 23, 25–26, 37, 42, 48, 57, 62–64, 67, 70–71, 73, 75, 101–2, 143–44

Mother Israel, 67–68, 114, 158, 160
Mount Sinai, 10, 19–20, 23, 26, 34, 41, 46, 48, 52, 61–62, 68, 142–43, 145
Mount Zion, 13, 47, 58, 124, 160
Muratorian Canon, 141

Nebuchadnezzar, 40–41, 69
Nero, Caesar, 90–96, 104–5, 109–13, 148, 151–52, 155
New Jerusalem, 30, 53, 76–78, 103, 119, 124, 132, 143, 159–60
New Year, 43, 49, 60
Nicolaitans, 127, 154–55
Nimrod, 102, 107–10, 123–25
Noah, 11, 14, 17–19, 34, 62, 143
numerology. *See* gematria.

oaths, 2, 11, 14, 22–24, 62–63
Octavia, 95–96
olive oil, 47, 49, 74
Ordo Lectionum Missae, 141
Origen, 140–41
Otho, 92, 95, 104–5, 121, 148, 152

palms, 55–56
Papirius, 134
Parthian Empire, 16, 116, 147, 161
Pascha, 82, 134–35, 141
Passover, 12, 14, 19, 22–24, 30, 40, 43, 51, 59, 88, 90, 135, 153
Patriarchs, 11, 46
Paul, apostle, 3, 26, 61, 82, 155
Pergamum, 126, 129, 154
Perrot, Charles, 27–28, 46
persecution, 8, 91, 99
Pesikta de Rav Kahana, 27
Peter, the Apostle, 20, 60, 133
Pharisees, 21, 25, 101

Phasael, 88
Philadelphia, 132, 154
Philip, 133–34
Philistines, 65
Philo, 3, 14–15, 21, 25, 27, 55, 57, 59, 70, 82, 89, 101, 116, 130, 139
plagues, 2, 59, 63, 73, 84, 145, 156, 158, 161
play on words, 2, 5, 18, 115–16, 127, 135, 139, 155, 162
poison, 93, 105, 116, 156
political context, 5, 8–9, 14, 24, 38, 55, 86–105, 109, 111, 138
Polycarp, 134
Polycrates, 132–35
Pompey, 87, 91
Potin, Jean, 25–26, 38, 44, 67–68, 89
prediction, 7–8, 13, 18, 97–98, 105, 126, 128
priestess, 94
priests, 2, 14, 24, 45–46, 48, 52–53, 64, 77, 82, 86, 90–91, 94, 101–3, 118, 120, 129, 132–34, 138, 143, 151, 160
prophecy, 7–8, 13, 15
punishments, 9, 49–50, 73, 118, 143, 145–46, 161

qsr, 109–11, 139, 162
qtsr, 110–11, 139, 162
Quartodeciman, 134–35
Qumran, 1, 4, 10, 14–15, 17, 20–21, 23, 25–26, 30, 51, 57, 78, 90, 102–4, 129, 140

rainbow, 19, 35, 61–62, 145
ram, 115–16
Raphael, 53
reaping, 13, 17, 39, 45, 65, 72–73, 102, 158, 161

Subject Index

redemption, 13, 37, 44–45, 47, 56, 70, 73, 80, 122–25, 143
redivivus, 87
remnant, 9, 57–58, 77, 123
Resh Lakish, 49, 60, 107
restoration, 9, 12–14, 53, 130, 132, 143, 146
resurrection, 3, 9, 80–81, 134
Revelation, Book of
    authorship, 3–4, 32, 35, 41, 78–79, 85–86, 100, 102–4, 118, 135–36
    composition, 32–35, 37, 42, 44, 46, 63, 66, 68, 73, 103
    context, 86–102
    date, 15, 104–5
    epilogue, 3, 78–79, 82–85, 96, 105, 129, 131–32, 139–40, 162
    Jewish apocalypse, 3, 106–25, 139–40
    prologue, 34, 78–82, 96, 105, 125–33, 139–40, 162
    redactor, 32, 78, 82–83, 85, 98, 100–104, 118, 125–26, 136, 139, 143, 162
revelation, divine, 1, 3–4, 7–8, 10–12, 19–21, 61–62, 66, 79–81, 83–84, 103–4, 115, 138
rhomphaia, 127, 129
Robinson, John A. T., 91–92
Roman Empire, 38, 41, 87–91, 96, 99, 109, 114, 126, 145, 148
Rome, city of, 91–93, 95–96, 104, 112, 114, 133, 141, 152
Root of David, 36, 42–44, 49, 64–66, 84, 102
Rosh Hashanah. *See* New Year.
Ruth, Book of, 29, 42, 146

Sabina, Poppaea, 95
Sabinus, 88, 91
Sadducees, 21
Sagaris, 134
saints, 8–9, 36, 53, 72, 75–76, 99, 144, 157, 161
sanctuary. *See* temple.
sapphire, 61, 67–68, 77
Sarah, 19
Sardis, 134, 154–55
Satan, 11–12, 69, 85, 99, 128–30, 154
scroll, 36, 42–45, 48, 52, 61–63, 115, 120, 139, 156–57
Sea Monster, 68, 105, 122
Seleucid Empire, 14, 87, 147
serpent, 68, 143
sets of seven, 2, 4, 10, 12–13, 15–16, 24, 35–36, 39–40, 42–48, 50, 52–54, 59–60, 62–66, 71, 73, 77, 80–82, 87, 91–92, 95–96, 99, 105, 117, 119–20, 125–26, 130–31, 137–38, 142–43, 145–46, 154, 158–62
sex, 12, 70, 93, 95–96, 111, 125–26, 138, 155
Shekinah. *See* Glory, divine.
shevu'ot. *See* oaths.
sickle, 72, 115, 139, 145, 158, 161–62
signs, 19, 23, 66, 81, 114–15, 124, 159–61
silence, 52, 156, 158
Simeon ben Eleazar, 28, 49
Sinai, Mount. *See* Mount Sinai.
Skehan, Patrick, 111
Smyrna, 134, 154
Snyder, Barbara, 2, 55
Sodom, 100
Solomon, 68
Son of Man, 17–18, 72, 81, 115, 129, 131–32, 141, 158, 161

song. *See* hymns.
Spirit(s) of God, 35–36, 39, 41, 43–45, 71, 80–81, 83–84, 86, 99, 134, 140, 146
stars, 2, 51–52, 81, 84, 126, 129, 131, 156, 160
Suetonius, 93–94, 155
suicide, 90, 92, 105, 152
Sunday, 55, 82, 132, 141
sword, 49–50, 127, 129, 131, 145, 156
synagogue, 4, 26–27, 29, 31, 82, 85, 128, 154

Tabernacles, Feast of, 2, 14, 55–59, 97–98
Tacitus, 91, 112
temple, 2, 13, 26, 28, 41, 45, 47, 52, 55–56, 63–64, 72, 74, 86, 88, 97–98, 101, 103, 119–20, 132, 139, 142–43, 151, 156–58
temple, destruction of, 26, 28, 41, 46, 90–91, 97, 101, 104, 132, 138, 153
terebinths, 25, 56, 74
theophany, 19, 38, 41, 48, 52, 54, 61, 62, 66, 120, 142, 145–46, 156
Therapeutae, 15–16, 51
thousand years, 100, 126
Thraseas, 134
three and a half years, 5, 27, 63, 68, 86, 98–99, 138
threshing floor, 16–17, 48
throne, God's, 35–37, 40–43, 46, 53–56, 58, 61–63, 67–68, 76, 80, 115–16, 120, 141–42, 145, 156–57
Tiberius, 91, 93, 148
timetable, 4, 9–10, 13–14, 16, 135
Titus, Emperor, 82, 90–92, 104–5, 148, 152–53
Tobit, Book of, 29–30, 53–54, 77

Torah, 2–4, 10, 12–13, 15–16, 23–27, 42, 48, 57, 61–62, 67, 70–71, 73, 75, 101, 126–28, 132, 136, 138, 143, 160
Tree of Life, 76, 84, 118, 131, 143
trees, 25, 51, 54, 56, 118–19, 138
trumpets, 2, 24, 35, 52, 53, 59–66, 138, 145, 156, 158
twelve, 16, 46, 54, 76–77, 118–19, 160
Twelve Tribes, 16, 54, 58, 70, 77, 119, 121–24, 143, 160

Ulfgard, Håkan, 2, 55, 58
uncleanness, 12, 76, 128, 134, 155
Uzziah, 64

Vayikra, 68
Vespasian, 90–92, 95, 104–5, 112, 121, 148, 152
Victor, 133–34
virginity, 70, 122, 134
Vitellius, Emperor, 92, 95, 104–5, 112, 121, 148, 152
voice, divine, 35–36, 48–49, 54, 62, 72, 76, 81, 91, 97–98, 138, 146, 153

Wacholder, Ben, 27–28
Weinfeld, Moshe, 26
wheat, 17, 47, 49, 60, 64–65, 72–74, 119, 125, 161
white horse, 49, 111, 159–60
white robes, 15, 35, 47, 51, 55, 57, 70, 138, 145, 154–55, 157
Whore of Babylon, 75, 93–95, 99, 111–15, 122, 159, 161
winds, 52, 54, 97–98
wrath, 44, 72–74, 158, 161–62

Zeus, 86
Zion, Mount. *See* Mount Zion.

Ancient Document Index

JEWISH SCRIPTURES/ OLD TESTAMENT

Genesis
10:8	108, 123
10:10	123
14:9	108
14:14	108
15:6	108
17:1–16	11
41	30

Exodus
15:13–18	63
19	29, 37, 57, 68, 71
19–20	28, 34, 63
19:1—20:23	28
19:1	23, 34
19:4	68
19:6	34–35, 37, 44, 46, 48, 57, 80, 87
19:7	81
19:14–15	70
19:14	57
19:16–19	62
19:16–18	53
19:16	46, 120
19:17	75
19:18	60
20:11	63, 71
23:16	22
24	67, 116
24:1–8	42
24:5	67
24:10	67–68
29	48
34:22	22
39:10–12	77
39:14	77

Leviticus
11:22	116
23:9–22	22
23:9–16	21
23:10–12, 14c–15	45
23:18	43
25:8–46	12
26	29, 43, 48–50, 54, 59
26:9	76
26:10–12	76
26:14–46	49
26:18–20	50
26:21–22	50
26:23–26	50
26:27–33	50
26:42–43, 45	50

Numbers
22–25	130
22:2—25:9	130
22:22	128, 130
24:5	128
24:17	126, 129, 131
28:11	43
28:19	43
28:26–31	22
28:26	22
29:2	43

Numbers (cont.)	
29:8	43
31:8	127, 129

Deuteronomy	
16:9–12	28, 34
16:12	22
26:1–11	22
26:5–10	23
26:3	22, 25
26:6	26

Joshua	
3:3, 11	120

Ruth	
4:17–22	37, 42

1 Samuel	
4–6	65
6:13	65
6:20—7:1	65

2 Samuel	
6	65
6:6	64
6:11	64

1 Kings	
18	130
19	130–31

1 Chronicles	
13:9	64
13:14	64
15:12–14	12
15:24	64
24:1–9	46

2 Chronicles	
15:1–15	24

Nehemiah	
12:41	53
12:44	53

Psalms	
1	29
2:8–9	129
29	29, 62–63
68	29, 69
68:7	75
68:30	69
89:27	81
89:37	81
119	29
150:6	37, 46

Proverbs	
19:17	100

Isaiah	
1:9–15	100
3:9	100
4:2	58
4:3–6	58
4:5–6	57
7:11	114
7:14	114
9:5–6	123
10	123
10:20–21	123
11:1–2ff.	45
11:1	42, 44
11:2	44
11:10	42, 44
34:4	52
40:28	142
46:4	142
49	130–31
49:2	131
49:16	131
50–51	130–31
50:4	130
50:11	130
51:1	130
51:3	130–31
51:4	130
51:6	130
51:7	130
51:8	130

Isaiah (cont.)

51:9	131
51:13	131
51:14	131
51:15	131
51:16	131
51:17	131
54:11–12	77
63:1–6	73

Jeremiah

2:3	58
5:21	118
5:23–25	118
5:24	117–18
5:31	118
7:34	98
8:16	121
22:8	100
23:14	100
50:29–34	100

Ezekiel

1–2	29, 41
1	29, 37
1:3	41
1:4	52
1:26–28	61
1:26	68
2	63
2:2	41
2:9—3:3	63
7:2	56
7:5–9	63
7:5–6	60
9:4	56–57, 70
16:23–57	100
29:2–5	69
36:24–30	41
37:27	76
39:7	100
39:17	76
43:2	81
47:12	119

Daniel

2:28	37, 40, 80
3:4	56, 71
3:5–7	69
3:7	71
4:27	114
4:30	114
4:31	142
4:34	41
5:4	61
7	57
7:7	69
7:10	46
7:13	81, 129
7:14	63
7:25	69, 86, 100
8:10	69
10:13ff.	69
12:4	42, 62–63
12:9	42, 62

Joel

1:11–12	60
3:13	72
4:9–17	17
4:13	73

Amos

4:10–11	100

Habakkuk

2:2–3	81
2:20	52, 54
3	29–30, 38–40, 52–53, 87, 89, 109, 114
3:2	89
3:17	38

Zephaniah

3	29
3:13	71

Zechariah

4:2	82
4:10	43, 82

Zechariah (cont.)
12:10	129
12:14	129

APOCRYPHA

Tobit
2:1	22, 30, 53
12	53–54
12:12	53
12:15	53
13–14	53
13	77
13:9	78
13:17	78
13:16–18	77

Wisdom
19:14–17	100

Sirach
45:25	43

Baruch
4	142

Bel and the Dragon/Daniel
14	39–40, 69
14:23–42	69
14:33–39	39
14:37–38	39–40

1 Maccabees
13:51	55

2 Maccabees
2:4–8	64
10:7	55
12:32	22
14:4	55

PSEUDEPIGRAPHA

1 Enoch
31–71	16
56:6	16
91:11–17	16
93:1–10	16

2 Baruch
6	64

2 Enoch
68:1–3	20

3 Baruch
3:5	68

4 Ezra
4:26–39	17
14	17
14:48	20

Jubilees
1:1	10–11, 20
1:26	12
1:29	11–12, 14
6:1–18	18
6:11–14	11, 20
6:15–17	19
6:17–22	11
6:18	11, 14
6:20–22	11
14:20	11
15:1–16	34
15:1–10	19
15:1	11
15:11	11
15:33	11
16:12–13	19
16:13–14	34
16:13	11
16:18	11, 34
22:1—23:10	11
22:1–24	19

Jubilees (cont.)

28:15	11
44:1–6	12
44:4–6	19
49:1–23	12
50:4–5	12

Sybilline Oracles

5:12–42	121

CHRISTIAN SCRIPTURES/ NEW TESTAMENT

Matthew

3:12	17
9:37—10:36	18
11:2–19	103
13:24–30	17
13:36–43	17
21:1–11	56
24:37–41	18

Luke

3:17	17
4:16–28	26
7:18–35	103
10:1–16	18
24:25–27	83
24:44–45	83, 144

John

4:34–38	18
4:34–35	18–19
12:12–16	56
18:15–16	133

Acts

2:1–41	20, 82, 140
2:17–21	60
2:2	52
7:38	61
13:15	27
13:27	27
15:21	26
18:2	93
19:1–7	103
20:16	82

1 Corinthians

16:8	82

Galatians

3:19	61

Hebrews

12:18	52

1 Peter

1:10–11	83

2 Peter

2:15	126
3	126

Jude

11	126

Revelation

1–3	34, 78–83, 96, 103–4, 125, 128, 130–33, 141
1:1–9	78
1:1–2	79
1:1	80, 84, 103
1:3	144
1:4	80–81
1:5–6	80
1:6	34, 80
1:7	81, 129, 131
1:9—3:22	131
1:9	79
1:10	82
1:12–15	129
1:12–13	82, 130
1:12	81
1:13	81–82
1:15–16	81, 131

Revelation (cont.)

1:19	81
1:20	81, 131
2–3	81, 127, 129–31, 135
2:1	130–31
2:2	85
2:4	131
2:6	127
2:9	85, 128, 131
2:12	131
2:14–15	85
2:14	125–26
2:15–16	127
2:16	131
2:17	131
2:20–24	85
2:20	125
2:26–28	129
3:2–3	131
3:2	80
3:4–5	130
3:9	85, 128
3:12	80, 131–32
3:14	131
4–22	79, 84, 125
4:1—22:7	132
4–11	66, 84, 100–101, 103–4, 119, 132, 138–39
4–5	29, 35–48, 80
4:1—5:14	35–37
4	34, 142
4:1	37, 40
4:2–4	10–11, 141
4:2	40
4:4	46
4:5	46, 120
4:8	142
4:9	41
4:10	41, 46, 141
4:11	47, 141
5:1	120
5:5	37, 42, 44
5:6–7	115–16
5:6	42–43, 115
5:7	44
5:8	46
5:9–10	45, 80, 140
5:9	47
5:10	44, 70
5:13	37, 46
5:14	46, 52
6	48–52
6:1–8	50
6:11	50
6:13	51
6:14	52
7	47, 54–59
7:1–3	56
7:5–8	121–22
7:9	56–57
7:13	57
7:15–16	58
7:15	56, 58
8	52–54, 59–60
8:2–4	53
8:2	52–53
8:13	60
9	60–61
9:1–12	116
9:2	60
9:20	61
10	61–63
10:2	62
10:3–4	62
10:6–7	66
10:6	62
10:7	84
11	63–66, 120
11:2–3	86
11:8	100
11:15–18	63
11:16–18	48
11:17	142
11:18	84
11:19	64, 120
12:1—22:7	66, 78–79, 84, 96, 98, 103–5, 139
12–19	102

Revelation (cont.)

12–13	66–69
12	66–69, 125
12:1	114
12:2	67
12:5	67, 116
12:6	86
12:14	68, 86
12:17	99
13:5	86
13:15	69
13:16	111
13:17	112
13:18	106, 109
13:18—14:1	124
14	70–73, 137
14:1–5	58, 71
14:3	122
14:4	47, 58, 70
14:5	71
14:5–16	141
14:6	71
14:12	72, 99
14:13	71
14:14–19	72
15–22	73–78
15:2–3	73
17	114
17:4	94
17:5	111, 114
17:6	99
17:8	122
17:9–10	91
17:9	111
17:10–11	105
17:14	111
17:18	112
18:8	112
18:13	74
18:14	74
18:21	74
18:22	74
19:5–9	98
19:6–8	75
19:10	98
19:11–21	131
19:11–16	111
19:16	111, 117
19:17–18	74
19:17	76
20:4–15	76
20:4	99–100
21	77
21:1	76
21:2	78
21:3	76
21:10–21	53
21:12	77
21:17	119
21:19–20	77
21:21	78
21:27	76
22:2	118–19
22:6	78, 84
22:7	83
22:8–21	78–79, 82–85, 104, 132–33
22:8–9	83
22:8	82
22:10	83
22:16–21	96
22:16	84, 129
22:18–19	84
22:21	144

DEAD SEA SCROLLS

CD

19:12	57

OTHER SECOND TEMPLE LITERATURE

Josephus

Ant.

13.8.4	87
14.13.4	88
14.53–54	87

Ant. (cont.)		*m. Pesaḥ.*	
17.10.2–6	88	94b	107
20.6.3—7.1	95	*m. Šabb.*	
B.J.		15c	29
1.13.3	88		
1:149	87	*m. Yoma*	
2.3.1	88	4b	25
2.3.2—4.2	88		
6.5.3	90, 97	*Midr. Cant.*	
		4.4.1	71
C. Ap.		8.4.1	72
2:18	27	*Midr. Eccl.*	
Philo		1.3.1	101
Somn.		*Midr. Exodus*	
2:127	27	15:28	62
Spec.		19:7	81
2.177	116	28:6	62
Pseudo-Philo		*Midr. Gen.*	
11:1–3	25	97	81
23:1–13	21, 101	*Midr. Lev.*	
23:2	25	28:4	102, 107

RABBINIC WRITINGS

b. Meg.		*Midr. Ruth*	
31ab	28, 34	3.2	68
31a	29, 38, 69	*Midr. Tanḥ.*	
b. Sanh.		Exod 29	48
105a	127	*Pirqé de Rabbi Eliezer*	
Bik.		48	67
1:1–8	47	*Roš Haš.*	
m. Hag.		1:2	51
2.1	29	*Sop.*	
m. Meg.		18.3	29, 62
3.5	28	29	29
4.10	29	*t. Meg.*	
31b	29, 49	3.5	28

t. Meg. (cont.)
4.5	34
4.34	29

y. Meg.
74b	28, 34

y. Ta'an
68d	126

GRECO-ROMAN WRITINGS

Dio
Hist.
61.12	95

Juvenal
Sat. 4.37ff.	105

Martial
Epigrams 11.38	105

Suetonius
Cal. 24	93
Cl. 26, 39	93
Dom. 1	92
Gal. 5	95
Nero 39	94, 113

Tacitus
Ann.
12.3	93
12.5	95
12.37	94
12.42	94
12.56	94
14.2	95
14.8	113
14.9	112

Hist.
2.8–9	92
3.71–73	112
4.2	92
5.13	91

EARLY CHRISTIAN WRITINGS

Acts of John by Prochorus	133

Eusebius
Hist. Ecc. 5.24	134

The Geneaologies of the Twelve Apostles	134

Hippolytus
Odes	133

Irenaeus
Adv. Haer.
3.17.2	
5.30	104, 106, 110, 121
5.30.2	
5.30.3	140
5.33.3	119

Justin Martyr
Dial. Trypho 81	104,

Origen
Comm. Joh. 5.3	141
On the 150 Psalms	140

Polycrates
Letter to Victor	132